Song of the Snow Lion

MĀNOA 12:2   UNIVERSITY OF HAWAI'I PRESS   HONOLULU

Song of the Snow Lion

Frank Stewart

EDITOR

Herbert J. Batt
Tsering Shakya

FEATURE EDITORS

Lama Champa Regzin, Lamayuru, April 26, 1987
Photograph by Karl-Einar Löfqvist

Editor   Frank Stewart

Managing Editor   Pat Matsueda

Production Editor   Michelle Tyau

Designer and Art Editor   Barbara Pope

Fiction Editor   Ian MacMillan

Poetry and Nonfiction Editor   Frank Stewart

Associate Fiction Editor   Susan Bates

Abernethy Apprentice   Natalie Asturi

Staff   Tia Ballantine Berger, Jenny Foster, Brent Fujinaka, Kathleen Matsueda, Candice Nii, Linda Sueyoshi

Corresponding Editors for North America
Fred Chappell, T. R. Hummer, Charles Johnson, Maxine Hong Kingston, Michael Ondaatje, Alberto Ríos, Arthur Sze, Tobias Wolff

Corresponding Editors for Asia and the Pacific
CHINA   Howard Goldblatt, Ding Zuxin
HONG KONG   Shirley Geok-lin Lim
INDONESIA   John H. McGlynn
JAPAN   Masao Miyoshi, Leza Lowitz
KOREA   Kim Uchang, Bruce Fulton
NEW ZEALAND AND SOUTH PACIFIC   Vilsoni Hereniko
PACIFIC LATIN AMERICA   H. E. Francis, James Hoggard
PHILIPPINES   Alfred A. Yuson
WESTERN CANADA   Charlene Gilmore

Advisory Group   Esther K. Arinaga, William H. Hamilton, Roderick A. Jacobs, Joseph Kau, Glenn Man, Franklin S. Odo, Robert Shapard, Marjorie Sinclair

Founded in 1988 by Robert Shapard and Frank Stewart.

"The Glory of the Wind Horse" by Tashi Dawa, "An Old Nun Tells Her Story" by Geyang, and "A God without Gender" by Yangdon are printed by permission of the publisher of Herbert J. Batt, editor and translator, *Tales of Tibet: Sky Burials, Wind Horses, and Prayer Wheels* (Rowman & Littlefield, 2001).

Mānoa is published twice a year. Subscriptions: U.S.A. and Canada—individuals $22 one year, $40 two years; institutions $30 one year, $54 two years; single copy $16. Other countries—individuals $25 one year, $46 two years; institutions $35 one year, $63 two years; single copy $17. For air mail add $18 per year. Call toll free 1-888-UHPRESS. We accept checks, money orders, VISA, or MasterCard, payable to University of Hawai'i Press, 2840 Kolowalu Street, Honolulu, HI 96822, U.S.A. Claims for issues not received will be honored until 180 days past the date of publication; thereafter, the single-copy rate will be charged.

Manuscripts may be sent to *Mānoa*, English Department, University of Hawai'i, Honolulu, HI 96822. Please include self-addressed, stamped envelope for return of manuscript or for our reply.

www.hawaii.edu/mjournal
www.hawaii.edu/uhpress/journals/manoa/

CONTENTS

Special Focus 🐚 **New Writing from Tibet**

Editor's Note

Twice a year, *Mānoa*'s editors gather significant new writing from throughout Asia, Oceania, and the Americas and highlight authors of a particular country or region. *Song of the Snow Lion* features prose and poetry of Tibet —a nation now subsumed within the borders of China. The volume marks the fiftieth anniversary of Chinese military occupation and the ascendancy of the Dalai Lama to leadership of the Tibetan people. The title refers to the snow lions that appear on the Tibetan flag, representing among other things the country's ancient unity. All but a few of the Tibetan writers featured in *Song of the Snow Lion* reside within Tibet. About half of the pieces were originally written in the Tibetan language; most of the others first appeared in Chinese-language publications.

As a result of China's seizure of Tibet—and the Communist Party's insistence, backed by its armed forces, that the country has always been part of China—many Tibetans and non-Tibetans alike feel that Tibet now exists freely and openly only outside its former national borders. In referring to the oppression of Tibetans within China and to the more than 100,000 living in exile, Kasur Lodi Gyari, the Dalai Lama's special representative in Washington, D.C., has said, "Today, everything that is Tibet—the culture, the religion, every aspect of Tibet—lives outside."

In the eyes of the United Nations and other international bodies, Tibet has indeed lost its autonomy. But since 1950, Tibetans have demonstrated how a people and culture can maintain a national identity in the face of extraordinary circumstances. During the first twenty years of Chinese rule, one-fifth of the country's population was starved, tortured, imprisoned, and killed as a result of Communist policies; at present, the Party's control is tighter than ever, and it continues to launch campaigns to accelerate sinicization, villify the Dalai Lama's government-in-exile, and quash any hope for the restoration of Tibetan independence. Nevertheless, the people have refused to submit.

Literature has played a significant part in this struggle. After the Chinese military invasion, one of the occupying government's major tasks was to educate Tibetans in the social and political ideals of Communism; to succeed, the government needed a medium for mass propaganda. Soon, how-

Sharing Secrets, Pipiting, July 19, 1988
Photograph by Karl-Einar Löfqvist

ever, the Communists found that their worldview and its terminology were so alien to the Tibetans that the language of the newly occupied people had no lexicon to adequately express Communist theory. Indeed, both written and oral Tibetan were syntactically incompatible with such socialist notions as a classless society. Furthermore, there was virtually no literary tradition in Tibet appropriate for indoctrinating the masses in socialist materialism and the Party's version of Sino-Tibetan history.

The Chinese therefore set out to dominate and colonize Tibetans first by altering the language and then by introducing modernist literary forms—such as secular fiction, poetry, and drama—as well as socialist realist visual images. Strict control was imposed on all expression. However, when the Chinese briefly relaxed censorship in the early 1980s, Tibetans were able to use the new literary forms to discuss among themselves many aspects of their political crisis—including issues of national identity, modernization, and religious values.

In his overview essay, "The Waterfall and Fragrant Flowers," co–guest editor Tsering Shakya explains how secular fiction and poetry emerged during this time. "Clearly, writers in Tibet and China lack the freedom to explore individual sentiments and subjects explicitly. Nevertheless," Shakya writes, "we can see that their work does not always merely follow the diktats of the Party, even when it is written in Chinese and published under the eyes of the censors. . . . Although the line favored by the state and the Party is compulsory and all authors must seem to conform in order to be published, when we examine the writings themselves, their conformity is not quite so clear-cut."

Poet, essayist, and fiction writer Dhondup Gyal was one of the first and most important young Tibetan authors to demonstrate that modern literary forms could be used to debate social issues and express unorthodox opinions. In his overview essay, Shakya discusses Dhondup Gyal's significance; and we include in *Song of the Snow Lion* Shakya's translation of Dhondup Gyal's landmark poem, "Waterfall of Youth." When first published in Tibetan in 1983, the poem caused a sensation. As scholar and translator Janet L. Upton has pointed out, "Waterfall of Youth" uses the image of powerful cascading water not only to give the poem its form, but also to represent the potential young Tibetans have to transform their social situation. With the publication of this poem, as Shakya writes, the possibility arose that through literature a new discourse on Tibetan modernity could emerge. The hopefulness expressed in Dhondup Gyal's poem was soon extinguished, however; having lost hope himself, he took his life two years later, at the age of thirty-two.

Nevertheless, his work has continued to be influential. The issues raised in "Waterfall of Youth" and the metaphors used to express them are alluded to in the two poems that follow it in this volume. Upton points out that "Tears of Regret Flow Uncontrollably," by Lhagyal Tshering, is a comment on the social situation three years after the appearance of Dhondup Gyal's robust waterfall: the grip of the PRC government had tightened, and the powerful cascade of youthful energy and optimism had turned into a torrent of tears.

Three years after Tshering's "Tears of Regret Flow Uncontrollably," the poem "Snow Mountain Tears," by Dpa' dar, was published. The poem reminds Tibetans that fourteen hundred years earlier the dynasty of King Songtsen Gampo had extended Tibet north into present-day Xinjiang Province, west into Ladakh/Kashmir, and east into present-day Gansu, Qinghai, Sichuan, and Yunnan Provinces. In the poem, Dpa' dar calls on Tibetan youths to dry their tears and emulate their ancestors' boldness and glory—even if it means that blood, rather than tears, will spill like a waterfall from the Land of Snows.

Similar references to Tibet's long history of nationhood and greatness appear in the three poems by Meizhuo. "Songtsen Gampo: Statue of the King of Tubo" evokes, as in Dpa' dar's poem, the first of the three religious kings of the sixth-century Yarlung dynasty and uses Tubo, the ancient name of Tibet, rather than Xizang, the name preferred by the Communists. "Tseyang Gyatso: My King" is based on the life of the Sixth Dalai Lama, who was deposed by the Qosot Mongols in 1706. "Milarepa: Song of a Saint" celebrates the twelfth-century mystical poet and ascetic whose body is said to have shone with a green light.

Among the fiction pieces in *Song of the Snow Lion* are two works by Tashi Dawa, one of the most prominent Tibetan writers in China. His story "Chimi, the Free Man" presents a feckless, downtrodden hero who eventually gets the best of his police pursuers, despite their wolf-tooth handcuffs. Chimi escapes captivity so frequently that his jailors finally give up trying to hold him. Tashi Dawa leaves it for readers to ponder the implications of this story and to reach their own conclusions about the fact that the character Jin Waji is Han Chinese. At the end of the story, when Chimi cannot wrangle a valuable bowl out of Jin Waji, he goes to visit Melong, a Tibetan tailor who is also a "superb machinist." The story ends with Chimi's climbing the stone steps to Melong's outhouse, which is "built like a concrete pillbox." From here, Chimi can survey the village, and he sees that it, like him, is still in its native state.

On the most literal level, the title of Tashi Dawa's "The Glory of the Wind Horse" refers to verses of Buddhist scripture or prayers written on paper and released into the wind. The narrator, Ugyen, is on a quest for revenge but finds that his enemy cannot be killed. The story's fantastic elements evoke the eternal Buddhist circle of reincarnation; cosmic justice operates against the backdrop of secular justice and amidst the Chinese presence in Tibet.

A number of other pieces in *Song of the Snow Lion* also emphasize a Tibetan Buddhist worldview, in contrast to a Chinese one, thereby identifying Tibetans as a separate and unique people. In a note preceding Sebo's "Get the Boat Here," co-guest editor Herbert J. Batt unravels the Buddhist allusions (and political implications) in this allegory of four travelers in search of the boat that will take them back across a wide river to their hotel. Yangdon's young narrator in "A God without Gender" is a Buddhist nun whose view of life is deepened by her contact with the marginal members of her family's large household. Geyang's "An Old Nun Tells Her Story" presents the life of a nun who has been compelled by the demands of her family to leave her faith behind and lend her strength to loved ones. And Palden Gyal's essay, "Your Birth Day," describes the tragic consequences of a father's decision—during the Cultural Revolution—to announce his son's birth in the traditional religious manner.

In Tashi Pelden's "Tomorrow's Weather Will Be Better" and Tonga's "Room 218, Hurrah!" the Tibetan protagonists struggle against overwhelming obstacles. In the first story, a farmer attempts to provide for his family during drought and flood; and in the second, a young Tibetan student strives to overcome the prejudices of his Han Chinese classmates.

Among the American work in this issue are stories by Kevin Bowen, Andrew Lam, and Olen Steinhauer, and essays by Lenore Look and Virgil Suárez. Bowen's narrator is an American soldier stationed in Viet Nam during the war, and Lam's is a Vietnamese writer who is living in the United States but is not at peace in his adopted home. Look's memoir, "Facing the Village," takes us to China with her parents for an emotional homecoming, postponed for decades. Suárez's two short pieces describe the world from the point of view of a boy too young to make sense of conflicts and compromises but sensitive enough to be affected by them.

The black-and-white photographs by Karl-Einar Löfqvist are of Tibetan communities in Ladakh, a region now part of Kashmir. Löfqvist's color image of *mani* stones, found on our back cover, was taken in the village of Choglamsar, established in 1963 by Tibetan refugees who were given the land by the Indian government; covered with Buddhist mantras, stones such as these are mentioned in several of the Tibetan works in this volume. The color image of Buddhas on the front cover was taken in the village of Alchi. The inner walls of the village's smallest temple are painted with thousands of such images, according to Löfqvist. The Tibetan monastery in Alchi dates to the eleventh century.

Many people have helped make *Song of the Snow Lion* a reality. The Chiang Ching-kuo Foundation and an anonymous donor contributed funds to support production of this volume. Translator Lauran R. Hartley thanks Pema Bhum for his patient assistance with her translation and Dr. Breon Mitchell for his advice and encouragement; translator Janet L. Upton thanks Larry Epstein and Pema Bhum for their help and advice in rendering the poems of Lhagyal Tshering and Dpa'dar.

Lighting the Lamp, Nurla, January 27, 1988
A boy lights a paraffin lamp.
Photograph by Karl-Einar Löfqvist

Chimi, the Free Man

This time, as Chimi walked the dirt road into town, the pebbles branded his feet. As he walked, he kept turning backwards to admire the crooked footprints he'd left behind. His head slammed into a tree limb, he bumped into people coming toward him, he almost slid into a ditch.

The people of Lhodrak Village believed in a goddess called Boka. They would piously vow, "In the name of Boka." The main street of Lhodrak was lined with shops, little taverns, the tailor's, and the blacksmith's. Chimi stopped in front of a shop. People kept their distance from him, but he wasn't bothered. He nodded and called to folks he knew. Passersby started whispering to each other. *Chimi's escaped again . . . The seventh time? . . . No, the eighth!*

In Lhodrak Village, you would usually see a policeman appear at the corner of the square, casually walking down the street, hands behind his back.

Chimi knew he shouldn't come back to Lhodrak every time he escaped. He knew he should run somewhere else, but he couldn't imagine where to go. There was no place like Lhodrak, where he could talk freely and hear cordial voices call his name.

Lhamo, the food shopkeeper, folded her arms and said, "So, Chimi, back again!"

"Back again. Not bad, eh?"

"Well . . ." She hardly knew what to say next. "They didn't let you out, did they?"

"No—the same as always." He sat down on Lhamo's front step, took the snuff pot she handed him, and shook a pinch onto his thumbnail. Other shopkeepers began to call their greetings.

"If that's how it is," Lhamo said in a low voice, "they'll catch you and take you back before you can finish that pinch of snuff!"

Chimi paid no attention. "Who's boiling mutton?" He could smell it.

"Melong—across the way there. I saw him come back this morning with a side of fresh mutton. If he knew you were back, he'd invite you."

"Hmm . . . ," Chimi said, wiping his lips.

Suddenly all the heads on the street turned north.

Then all the heads turned back to Chimi.

Along came the policeman, hands behind his back. Chimi inched his way out, craned his neck, and peered . . . The policeman spotted him. Chimi shifted nervously, ready to bolt. But the policeman just walked past, nodding to Chimi as if to say hello, and carried on straight down the street, looking as if he were pondering some mystery.

Everybody breathed a sigh of relief.

"Did they really release you this time, Chimi?" someone asked him.

"I got out just like before," he replied.

And so they all returned to their own affairs.

Chimi didn't trouble himself with wondering why the policeman hadn't rearrested him. He said good-bye to Lhamo and walked into a tea shop near the square. There was nobody inside. He rapped an empty cup. A girl came out and poured him some tea.

A young man sat down opposite him and looked out the window. It was Jin Waji, a younger son of the Jin clan. He rarely appeared in town because, people said, his health was bad. His family kept him deep inside the walls of the Jin family mansion. A lonely figure, he had attractive melancholy eyes.

"Young master." Chimi nodded to him.

"You're back!"

"Yuh."

"How's it going?"

"Everything's good. Boka blesses me."

Jin Waji gave a pleased nod and looked back out the window, all the way down the street to the very end of town, where the old walnut tree clung to its last few, dried leaves. The people on the street were all from Lhodrak, and knew each other.

"Now that you're back, what are you going to do?" Jin Waji asked.

"Time will tell."

"Why not go back to your old job?"

"I can't. They won't let me. You know, these two hands of mine were just made to polish sacrificial bowls and bronze buddhas in the temple." Chimi held out his hands.

Indeed, they were beautiful, lithe, elegant hands. It was impossible to imagine them at the end of the arms of someone like Chimi. Their skin was smooth, lustrous, impressionable as butter, as if the slightest touch would leave its imprint on them. They were covered with soft, downy hair, with an intricate network of blue veins showing through. Chimi admired his hands a moment, then hid them between his legs. "It looks like you're waiting for someone," he said.

Jin Waji didn't answer.

"Or maybe waiting for some miracle," Chimi muttered to himself. "You can dream what you like, but when you open your eyes, there's no miracle. Is there?"

"What I want to know is how much those red-elm bowls in our house are really worth. They must be symbols of something. Maybe some wandering lama could tell me."

"I've got a hunch . . . Could those bowls be reincarnations of women?"

"Women? Good! Go on."

"Oh, it's just nonsense, young master."

"Then go on with the nonsense—don't stop!"

"Haven't you heard that song?"

> *I can't take you with me,*
> *Can't bear leaving you behind.*
> *If I could turn you into a wooden bowl,*
> *I'd tuck you in my shirt*
> *And take you everywhere I go.*

"Ah-ha. That's how you explain it!"

"It's just nonsense."

"Women . . ."

"How many of those wooden bowls are there in your house, young master?"

From time immemorial, Jin Waji's family had been feuding with another rich, powerful clan, and the two families had each drawn a line for a boundary in front of their doors, which faced each other. Neither side was permitted to step across the other's line, a rule that had been passed down from generation to generation. Once, a maidservant from the other family got drunk, took the wrong turn, and wound up in the Jin family's courtyard, where one of the stablemen pulled her down on the firewood pile behind the kitchen and raped her.

There was no court system in Lhodrak then, so to settle the matter, the two families sat on their respective sides of the line and prayed together to Boka. They laid the whole thing before her, and asked her to take pity on them and render judgment on the unfortunate affair that had befallen her subjects. The villagers crowded round to watch. People climbed up on courtyard walls, some sat in trees, some stood on rooftops. All they could see was the two disputing families sitting opposite each other with their eyes closed. The whole town held its breath. The crows stopped cawing, waiting for a miracle. There was a clap of thunder. Nobody dared raise his head. The story goes that a few impious, rash youths who looked up were immediately blinded by a dazzling rainbow-colored ring of light, and couldn't speak for a long while after. From the invisible heavens came Boka's voice with the verdict: Jin Suotang (Waji's ancestor) must compensate Palo Kunsang Gyalpo (the maidservant's master) with a bowl carved of red elm.

No other goddess could issue such a just verdict as Boka.

Everyone was wholeheartedly satisfied.

From then on, whenever the Jin family had to bear the responsibility for anything, they would give as compensation a red-elm bowl commensurate in size with the offense.

And everyone was wholeheartedly satisfied.

This was a legend from ancient times.

"Smack me on the head," Chimi said.

"What?"

"Smash me on the head. Knock me out."

"You want a bowl, eh?"

"I'll be honest. I've wanted one for years."

"Wouldn't that be giving you one for nothing?"

"Well . . . never mind."

"Why not go back to your old job?" Jin Waji asked.

"I can't. I'd rather polish the sacrificial bowls and the bronze buddhas in the temple. I don't know why, but the lamas wouldn't shave my head and take me in as a monk."

"Why did they send you away?"

"I don't know. Anyway, what good would it do me to know?"

"Now you're a free man."

"Right—as free as the wind." When the word "free" passed his lips, Chimi felt empty as the wind.

"Come on, let's drink our tea," Waji said.

They finished one cup, and another was poured.

Chimi didn't have any money. He knew Waji had money and would pay for his tea.

And indeed, the young man paid for Chimi without a thought.

"So, what work did you do after the monks sent you away?" Waji asked in a low voice.

"You don't know?"

"Don't stare at me with your eyes like walnuts."

"In the name of Boka! He doesn't know what my last job was!"

"Stop yelling and tell me."

"But if I . . . if I tell you, maybe you'll think it's boring."

"If you tell me, I'll give you a bowl."

So Chimi told him.

Chimi had taken care of the barn at the edge of town. Every harvest, the people brought all the straw left over from the threshing ground and piled it into the barn. All winter the villagers relied on this straw to feed their livestock. Chimi's job was to keep accounts and prevent fires.

All autumn Chimi was busy. The straw in the barn rose into a little mountain. When fall was over, he had nothing to do. He went to bed early, bored. One night there was a knock at the door. It was a vagrant begging for a cup of hot tea. Chimi gave him a warm welcome, asked him in, boiled a big pot of beef, made a pot of strong yak-butter tea, and dug up the bottle of fiery liquor he'd buried by the sheepfold. The two of them sat down face to face, crossed their legs, and clinked glasses. Chimi hadn't had such a good time in ages—he'd spent so many evenings all alone. When the liquor was gone, the two of them fell asleep, dead drunk. In the middle of the night, somehow or other the barn caught fire. At midnight one of the villagers went out to take a piss, heard the dogs barking in a funny way, and looked east. At first he thought it was dawn. Then all of a sudden he realized what it was and yelled, "Fire!" A fierce red glow engulfed the village. Villagers running out of their houses a mile away felt waves of heat hit them in the face. Everyone rushed to the fire, but nobody tried to put it out. Girls admired each other's complexions, turned ruddy in its light. Someone skewered some meat on a long metal pole, thrust it into the flames, and turned it quickly. In a flash it was done, juicy and delicious. *Blow on it. Quick, pull off a piece and put it in your mouth!* Most people just stood at a distance, chatting casually. Everybody knew it was useless to try to put out a blaze like that. It's not so easy to be reincarnated as a human, so why throw your precious life into a roaring fire? The flames exploded and thundered till people's eardrums hummed. A dense cloud of sparks danced in the sky like a mass of stars—a once-in-a-century spectacle.

As the little shed that stood on the side of the barn was starting to catch fire, a few robust, generous-hearted men risked their lives to break in and carry out two fellow humans. Chimi and the vagrant were still passed out. When they were laid down in the ditch, they didn't even come to.

By the next morning, the barn and the hundreds of tons of cattle feed inside it had burned clean to the ground. A few last wisps of smoke curled up from the blackened remains of the great stack of straw. A whole winter's fodder had been incinerated to a white ash, but nobody blamed Chimi. They knew he hadn't set the fire. He just hadn't done his job as a watchman. They got the befuddled vagrant drunk all over again, then four men picked up and carried him off. A big crowd of men and women of all ages followed after, singing merrily. They carried the vagrant to the banks of the Machu River, not far from town. One man grabbed his arms, another took his feet, and they swung him back and forth. "One, two, three!" the crowd shouted, and the men heaved him in a big arc. An enormous splash, then everything was quiet. They'd seen him come into town from the east, so they let the river carry him eastward, back home. The vagrant wasn't a Lhodrak man.

The crowd returned just as they came, singing merrily, but they wouldn't have been fulfilling their duty as responsible townsfolk if they hadn't somehow dealt with Chimi. When he finally woke up, they helped him to his feet, reassured him, and then, as silent as a funeral procession, they took him to the police. What else could they do?

Chimi escaped seven times. After the fourth time, the police had to bring out their secret weapon. They put him in the wolf-tooth handcuffs.

The instant a criminal struggled, a ring of steel teeth automatically pierced the skin of his wrist, straight to the bone. The police had only put this set of handcuffs on two other prisoners. There were bloodcurdling stories about what happened to these two. But Chimi had a marvelous, matchless pair of hands. His wrists and fingers were as supple as rubber, his skin as slippery as oil. He got out of the wolf-tooth handcuffs in three minutes. Then he waited quietly. When night came, he used the handcuffs as a handy tool to dig a hole through the jail wall. Chimi crawled out, took a deep breath of the early-morning air, and headed for Lhodrak Village.

Jin Waji had already heard about the burning of the barn, so he didn't reckon Chimi's story was worth a wooden bowl. Chimi still hadn't explained why the police weren't arresting him again.

"Ask them. How should I know?"

Chimi really didn't know. And just because he didn't know, he didn't get a red-elm bowl. He was crestfallen, but what could he do?

Resentfully, he walked out of the teahouse, then bumped into Melong. Sure enough, Melong invited him to share some juicy roast mutton.

Of course, Chimi couldn't refuse.

Melong has a beautiful, promiscuous older daughter and a beautiful, imaginative younger daughter. As everybody knows, he is a superb tailor, but, unknown to most people, he is a superb machinist too, having designed a gun to pierce heavy armor.

The internal directives of the Lhodrak police are classified information, but afterwards this leaked out: the local police have handcuffs, but no shackles. Therefore, a new article has been added to the regulations to the effect that the rare criminal—like Chimi—who cannot be restrained with handcuffs and who repeatedly makes good his escape shall not be rear-rested.

As dusk was about to fall, Chimi walked out of the house and climbed the stone steps to Melong's outhouse, which was built like a concrete pill-box.

As he climbed, Chimi looked out over the village, covered in the hazy smoke of evening cooking fires. None of the buildings was limed or white-washed. They all showed their original color: earthen yellow.

Lhodrak is a yellow-earth village.

Translation by Herbert J. Batt

Yelchung, July 26, 1997
The small village Yelchung is surrounded by high mountains.
The walk to the village from the nearest road takes five days
and includes travel over the pass Singi La, five thousand
meters above sea level.
Photograph by Karl-Einar Löfqvist

Man and Boy, Leh, September 27, 1991
An old man and his grandson enter Leh Palace.
Photograph by Karl-Einar Löfqvist

DHONDUP GYAL

Waterfall of Youth

The clear blue sky,
The warmth of the sun,
The fragrant flowers,
The majestic mountains—

Ai ma!

But even more beautiful than these,
a cascading waterfall
before a steep cliff,

Look!

Brilliant rays, pure white, spread like a
peacock's feathers,
parrot's plumage,
patterns on silk brocade,

Listen!

The sound of the gushing water, clear and pleasing,
The music of the angels,
unblemished melody,
music of the gods,
pure in origin,

Kyi!

This is not an ordinary waterfall—
It possesses a majestic quality,
a fearless heart
incomparable in its pride,
a strong body
adorned in finest jewels,
most melodious music,

This!

The torrential waterfall,
the glorious young people of the Land of Snows,

This!

In the year 1980,
the heartfelt power and creativity of the youth of Bo,
The dignifying struggle,
the music of youthfulness,

Kyi! Kyi!

Youthful waterfall,
waterfall of youth,

Where did you obtain
the fearless heart,
immeasurable confidence,
unbending pride,
limitless strength?

Yes!

The rainfall during the three months of spring,
the new growth during the three months of summer,
the nourishment of hail and storm during the three months of autumn,
the ice and snow of three months of winter,

And more!

Water from the snowy mountains, meadows, valleys, ravines,

In short!

Water of auspiciousness,
water of prosperity,
water of fulfillment,
water of perfection
possessing the Eight Purities of water,

The hundreds and thousands of different qualities of water,

You are the water of friendship,
daring to leap from the ferocious cliff—
you are the water of the universe,
Courageously leaping into the valley below,
Proud to take on what is new

You have an open mind, strong body, and majestic appearance,
without arrogance or defilement,
your origins are deep,
having cast aside all impurities,
you have an unblemished mind, a splendor in your youthfulness,

Waterfall!

You are witness to history,
the way of the future—
the breathing and lifting of the snow land are written
on every droplet,
the rise and development of the Land of Snows
shine in each of your rays,

Without you!

Where can we whet the sword of language?
Where can we sharpen the sword of our skills,

Without you!

The tree of medicine cannot bloom,
philosophy and Buddhism will not bear fruit,

Possibly!

Lingering in your crystal mind
may be wounds of history,
scars of old battles fought,
lesions of ignorance,
the clotting of conservatism—
these are not possible,

The reason is!

You possess pride, majesty, and strength of youth,
will never let the winter ice stop you or
numb your mind—
a hundred slashes from a wrathful sword
cannot halt your flow,

The reason is!

The waterfall's source lies in the deep snows,
its end is joined with the vast ocean—
your history is long,
it generates pride and dignity,
how melodious your chorus of time,
our inspiration and potency,

Have you heard? Waterfall!

The questions of the youth of the Land of Snows,

How can you let a poet's horse suffer from thirst?
How can you let composition's elephant suffer from heat?
How can you let metaphor's snow lion be covered in dirt?
How can you not nurture the orphan of dance and music?
Who will preserve the heritage of astrology?
Who will welcome the groom of science?
Who will wed the bride of technology?

Alas! Waterfall!

Your clear, bright, and harmonious answers will reach our ears,
they are incised in our minds as a carving on a rock,

In truth!

The thousand brilliant accomplishments of the past
cannot serve today's purpose,
yesterday's salty water cannot quench today's thirsts,
the withered body of history is lifeless
without the soul of today,
the pulse of progress will not beat,
the blood of progress will not flow,
and a forward step cannot be taken,

Kyi! Waterfall!

Your gentle ripples,
droplets from your splashing water,

You symbolize the strength of the new generation of the Land of Snows,
your torrent and thunderous sounds,

Ours!

You show the hopes of the new generation—
our generation must not tread these paths,
conservatism, isolationism, ignorance, slothfulness—
backwardness, barbarism, darkness, and reactionism,
these have no foundation in our land,

Waterfall, waterfall!

Our minds will follow your course,
our blood will run like yours,
in the currents of times to come,
however difficult the way,
Youth of Tibet, relinquish fear,

Our people!
A new path is opening in front of you,

Look!

The new generation of the Land of Snows,
we are marching together,

Listen!

This harmonious song
is the anthem of the youth of the Land of Snows,
the bright road,
pride in responsibility,
joyous life,
song of struggle,

The youthful waterfall will not diminish,
the water will never become impure,

This is!

The waterfall springs from the voices of the youth of Tibet

This is!

The waterfall flows from the mind of the youth of the Land of Snows.

Translation by Tsering Shakya

Tears of Regret Flow Uncontrollably

When a girl of fifteen is not sent to school but is given over
    to the milk cows;
When a charming, slender girl does not marry but is used by
    a swindler;
When a beautiful bride does not fit into her new household
    and is abandoned to roam in unknown, distant lands—
Oh—how tears of regret flow uncontrollably from my eyes!

When a white-haired old man does not know the alphabet
    but recites mantras for this life and the next;
When a white-toothed young man does not know the four vowels
    but adorns his chest with gold ornaments;
When a pure-hearted monk does not know how to punctuate
    sentences but conducts rituals in the home—
Oh—how tears of regret flow uncontrollably from my eyes!

When the children of farmers and herders aren't sent to school
    but spend their time with flocks of goats and sheep;
When the schoolyard is empty of students but full of
    grass and weeds;
When the classroom walls crumble in the rain while the teacher
    revels in drink—
Oh—how tears of regret flow uncontrollably from my eyes!

When the field of culture is trampled under the hooves of those
    who disparage it;
When the flower garden of education withers in the drought
    of conservatism;
When the peachlike face of literature is infested by swarms
    of ravenous insects—
Oh—how tears of regret flow uncontrollably from my eyes!

When the broad heart of the snowy mountains is covered with
    filthy dust and sand;
When the courageous peaks of the rocky mountains are split apart
    by black-beaked crows;
When the wisdom of the grassy mountains' fertile slopes
    is undermined by thousands of gophers—
Oh—how tears of regret flow uncontrollably from my eyes!

When the stallion of progress and knowledge is bound tightly
    by the hobbles of domination;
When the white yak of freedom is chained by the nose
    to a hybrid yak-cow and made subservient to her;
When the sheep of peace and happiness are exploited for profit
    and sheared again and again—
Oh—how tears of regret flow uncontrollably from my eyes!

When incomparable geniuses wander as beggars in foreign lands;
When unprecedented idiots sit upon the thrones of brilliant scholars;
When savages control the wise and knowledgeable—
Oh—how tears of regret flow uncontrollably from my eyes!

When the pure river of an untainted history is contaminated
    with the salty water of distortion;
When the unblemished vow on the face of a stone monument
    is defaced with one-sided views;
When the incomparably white pool of the five sciences becomes
    the playground for lying frogs—
Oh—how tears of regret flow uncontrollably from my eyes!

Translation by Janet L. Upton

Snow Mountain Tears

Don't know when it happens:
A boisterous nation
Suddenly loses its voice, loses its breath.
People forget its vigorous story,
Leaving only an endless expanse of snow
And the offering
of a sky-blotting, earth-covering white scarf.

Diligent   Brave   Unsophisticated
  Wild   Ignorant   Backward
The offhand comments of thoughtless people.

A thousand years of labor and suffering
Obscured by the mists of history,
Now lie motionless beneath the deep, deep snows,
A reminder of acts of boldness long since past.
The roars of those who fought for the Central Plains,
The force of those whose horses drank from the Yangtze,
The majesty of those who held sway over Ba and Shu,
The magnificence of the colored-pottery culture,
All are now so distant.
Your soul is trapped in chasms in the frozen snow,
Exhausted.

History—ah, history!
Why have you laid your head down to sleep here?
If the ascendance of the Tibetan empire
Had continued to spread into the heavens like the stars
It would have been absorbed into the vast emptiness of the night.
The Land of Snows is like a fur coat torn from a rabid dog
Faded and fallen in a desolate corner of the universe.

Ah—there is only a clay princess
In the smokey mist of the incense flame
Eternally staring at her distant homeland.
An endless expanse of wilderness, without change.
Civilization lies in the difficult trek through the snowy peaks.
My emaciated male elders
Light a hundred thousand butter lamps,
Walk out of the temple full of brilliance
And begin to shudder on the dim and winding path.

Ah—compatriots!
You have probably thought before
Sakyamuni's hometown was as poor as yours.
Beneath the pilgrims' feet the foundation has been worn away,
Changed again and again.

Ah—the wisdom of our alphabet's thirty letters!
Why don't they point the way out of the three narrow
    paths of pilgrimage?
The cold wind plays a bitter symphony.
In their crow-colored tents
The descendants of the Land of Snows curl up on goat skins
While the people next door sleep on Simmons mattresses.
A warhorse cannot catch a spaceship.
Humanity moves toward the space age
But on your waist you carry only a shepherd's staff for
    fending off dogs.

Ah—Snow Mountains!
You bring forth snowy lotus and glossy genoderma
    in an endless cycle of death and rebirth
But have no medicinal herbs to cure these intense contradictions.
Flowing beneath the wrinkled brow of Majiaogangri
The inexhaustible currents of the Yellow River and the Yangtze
Are the tears of the Snow Mountains,
So people say.

No.

The Snow Mountains spill blood, not tears.
Let us not use tears to welcome the dawn of a new era.

Translation by Janet L. Upton

Man with Horses, Pangong Tso, December 22, 1997
On their way home, a man and his horses pass the
salt-water lake, Pangong Tso, at the Tibetan border,
four thousand meters above sea level.
Photograph by Karl-Einar Löfqvist

Journal of the Grassland _____

Written in Serzang Tang in X, on the x day of x 198x

1

"Now if you wanna talk about the old days . . . Our yak-hair tent back then was cured with smoke! We had a huge iron pot—soot-black we used it so much! *Hmmph.* And who was that, you ask? That was *my* family . . . Wa Tar's family in Logor. I'm the son of an outstanding man! The hide of an excellent yak! Who else but *me,* Norbum, was raised reining in wild horses, leading wild yaks by the nose, seizing the chests of charging tigers, and grabbing the horns of rampaging yaks?! *Hmmph.* And why do I mention this? . . ." By this time, Akhu Norbum's eyes were bloodshot, and his strength having waned, he could no longer hold himself steady. A long strand of drool wound its way to the ashes below.

"Ano! . . ." called Norbum's younger brother, Tsewang, who was seated across from him and was now quite concerned. He tried to quiet Norbum. "Ano, now you're drunk!"

Akhu Norbum simply ranted all the louder. "I'm *not* drunk! Ever since the world began, people have had to pay for brides and the mother's milk that nourished them. Especially these days—now that Party policy has improved . . . Besides, this daughter of mine is our firstborn, the first pup of the litter. We need *something* to tell our relatives, no? Something to show up our enemies, right?"

Akhu Tsewang looked uncomfortable. He repeated, "Ano, you're drunk."

But the guests who had been asked by their relatives to arrange this marriage hastened nervously to defer. "Of course! You're absolutely right." Showering Akhu Norbum with such remarks, they adorned with ornamental laurels the worthy points he'd just made.

It was nearly midday. Ama Dzomkyi was seated in the doorway of the tent she shared with Akhu Tsewang, sunning herself, as she did every day. One end of the wide sash at her waist was draped over her head to shield her from the sun's bright rays. Under her *chuba* of navy-blue wool, she wore a tattered, white silk shirt. Where its collar button was left unfastened, one could see the string of her amulet pouch and a soiled, red silk cord blessed for her protection. Ruddied by sun and oil, her face was flushed and happy. While her fingers kneaded the time-worn prayer beads, Ama Dzomkyi peered out lazily towards the grassland. Her glance fell upon the young woman who was spreading out wet dung to dry in Akhu Norbum's yard. It was her niece, Drolkar. Ama Dzomkyi continued to recite under her breath, concluding, "I dedicate any merit accumulated now and always to the Buddhahood of sentient beings who have all once been my mother."

With these words, she turned around slowly toward her husband, Tsewang, who was busy arranging the cloth that covered the *thangka* painting of Sakyamuni Buddha. "Why give that girl to a family who lives so far away? It will be difficult for us to visit each other even once."

"Who? Oh. Drolkar?"

"It's not like there aren't other families. What about giving her to Uncle Sonam Tsering's family? Our nephew is practically a young thoroughbred. He's from a good family. And in terms of property, while they might look flashy on the outside, down deep they're as rich as dark earth. Or you could give her to Yangbum Jyal's family. They're respectable—and rich too! That's for sure. Why give her to some farmer?" She sat with her head turned away in disapproval, but Akhu Tsewang's attention was wholly fixed on covering the *thangka* and he didn't respond.

Ama Dzomkyi drew the wrinkles of her brow into a single furrow and placed around her neck the prayer beads she'd been holding. "*Nama!* How about making some tea? We've missed teatime again." She stretched her legs out, then folded them back to the other side and continued, "It's too cheap, sending her to some old farmer. If you're going to buy, then buy right. If you're going to sell, then sell right."

Akhu Tsewang stopped what he was doing and glanced down at her. "Hold your tongue! You're a woman. What would *you* know about it?"

Ama Dzomkyi snorted in disgust. "*Ho ho, ya!* Oh, my! If it wasn't me, then *who* let golden light into your starving valley? *Who* allowed greasy pools of fat to form on your deprived family's meals? We know perfectly well how your family used to live! I took care of *everything* for our eight children and managed to find three daughters-in-law. Was all *this* the fault of my ignorance and the virtue of your knowledge?"

"You?! . . . My background, this business about Drolkar . . . What's it to you? Why not chant some *mani* instead, and that will be your virtue!"

Ama Dzomkyi yanked the sash from her head, infuriated. "I am the very blood of your flesh, the stuff of which your bones are made! Do you think I want to bring your family down?! Don't I have any right to discuss Drolkar's business? *Pfft!* That old farmer is a donkey racing against horses, a goat trying to outdo sheep. Is he not?"

"What difference is there between farmers and nomads except a few fields and yaks? If you'll recall . . . our families were also farmers once. It's just that they left Rebgong Gartse. Now be quiet. Hush."

"*Ya!* And if I don't, so what?! I've a mouth on me. Fruit hangs on a tree! Don't I even have the right to speak these days?!"

"*Aarrgh,* women!" As Akhu Tsewang's anger flared, his tone grew harsher. "Have you gone mad?!"

"Your face just looks stonier the older you get! If you can't agree to my having a happy life here with our son and daughter-in-law, *you'll* be the one to suffer. Even if the sky ripped open with your anger and the dragon up there fell to earth and died . . . *I would speak!* I'd be *happy* even."

Akhu Tsewang was incensed. With a rage from somewhere deep inside, he grabbed the poker off the hearth and rushed towards Ama Dzomkyi.

Ya, ya. *That's it. I'll end my writing here for now. Anything further surely wouldn't bode well for this old couple.*

3

And whose tent have we here? Oh. It belongs to Akhu Norbum's older sister. So sad. I first heard a bit about this woman's story some time ago, but it's too long to tell here now. Anyway, her karma *isn't good. She was married four times and had three young boys, like tiger cubs. But it was all as if a magician had performed some sleight of hand. She alone remains after so many have died, abandoned like the adobe stove of a deserted nomad camp. It's truly difficult to take one's life when, even after several attempts, the Lord Death won't come.*

Again today, when Ama Huamo had performed all the chores a nomad woman must, she looked up at the ray of sun streaming in through the opening in her tent and said to herself, "Oh, it's time for the midday meal." She fanned the fire in her stove, coughing as she blew.

One can tell by the dusty look of her dress, by the dried dung and milk stains on her padded clothes, that this is what she always wears. It's as if her dingy hair, bared shoulder, and many rows of wrinkles are meant to serve as fearsome warnings to folks that such is the twisted path of time. Just look. Who knows how many cups and such have been washed with those grime-eaten ends of her sash?

"*Ayi!* This meat is for you from Uncle Ano's family!" Akhu Tsewang's young son arrived with a share of freshly cut meat for his aunt.

"Oh, honey, you didn't need to bring that. I don't eat *nyinsha* [meat of an animal killed the same day]. Besides, today I'm on a fast." After a long sigh, she added, "I'm preparing the midday meal right now."

But what can a young boy know of an old woman's sigh? He placed the cuts of meat inside the tent and skipped off. Ama Huamo called out after him, "Lhakho! Tell Ache Drolkar that I need some help softening a sheepskin!"

A moment passed. Suddenly a sob rose and caught in her throat. Perhaps it was Drolkar's situation that came to mind. "Now my niece will have to go. How can that beast even think about giving his daughter away to some farmer? It's like they say: old people are powerless. Am I invisible to him? As if I haven't had experience with in-laws! Marrying her off without any choice! She may be a devoted daughter, but it will certainly crush her. It's never easy holding one's own under a mother-in-law's thumb. Had she agreed to it herself—farmers or not—it wouldn't matter *where* she went; she could stand any amount of her mother-in-law's ill will. Honestly! Are those two folks half-crazy? If they weren't planning to find a *mogwa* [a husband who lives in the home of his in-laws] for their only daughter, why did they send their two sons off to be monks? Oh my goodness! Now look, ignorant old woman that I am—reaping the bad *karma* of unmindful speech. It's a blessing from Kunchog Sum that I have so many nephews who are monks, right? But once they've given their daughter away, my sister-in-law will have to suffer what I did. And now they don't have any sons to get a daughter-in-law. *Uh, oh.* The tea has boiled over." She hastily removed the kettle from the stove, burning her hands as she set it on the ground.

Akhu Norbum's old dog is barking and rattling his chain. A visitor must have arrived. But I am drawn to look back at Ama Huamo. "Pity," I think. "Not until the day she dies will this old woman's lonely conversations cease."

4

Oh. The visitor is Akhu Norbum's younger brother, who was offered to a couple many years ago to be raised as their foster son in Dragmar Village. Really, it's just like the old saying: "Mistaking animals provokes a fight, but mistaking people—laughter." Just look. Akhu Norbum and his younger brother resemble each other in every feature: the strong but slightly stooped frame, the aquiline nose, broad forehead, jaunty chin, and long thick beard—even the way their lips twist to the right when they laugh. Nevertheless, one can be sure who's older and who's younger by the amount of white hair they have, the depth of their wrinkles, and their temperaments.

Looking exhausted, the younger brother took off his felt hat and laid it on the ground. He wiped his face several times and huffed. "*Ah, la la la!* It's so far! I rode that blessed horse nonstop."

Akhu Norbum inhaled from his pipe and asked, "How was your family's party? We couldn't go. The two of us were just leaving for Lhasa at the time . . . How old is your daughter-in-law anyway?"

"The party wasn't bad. She's sixteen."

"Good, good. It's good if there's someone who can take on the busy work."

Akhu Norbum's wife sat in the doorway stirring the *chura* that she'd laid out to dry. "It's hard to find such a daughter-in-law these days. Druglha Jyal gave that girl's family fifteen hundred *yuan,* a horse, seventy bottles of *chang,* and forty sets of clothes just to get her as a daughter-in-law. And then later, he still had to take more clothes, turquoise, coral, and whatnot for the girl herself. I heard that her father was saying that if the wager for the hand of Drugmo [heroine of the Gesar epic] was a horse race, then wealth could certainly win *his* daughter. He said that unless he got enough turquoise and coral to measure by the kilo and a beaver skin at least two handspans wide, then it would be meaningless to say he'd acquired any real wealth, and one might as well say, 'Drugmo was a nobody.' A family like ours—really!—we could never match that, even if we emptied our grazing yard out front. The Druglha Jyal family has relatives everywhere, enough wealth to fill the sky. Pride like that can't lose." She tossed a piece of dried cheese in her mouth and chewed on it while she shuffled inside and took her seat next to Akhu Norbum. "Now let's have tea. Never mind breakfast. I haven't had time to set this bum down since dawn."

Truly. Clearing dung from the yard, spinning and weaving—for women of the grassland, such endless work is fusing their flesh to their skin and distilling their bones. Yet, far from being bored, they feel these chores should be done in high spirits. See for yourself. Akhu Norbum's wife, Ama Drolma, is now sixty, but still she . . . Oh, it's too sad to talk about just now.

"Uncle, have some tea."

"*Ya,* such a sweet girl." Akhu Norbum's younger brother took the cup and set it on the ground. He glanced again at Drolkar and addressed his brother, "I came here today because of this business with your daughter. Ano, what kind of man are you?! We came from the same womb. Couldn't you have at least discussed it with me?"

Ama Drolma, who had never approved of the marriage, aired her frustration. "You're absolutely right! I can't even talk to him about this business! . . ."

The younger brother continued, "Our family is well known. We've always been highly regarded. If you don't uphold our honorable name and our father's estate, who will? Even if you can't decorate our good father's bones with gold, don't scatter his white hair to the bitter winds! I trust that a meat-eating hawk like our father didn't sire a shit-eating crow. You haven't consulted our uncles or said a word to our guardian aunts. Think about it! This is bound to start some serious quarrels."

"Whether I ask them or not, whether they agree to it or not, I *have* to give her to that family." Akhu Norbum puffed on his pipe as he made this pronouncement. "In the first place, the boy's father and I are sworn brothers. In the second place, we went to Lhasa together. And third, I have a lama's prophecy."

"A prophecy? Which lama's prophecy?"

Akhu Norbum took a large sip of tea and then tapped his horn-bone pipe against the bottom of his shoe. Once he'd cleared the ashes, he coughed and said, "It's not your fault you don't understand. This business started forty years ago. Drolkar, could you please get some *chang* for your father?"

> *I make this offering to the lamas, the* yidam, *and Kunchog Sum.*
> *I make this offering to the noble* dakini *protectors.*
> *I make this offering to the eight families of god,*
>   *the* nagas, *and the six spirit families.*

For a few moments, Akhu Norbum's tent was filled with the aroma of *chang* and the murmur of his chanting. "Of course, only an old couple like us knows about this stuff. Again, it's like that old saying: 'No one has faith when the lama's present, but when your faith is there, the lama isn't.' He was *so* compassionate—my lama—but now he's already passed away." He gulped down some *chang* and stared at his younger brother. "*Ya*, I forget. How old were you when they sent you to live there?"

His brother replied, "I must have been about eight."

"*Ya*, that's right. That's right. It was four years after you left. Our father —bless him—he took me to Lhasa, on foot. Gompo Kyab, who's county governor now, and Kalbha—do you know him, director of the cultural bureau? We all travelled to Lhasa together. It took us a full year—there and back. Can you imagine? We certainly were something in the old days, huh?" A proud smile came over his face. He swallowed some more *chang* and continued, "I was eighteen at the time. So proud of myself—my long hair all braided and wrapped around my head. Of course, we *did* have to carry a sack and beg for food. *Heh, heh.* Kalzang's father—you probably don't know him . . . *Om mani padme hum.* That was when he and five other old people drowned—swept away looking for a place to cross the Drichu. Of course, with such a pure goal they must be in a higher realm now. Several of the people we met on the way we already knew. One of these was this friend to whom I'm bound by oath. I don't know why, but we felt really close to each other. On the way back, we met a famous lama from Kham and told him about our friendship. The lama said, 'You two are connected by good *karma*. It is really rare to have a son in the male tiger year and a daughter in the female dragon year, but . . . *ha, ha, ha.*' The way he laughed is still clear in my mind. Based on what the lama said, we made a pledge then, but never entirely believed that anything like this would actually happen. We met again, because of our *karma*, shortly after the Cultural Revolution. Only then did we discover that everything the lama had predicted had come true—his son, my daughter, even their birth years and signs. But the lama was killed many years ago in a struggle during the Cultural Revolution. I've never met a Buddhist like him. He knew exactly what would happen." Whether Akhu Norbum lost himself in reminiscences about his pilgrimage or had come to the end of his story—I don't know. But it goes without saying that he sat sipping his *chang* for some time.

As she wiped the tears from her eyes, Ama Drolma turned to her brother-in-law and asked, "Now what to do? Never mind how different farming is compared to a nomad's life—we won't be able to see her even when we're on our deathbed."

"I won't give her away. No, I just won't do it. This niece means as much to me as the moustache on my face or the hair on my body. Don't *I* have any rights in this?"

Kunchog Sum! This younger brother is emphatic too! Perhaps alcohol, which fortifies tongues and emboldens hearts, caused a quarrel to explode between these two brothers—like the sparks that fly when metal strikes metal. But, after all, what significance do farts have if everyone's asleep? What meaning is there in chang-*laced speech?*

5

While they were milking together, Ama Drolma took the opportunity to say, "Drolkar, I heard that Akhu Hualo's family has just returned and set up camp again this year on the back slope of the mountain. I'm sure their son Wema Dorje will visit you tonight, but it would be good if you kept this marriage matter to yourself for a while. Otherwise . . ."

Even as her mother spoke, tears began to fall like a string of pearls from Drolkar's eyes, onto her turquoise and coral necklace—only to sink into her heart again. The sight pierced Ama Drolma's own heart with a thorn of anguish, since she herself had endured much and had few happy tales to tell. Wiping tears from her own eyes with the backs of her milk-caked hands, she continued, "It's like they say: 'A woman—tressed and to be wed—should leave her father behind, however good his name, for her husband ahead, however poor his name.' What is there to do but go?"

Ama Drolma spoke more or less decisively, but when she saw the broken hope in Drolkar's eyes and the tears she shed and heard the sound of her daughter's listless milking, the mother's heart was suddenly gripped with fear. She thought of the saying "The fox smoked out of its lair escapes only to sacrifice its life." Might her daughter look for a way to take her own life if her mental suffering grew too painful? Ama Drolma quickly added in a softer voice, "Honey, don't cry. Look, it's not your father's fault. And even though all of this is the fate given to you by Kunchog Sum, we still have to discuss it with the elders. It's possible that you won't even be given away."

Drolkar. Where did Drolkar go? Oh, she's finished milking the *drimo*, Blaze. Now she's milking Chestnut. Though from her size the *tulma* looked young, her horns had grown sharp and held a certain strength, a boundless, untamed spirit. Her body, strong and fleshy, evoked autumn's abundance. From time to time, the *tulma* would toss her horns with displeasure, switch her tail sadly, or even give some warning kicks. Nevertheless, Drolkar had laid her head upon the *tulma*'s haunch, crying softly with frustration— perhaps she was listening to her mother. She wanted to tell this *tulma* with silent, gentle words all the stories she had strung on the ribbon of her mind —stories of women who had come from other plains, stories of the countless brides who had left this grassland home. But—*bang!* The *tulma* unleashed a frustrated kick straight at the small milk bucket. She turned towards her calf and lowed, then ran off, leaving milky hoofprints. As Drolkar watched the retreating *tulma,* she was overwhelmed with intense anger. Gradually, the sense rose in her that this anger had several causes. At the same time, she felt admiration for the *tulma*'s youthful courage to resist. But with a deep sigh and eyes that had turned again into pools of sorrow, she stared at the milk for a long time—watching it seep into the grass. Then she slowly wiped up some milk with her hand and smeared it respectfully across her forehead.

Usually, Ama Drolma would let out an endless string of curses if even a cup of milk were lost. But today she needed to be absolutely patient.

Akhu Norbum's yard was gradually suspended in particles of darkness. Mother and daughter remained, breathing in the air, each sitting with her own recollections and tears. There was nothing left to say. And yet still there sounded in the dark the endless milking of the grassland—*sshh, sshh, sshh, sshh . . .*

Translation by Lauran R. Hartley

Silhouette, Lamayuru, April 27, 1987
From a rooftop, a young lama awaits the procession.
Photograph by Karl-Einar Löfqvist

The Waterfall and Fragrant Flowers: The Development of Tibetan Literature Since 1950 ———————————

Modern Tibetan literature is largely unknown in the West, and has been ignored by the field of traditional Tibetan studies, which considers it of little interest. Over the past four decades, however, the Tibetan language and literary production have diverged from the usages and genres of the literature of the past, and thus there is a need to study and read it in light of the many fundamental changes that have occurred.

Traditionally, Tibetan society has always been highly literate and has placed great value on literary activities and creation; part of the reason is that much of the literary production in the premodern period focused on Buddhism and was composed mainly of philosophical texts and liturgical and biographical accounts of lamas. Although there was also a body of secular texts comprising various types of histories *(lo rgyus, rgyal rabs, chos 'byung)*, biographical literature *(rnam thar)*, aphoristic writings *(legs bshad)*, oral folk songs *(glu gzas)*, bardic tales, and folk stories *(sgrung gtam)*, Buddhism cemented all literary creativity in Tibet.

Poetry *(snyen ngag)* dominated the secular literary tradition, inheriting both content and style from Indian Sanskrit conventions. *The Mirror of Poetry (snyen ngag me long),* by the seventh-century Indian scholar Dandin, served as a paradigm. As a consequence, contemporary Tibetan critics such as Ju Kalzang *('ju skal bzang)* and Dhondup Gyal *(don grub rgyal)* have been scathingly derisive about traditional poetry, condemning it as nothing more than eulogy *(bstod pa)*.

The sole example of a premodern secular novel is an eighteenth-century work, *The Tale of the Incomparable Youth (gzhun nu zla med kyi gtam rgyud)*, written by Do Khar Tsering Wangyal *(mdo mkha tshe ring dbang rgyal)*. The novel is composed in verse in a classical style drawn from such Indian epics as the Ramayana. The primary focus of the secular narrative, however, has been shifted from religion to romantic adventure. For the first time, the adventures of the protagonist are at the center of the story, with religion forming only the subtext.

Despite the existence of such secular works, fiction as modern Western authors would define it—that is, work of an author's imagination, in the form of short stories and novels—had no place in traditional Tibetan literature. Indeed, if we use a modern Western definition of literature, virtually no secular literature existed in Tibet until very recently. In fact, most critics in Tibet would tend to say that such a literature began only in the early 1980s.

A new Tibetan literature emerged only after the establishment of Communist Chinese rule in Tibetan-speaking areas. The Chinese government established not only Communist political and administrative control of Tibet, but also brought about Tibet's first encounter with the modern world—specifically, an engagement with a technologically advanced society imbued with a modern and materialistic ideology. The missionary zeal of the new Communist regime was focused on incorporating Tibet into the great "motherland," and in doing so to "civilize" this underdeveloped, backward region. In this regard, there are many similarities between Western colonial rule and Chinese colonization of Tibet. In both cases, colonialism caused a dislocation of identity and traditional epistemology in the indigenous social system and culture. Like other colonial rulers, China not only asserted territorial claims but also set out to control the minds of the natives.

The notion of underdevelopment (rjes lus) is crucial to understanding the nature of Chinese rule in Tibet. The term implies that Tibet lagged behind in technology and, more important, that it was culturally stagnant and backward. Therefore, "liberation of the serfs" was intended to result in both economic emancipation and the cultural empowerment of the people. In this process, language and literature became the focus of colonial exchange. And it was in this context that a new literature emerged in Tibet.

Chinese rule had an immediate and striking impact on the Tibetan language at every level because initially it was the principal medium used by the Communists to convey their message. At this stage, Tibetan intellectuals were recruited as "important patriotic personages"—a class that would mediate between the past and the present. Because many of the early literary elite came from monasteries and the religious community, the Chinese assumed that they would be trusted by the masses. The Communists used them and their literary skills not only to mediate but also to articulate the new course for Tibetan society, and so literary discourse in the early stages was narrowly focused on the question of a new lexicon and terminology (tha snyed). A new Tibetan lexicon was needed to translate the Communist propaganda and Marxist ideology that had driven the Communist revolution in China. It's worth noting that, unlike Western colonialists, who generally did not intend to overthrow the traditional ideology of their subjugated territories, the Communists came to Tibet with the explicit intention of replacing the existing socio-ideological system.

Modification and reform of the Tibetan language was therefore considered necessary to mold the thoughts and actions of the people. In the early 1950s, the Communists acted with the belief that the social transformation would be gradual, and that it would proceed with the consent of the people. Change was to be introduced slowly by both overt and covert means: overtly by appropriating existing institutions and ideology to win over the people; and covertly by undermining the ruling order. The knowledge and skills of the traditional literary elite could be exploited for the revolutionary cause; ironically, the class position given to these writers also made them targets for attack. Indeed, the literary production of the Tibetan elite was soon used against them, to undermine their privileged position in society.

Initially, then, the Communists' concern with the Tibetan language was primarily related to the practicality of governing a country that—whatever China's historical and legal justification for claiming Tibet to be a part of China—had been and wished to remain fundamentally separate. At this time, literary activities involved publishing translations of Communist propaganda, and so the literary elite debated how to translate into Tibetan such concepts in the Communist lexicon as *people, democracy, class, liberation,* and *exploitation.* They also discussed whether there was a need for a written textual basis for coining new terms, or whether the new terms should be derived from colloquial usages. Clearly, printing technologies and presses were not brought into Tibet by the Chinese in order to promote literary creativity; rather, they were there for the Party and its propaganda needs.

During the Cultural Revolution (1966–1976), the Chinese emphatically denied the existence of a separate Tibetan identity, and under the Communist slogan "destroy the Four Olds," all aspects of Tibetan life and custom were attacked. The Party imposed total uniformity on culture and lifestyle throughout China. In Tibet, almost all publishing in the Tibetan language ceased, except for Party propaganda and translations of articles from Chinese newspapers. Consequently, the sole marker of distinction that remained for the Tibetan people was the spoken language.

Only after the death of Mao and the subsequent emergence of new leadership under Deng Xiaoping did unprecedented change come to China. The Party's policy towards intellectuals underwent a transformation, and at the same time the Party's policies toward so-called minorities began to change as well. The policy of overt assimilation was abandoned, to be replaced by policies of cultural autonomy. These changes had far-reaching consequences for Tibetans.

Tibetans generally agree that when the authorities started to allow Tibet some degree of autonomy in expressing its cultural identity—shortly after the Third Plenum of the Eleventh Central Committee, in 1979—modern Tibetan literature began. Tibetan Buddhism, suppressed for over twenty years, was also revived.

In 1980, the first journal devoted to new writing was *Tibetan Literature and Art (bod kyi rtsom rig rgyud tsal).* Published by the Tibet Autonomous Region (TAR) Writers' Association, the inaugural issue comprised four short stories: "Auspicious Flower" *(skal zang mi tog),* "Yangchen" *(dbyang chen),* "Soil of the Native Land" *(pa yul gyi sa),* and "Honored Person" *(sdi dbang gis gson pa'i mi).* These stories had been written several years earlier and had already been published in Chinese magazines; all were about Tibet and had been written in Chinese by Tibetans. Their primary aim was to persuade Chinese readers of the moral justification for the "liberation" of Tibet by portraying the People's Liberation Army as freeing Tibetans from the "dark period" of feudal exploitation that had previously prevailed. The fact that the stories were written by Tibetans—the muted voice of Tibetan serfs speaking against oppressive feudal lords—gave them an air of authenticity. All were published widely and used in schools.

The translation of these stories from Chinese into Tibetan implied that there were no Tibetans writing in their own language at this time. Indeed, in 1979 when a Swedish journalist arrived in Lhasa with the intention of meeting contemporary Tibetan writers, the Cultural Department of the TAR Government was unable to produce a single one. According to Tenzin Namgyal, a former editor of *Tibetan Literature and Art,* this had a great impact on Tibetans working in the Cultural Department and inspired them to encourage Tibetans to begin writing stories.

Later, critics realized that no Tibetans had been producing fiction primarily because they were unsure what was permissible under Party policy. A more cynical observation is that the four stories in the first issue of *Tibetan Literature and Art* were deliberately selected to establish precisely the guidelines on style and content favored by the Party; this seemed especially true since all four dealt with the crimes of the Tibetan "feudal" society and the miserable lives of the working class.

Whatever the motive for publication, the first edition of *Tibetan Literature and Art* initiated a burning debate. What is Tibetan literature? What should be the defining factor: the ethnic origin of the author, the subject matter, or the language? The first edition of *Tibetan Literature and Art* seemed to suggest that subject matter and the author's ethnic origin defined Tibetan literature.

A year later, a new publication called *Light Rain (sbrang char)* was issued in Amdo, in the far northeastern corner of the Tibetan-speaking world. The title suggests the nurturing of young seedlings and evokes images of fertility, luxuriance, and the regenerative power of rainwater. Aptly titled, *Light Rain* was to become the premier literary journal in Tibet. More than any other publication, it shaped and established the foundation of modern Tibetan literature.

The editors of *Light Rain* deliberately challenged the views of *Tibetan Literature and Art* by setting a policy of publishing only stories written in

Tibetan; furthermore, they would publish translated stories only if they had been written originally in Tibetan. This suggests that the editors felt Tibetan literature should be defined not by the subject matter or the ethnicity of the author, but by the language alone. The readers concurred. One reader insisted that if the journal published stories translated from Chinese, it would lose its unique nature and become neither "a goat nor a sheep" *(ra ma lug tu 'gyur).*

A number of magazines soon emerged, including *New Moon (zla zer), Tibetan Popular Arts (bod kyi mang tshogs sgyutsal), Youthful Sun (nye gzhon), Lhoka Literature and Arts (lho kha'i rtsom rig rgyu tsal), Kyichu River of Lhasa (lha sa'i skyed chu),* and *Snowy Mountains (gangs dkar ri bo).* In the words of one Tibetan poet, the magazines "blossomed like spring flowers."

These journals were never truly independent, but continued to fall under the control of larger associations. Current examples include *Tibetan Literature and Art,* published by the Tibet Autonomous Region Writers' Association; *Light Rain,* published under the auspices of the Qinghai Writers' Association; and such magazines as *Snowy Mountains,* published by the trade unions.

In addition to these journals, many unofficial publications and magazines—from colleges and even monasteries—began to circulate in local areas. In Amdo, there was a mushrooming of unofficial publications, such as *Song of the Blue Lake (mtsho sngon po'i glu dbyang), A New Shoot (myug gsar), Sound of a Sheep ('ba' rgra),* and *The Eastern Mountain (shar dung ri).* Published in cyclo style, the journals were poorly printed and were distributed only in local areas.

In this early period, the subject matter of a typical story was predominantly the evils of the old society. For example, "A Story of Three Sisters" *(bu mo spon gsum gyi rnam thar),* written by Kalsang Namdrol and published in *Tibetan Literature and Art,* tells of the sufferings of three sisters—Patok, Botrik, and Tsamcho—at the hands of a soldier, a son of an aristocrat, and a lama (these representing the three feudal lords of old Tibet). By describing the evil behavior of these three men, the story attempts to show the backwardness and oppressiveness of the old society.

Between 1980 and 1984, such stories condemning the evils of the old society and praising the benefits of the peaceful Chinese liberation were regularly published in *Tibetan Literature and Art.* They were intended to convince the younger generation of Tibetans, those born after 1950, that Communist policies in Tibet were justified. This was particularly important after 1980 because, by then, most people were complaining not about the evils of feudal Tibet but about the suffering they and their parents had endured during the Cultural Revolution.

Fiction writing at this time was confined to the short-story form because the only medium for publication was magazines. In 1982, however, the first full-length Tibetan novel was published: *An Auspicious Flower (kalsang metok)*, written by Jamphel Gyatso, an academic working at the Academy of Social Sciences in Beijing. From a poor family in Bathang in Eastern Tibet, Jamphel Gyatso had joined the invading People's Liberation Army at a young age and had been trained as a translator. *An Auspicious Flower* is written in the style of socialist realism and has stereotypical characterizations. Set at the time of the Chinese invasion, the novel celebrates the "unwavering service performed by the People's Liberation Army for the Tibetan people" in liberating the masses. In the epilogue, the author says that he wrote the book in order to depict the sacrifices made by the People's Liberation Army.

The book received much praise and won a prize for the best novel by a minority national in China. Among the Tibetan populace, however, the book was recognized as Party propaganda, and the author was criticized for denigrating Tibetan society while internalizing the colonizer's image of Tibet as "a hell on earth" before the Chinese invasion. Despite the novel's propagandistic style and content, it nevertheless made innovations in the use of simple and readable language.

In 1985, the second Tibetan novel, *The Turquoise Crown (gtsug gyu)*, appeared as part of the celebration of the twentieth anniversary of the founding of the TAR and was serialized in *Tibetan Literature and Art*. The author was Paljor Langdun, a great-nephew of the Thirteenth Dalai Lama. As a young boy, Paljor had studied in Darjeeling, India, and in the fifties had travelled to China to further his education. The subject of the novel is the internal rivalries among the aristocracy of the old Tibetan society. The story was intended to portray "the exterior beauty and the internal rottenness of the aristocracy and power holding classes," and readers were asked to empathize with the suffering of the working class. True to the Party line, aristocrats and landlords are once again represented as serving only their own class interests. The protagonist, Palden, is described as a slave with deep hatred for his oppressors. Through Palden's actions, we are shown that the overthrow of the ruling class is natural because the hatred of the working class cannot be suppressed.

Despite its very narrow and superficial theme, *The Turquoise Crown* was an instant bestseller. It is now out of print, and when I was last in Lhasa I was unable to find anyone who would part with a copy! Though propagandistic, the book was widely read and liked by Tibetans for its use of language and its portrayal of old ways of life. Readers tended to dismiss the obvious propaganda in the novel as simply a prerequisite for publication, and therefore focused on the language and how the narrative moved them. The plot has been described as a "turquoise rosary," meaning that it grips the reader.

While the novel follows traditional Tibetan grammatical and stylistic rules, *The Turquoise Crown* also manages to give everyday conversation a literary flavor. The mixture of colloquial speech and literary form made the novel accessible to the masses; thus it was able to meet one of the new literary criteria. *The Turquoise Crown* and *An Auspicious Flower* were thus landmarks in the development of modern Tibetan literature.

After 1985, a new theme began to emerge in Tibetan short stories. This, too, was not an accident but the result of Party policy to "expose the crimes of the Gang of Four and praise the Four Modernizations." The policy allowed Tibetans for the first time to write and speak about the painful period after the "peaceful liberation" of Tibet. A number of stories appeared depicting life during the Cultural Revolution and the suffering endured by the people. Gopo Lin, a critic from Kham writing in *Light Rain* in 1989, called these "the stories of the wounded mind of Tibet" *(bod kyi sems rma'i sgrung gtam)*. The popular term "literature of the wounded" had appeared in China in 1979. A typical story of this kind is "Old Man Tsering's Misunderstanding." The main character, Tsering, is persecuted during the Cultural Revolution for following the "capitalist road"; but afterwards his skill as an entrepreneur is appreciated and encouraged.

Most of these stories about the Cultural Revolution were not original and did not critically analyze or explore the deeper experience of that nightmarish period. However, two stories published in the early eighties in *Tibetan Literature and Art* were exceptional. While they lacked immediate identification as "scar literature," later commentators quickly saw in them representations of the Cultural Revolution. These two stories, "The Forest After a Storm" *(char shul gyi nags tshal)* by Namdrol and "A Dispute in a Garden" *(me tog ldum ra'i nang gi klan ka)* by Paljor, are written in an allegorical style and borrow much from folktales and traditional genres, such as the dispute between Tea and Beer.

The former is written in the style of a folktale *(sgrung)*. The narrative is in prose, but the speech of the main protagonists is in verse. In the story, a group of animals have to rebuild their forest dwellings after a storm, which evidently represents the Cultural Revolution. Remarkably, the characterizations of the animals are reminiscent of George Orwell's *Animal Farm.*

Paljor's "A Dispute in a Garden" is regarded as one of the finest works of prose written in Tibetan. The language and style of the story are significantly more sophisticated than those of comparable works, and the author makes little attempt to comply with the demand that the language be accessible to the masses. Using old-fashioned language, the narrative has flowers in a garden disputing who is the most beautiful; in order to claim the coveted title, each behaves selfishly and ruthlessly.

These two short stories resist the standard treatment of the Cultural Revolution in fiction. Rather than merely justifying the policies of the new leadership under Deng Xiaoping, the authors look deeply into their own experiences, questioning the nature of humanity and human relationships. The Cultural Revolution, like all traumatic events, brought to the surface the best and worst human emotions, including greed. By depicting allegorically how characters behave in an evil manner in order to achieve their own goals, the authors ask if human nature is inherently selfish or altruistic.

In essence, this opening of literature to other kinds of expression was an invention of the Chinese authorities, designed to serve a political need. For their part, the authorities saw a dual role for literature: extolling *(bstod bsnags byas)* the virtues of the revolution and exposing *(ther 'don)* the criminality of feudalism, perpetuated by enemies of the state. The literary revolution they designed was meant to sever the link with Tibet's past and usher in a new period of socialism under the tutelage of the Chinese Communist Party. To this end, the reforms were meant to leave no room for ambiguity or freedom of expression.

Ultimately, the authorities hoped that literature would establish a secular humanistic tradition to replace religion as the main discourse of public and private morality. And this educational function of literature—to mold people's thoughts and train citizens how to behave—was made a significant part of the burden that a writer under Communism was required to shoulder. The emerging generation of Tibetan writers was expected to be the vanguard of socialist modernization, and their work—through exemplary plots and appeals to rationalism—was expected to urge the people, by peaceful means, to open their mental horizons *(blo sgo phye)* and to embrace China's socialist modernism *(gsar rje).*

Of course, this is the official version of literature's function, and it is disputable whether all writers and artists agreed with it in the 1980s any more than they do today. It was clear, however—as it is now—that without conformity to Party policy there was no possibility for publication.

In the period after 1980, the Tibetan intellectual community—traditional scholars educated in the monasteries and a young generation of intellectuals trained in universities in China—emerged from the Cultural Revolution severely traumatized. They had witnessed attacks on every aspect of Tibetan culture and identity. Now, when the Party allowed even a small opportunity for expression, the intellectual community plunged into a debate on how best to make use of the degree of openness that the new policies allowed. Traditionalists in the community argued that the weight of intellectual labor should be directed towards restoring what had been lost and destroyed; this group embarked on a mission to salvage and reproduce damaged manuscripts. Consequently, during the eighties there was a renaissance in Tibetan publications, and a large number of rare manuscripts and texts began to enter the public domain.

At the same time, a group of young intellectuals believed that the main task facing Tibet was what they called "innovation." They believed that Tibet had suffered under the hands of the Communists not only because of the military and political might of the Chinese, but also because there was an inherent weakness in Tibetan culture: its inability to confront and integrate the forces of change.

Among the writers of the Tibetan intellectual community to emerge from this debate was a young man named Dhondup Gyal (1953–1985). Now considered the founder of modern Tibetan literature, he was born in a small village in Gurong Phuba in the Nangra district of Amdo in 1953, a few years after the Communists came to power. Dhondup Gyal was therefore from the first generation born after liberation—those who supposedly were the main beneficiaries of the Communist revolution. However, like that of so many of his generation, his education was to come to an abrupt end during the Cultural Revolution.

In 1979, Dhondup Gyal enrolled at Beijing Central Nationalities Institute and began to study under the prominent Tibetan scholar Dungkar Lobsang Trinley, who remembers him as a brilliant student with a perfect memory. "He would sit in the class without opening a notebook, but a few days later he would recall everything he had heard," Trinley has said.

In 1983, Dhondup Gyal published a poem called "Waterfall of Youth" *(lang tsho'i rbab chu),* which caused a sensation among Tibetans. The poem was like nothing they had ever read. Not only did it evidence literary innovation, but it contained a bold and nationalistic political statement. The poem fervently appealed to Tibetans to embrace modernism as a means of regenerating their culture and national pride, and beseeched the youth to shake off the past and march proudly towards their future.

This boldness in style and politics was characteristic of Dhondup Gyal's writings. For the first time, the possibility emerged that, through the medium of poetry and fiction, a genuine discourse on Tibetan modernity could occur. At stake were the future direction of Tibet and Tibetan identity in the latter half of the twentieth century.

Dhondup Gyal's work was a turning point because, while criticism was unacceptable to the Chinese authorities, he showed that it was nevertheless possible to speak implicitly about the "wound inflicted on the mind of the Tibetans" *(bod kyi sems kyi rma),* referring to the period under the leadership of the Gang of Four.

Furthermore, he was able to raise the issue of Tibet's status as subaltern, which was intrinsic to a debate about modernization. At this time, the founders of literary journals saw their task as nothing less than the regeneration of Tibetan culture and identity, and one of the phrases that dominated Tibetan literature between 1980 and 1987 was *mi rigs kyi la rgya,* which means "honor, pride, allegiance to nationality." Literature that raised this subject was possible because indigenous discourse on Tibet's alterity paralleled state-sponsored discourse on modernization—that is, the Four Modernizations. The authorities saw the emerging debate in Tibetan literature as conforming to the Party's will—thus lessening the Party's fear of a possible challenge to official definitions—but overlooked the larger issues being addressed in the writing.

The debate inevitably produced a confrontation between traditionalists and modernists. While the modernists saw tradition ("old habits") as impediments to change, others pointed out that tradition was the most significant marker of Tibetan separateness from the colonizer. Because of Party restraints, traditionalists could not make their counterarguments publicly. However, the actual process and practice of revitalization demonstrated that a large portion of the populace favored the use of tradition as a way to restore Tibet's selfhood and define it as separate from China.

Despite obstacles, this infant literature was audacious, and it is fitting that Tibetan critics compare the period to the May Fourth literary movement in China, which brought debates about modernity into the forefront of intellectual discourse in the twenties and thirties. While a characteristic of this early period of Tibetan literature was writers' condemnation of the "old society," the best work can be distinguished from the turgid style favored by the Party and from the stereotyped proletarian heroes and demonic feudal lords prevalent in propaganda. While condemning the past, Dhondup Gyal and other new writers made no attempt to provide a political justification for the present. Nor did they make a clear distinction between a "bad past" and a "good future." Significantly, they portrayed a more complex relationship between past and present; and the imperfections of the old Tibetan society were described along with its accomplishments.

In a number of short stories, poems, and articles, Dhondup Gyal championed modernism. However, his advocacy did not include the official characterization of Tibet as underdeveloped. In his poem "Waterfall of Youth," for example, he demonstrates that he feels the only path for Tibet to follow is embracing "the bride of science and technology." In this verse from the poem, he makes it clear that the past cannot be a guide to the future:

> The thousand brilliant accomplishments of the past
> cannot serve today's purpose,
> yesterday's salty water cannot quench today's thirsts,
> the withered body of history is lifeless
> without the soul of today,
> the pulse of progress will not beat,
> the blood of progress will not flow

Tibet's past is compared to "salty water" and a "withered body" that lacks the ability to regenerate itself. In a poem published five years later, "A Pulsating Heart at the Edge of a Cliff" (*'di na yang drag tu mchong lding byed bzhin pa'i snying gson po zhig 'dug*), he associates the old Tibet with conservatism (*rnyeng zhen*), isolationism (*bag 'khums*), and reactionary thinking. He asks, Why is it so difficult to plant new ideas, new habits, and new doctrines in the Land of Snows?

In short stories and articles as well as in poetry, Dhondup Gyal explored the urgent need for Tibet to modernize. His ideas crystallized in a brilliant polemical essay, "A Narrow Footpath" *(rkang lam phra mo)*, published in *Light Rain* in 1984. The essay begins with a group of old men in a village who are gazing towards a narrow footpath that leads away from the village. The footpath is full of historical significance, and the villagers are greatly attached to it. Legend has it that the mythical King Gesar once traversed the path and that Trehue Jangchup Sepa, the primogenitor of the Tibetan race, also travelled on it. Other villagers assert that the path was created by Lhalung Palgyi Dorji, a monk who assassinated the anti-Buddhist King Lang Dharma.

The narrator of "A Narrow Footpath" is a young boy. He walks on the path to school every day, wondering why the old people of the village do not use the new road below the village. For him, the ancient path evokes wonder at the courage, innovation, and bravery of his ancestors, but it also poses a question: If our ancestors could carve this path, why has the current generation failed to make any improvements and allowed it to fall into such a dilapidated state?

For Dhondup Gyal, the narrow path is a metaphor for Tibet's parochialism, conservatism, and confinement. The old people who venerate the past do not want to change. Rather than seeing history as containing the potential for innovation, the traditionalists insist that their way of life is immutable, and they fear progress. Dhondup Gyal concludes that the narrow path cannot teach contemporary Tibet much about the spirits of science and technology, that traditional cultural monuments cannot provide the Tibetan people with "nourishment and energy for the invention of a new culture." We can understand that it is Dhondup Gyal's own voice calling for change when the boy narrator declares that he will travel to school on the new road.

"A Narrow Footpath" was published under a pseudonym and was seen by many as an attack on traditional culture, which offended conservative sections of the Tibetan community. Dhondup Gyal reportedly received death threats after its publication. However, he remained undaunted and continued to explore the theme of tradition versus modernity. In each, he did not blindly condemn the "old society," but rather encouraged readers to question all power and authority, and this gave Tibetan literature a purpose different from that assigned to it by the Party.

Related to the question of modernization, another difficult subject for Tibetan writers was, and still is, religion. At a practical level, the Party's policy is to view religion as obstructing economic modernization and to regard religion's persistence and popularity in society as contradicting socialism. It is through their religion, however, that Tibetans have always found their identity. Consequently, the early Party practice of overtly denigrating Tibetan Buddhism was seen by the people as undermining Tibetan selfhood, and it gradually became clear to the Party that their direct attacks and coercive methods had completely failed. Therefore, in the new period, the Party decided to challenge the influence of religion indirectly—through literature. Writing that contested the authority of religion and portrayed religious figures negatively was encouraged. (This is why many Tibetan readers continue to see all modern literature as nothing but a tool of the Chinese Communist Party.)

Dhondup Gyal dealt with this question in a controversial story titled "An Incarnate Lama" *(sprul sku),* published in *Light Rain.* Set in a remote village in 1980, the first time after the Cultural Revolution that people were allowed to practice their faith freely, the story begins with the arrival of a stranger who proclaims himself to be an incarnate lama.

The form and content of the story appear similar to those favored by the authorities. The protagonist, an old man named Agu Nyima, embodies religious faith and is described as "honest and straight as an arrow." His faith is so strong that he distrusts his own knowledge. He sees evidence that the incarnate lama may not be who he claims to be—the lama contradicts himself and shows an imperfect knowledge of Buddhism—but Agu Nyima accepts the lama's explanations for these lapses and regards his own doubts as a lack of faith.

At the time of its publication, the story was seen by commentators as a good example of modern writing containing antireligious social-moral propaganda. The story appeared to warn people that religion could be used to deceive them. Whether readers interpreted it as attacking religion or merely reflecting a trend in society, the story became the subject of much debate. But Tibetans have always been well aware, of course, that there are people who wear the mask of religion in order to dupe the faithful. Therefore, a closer reading of the text—in light of the recent history of Tibet and China—might suggest that the figure of the incarnate lama represents the blind trust that people had placed in Mao and the Communist Party.

Such ambiguities are present in many modern Tibetan stories. For example, "A Sound of a Bell from a Monastery," published in *Tibetan Literature and Art,* tells of an old woman who is very sick. Her family consults a lama, who tells them that if the mother goes on a pilgrimage and hears the sound of a particular bell, she will be cured. The family makes the long journey. The old woman dies, but just before her death, she hears the sound of the gong. Describing her death, the author implies that as she hears the bell, she finds "laughter and peace" within herself. Rather than demonstrating that religion is false, the story may be suggesting that religion is useful in providing mental peace.

Clearly, writers in Tibet and China lack the freedom to explore individual sentiments and subjects explicitly. Nevertheless, we can see that their work does not always merely follow the diktats of the Party, even when it is written in Chinese and published under the eyes of the censors. Despite the constraints imposed by the state and the Party, Tibetan writers are able to bring burning issues into the foreground, and as we have seen, this stimulates politically charged debate. Although the line favored by the state and the Party is compulsory and all authors must seem to conform in order to be published, when we examine the writings themselves, their conformity is not quite so clear-cut.

Literature has become the main arena for intellectual confrontation among competing ideas in Tibet today. At the same time, literature emanating from Tibet is still in its infancy. Many works are repetitive and didactic and simply follow the Party's guidelines on art and literature. Since 1994, control over work produced by Tibetan writers has become increasingly strict. The creative energy that was released in the early eighties has been suppressed, making writers more cautious than ever.

Festival, Spitok, January 17, 1988
The annual festival at Spitok gompa *(monastery).*
Photograph by Karl-Einar Löfqvist

Get the Boat Here _____

Translator's Note

The structure of this parable is circular. Four Tibetan tourists cross a river by boat in the morning, disembark, and then wait for the boat to take them back to their hotel for the night. When the boat fails to appear, they search for it anxiously, even trying to climb a cliff so that they can see further. Finally the boat appears at the end of the day, and they return to their hotel. The circle is a fundamental symbol of Tibetan Buddhism. Human life moves in an endless round of reincarnations, and the characters' journey back and forth across the river is suggestive of one incarnation in this cycle.

The characters represent four types of people: the leader (Gangchen), the willing follower (Tenphun), the intuitive personality (the narrator), and the unwilling follower on the verge of despair (Yangnor, the lone woman). Their actions on the far bank of the river—disjointed, absurd, agitated, fearful, purposeless—reflect the Buddhist conception of human life as a meaningless illusion, inextricably bound up with suffering. The vacationers have no stake in the place where they find themselves. They poke around, pick things up, throw them away. They're on a lifelong vacation. The true nature of this meaningless existence is captured in Yangnor's vision of the gate of hell. Their preoccupation with finding a boat corresponds to a fear of not finding a conveyance to another mode of existence when life ends.

The real meaning of the story resides in the author's presentation of the paramount Buddhist virtue—compassion—in the midst of meaningless flux. After she hears a lama's mantra, Yangnor weeps, and the boatman, moved by her tears, casts into the river the huge fare he has forced the travellers to pay him—money representing attachment to the illusory things of this world. Gangchen, the group's leader, sets a destination for the next round of the travellers' circular existence: the hermit's cave, symbolic of the Buddhist struggle for detachment and illumination. The boatman repeats the lama's mantra as the group lands on shore.

Buddhism is a focal point of Tibetan resistance to the Han Chinese regime, so Sebo's Buddhist theme has political implications. Images of Han occupation—the army camp, the soldier on the boat, his rifle—are additional representations of the absurdity and suffering of daily life. But these images are fleeting. We see that Tibetan believers have torn a red strip from a Chinese flag to use as part of their five-color Buddhist prayer flag, and that the soldier of the occupying power is asleep. It is the lama on the passing boat who is awake—spiritually—and his mantra echoes across the falling night.—H. J. B.

The moment the cowhide boat touched shore, the boatman tossed the oblong paving stone on the rock-strewn bank and said, "On your way back, get the boat here."

Clay bodhisattvas lay among the rocks on the bank. Yangnor stooped down, picked one up, and put it in her pocket.

The rocks along the shore were covered with dark-green moss. Azure-green patches appeared where fish had licked the moss. The Yarlung Tsangpo River was broad as a lake, and desolate—no waterbirds flying or swimming. And no wind.

We had been wandering back and forth along the shore for hours now, seeing no sign of a boat.

"We'll never get back!" Yangnor moaned.

A line of *mani* cairns—rocks inscribed with the mantra *"Om mani padme hum"*—stretched up the ridge and out of sight. Prayer flags jutted up from each one, their staffs wound with yak hair, and from every cairn the smoke of a votive fire floated toward the sky.

"If this is the wrong place to wait for the boat, even better," Tenphun said, grinning.

"This way!" Gangchen snapped. "Come on." We followed him down a narrow path along the stretch of shore at the foot of the cliff. Sixty meters ahead, a narrow ridge jutted out into the water. We reached the foot of the ridge, then halted. Clumps of brush filled the crevices in its steep face. Carved in its smooth surface were buddhas, lines from the sutras, and wild animals.

"We'll never get back!" Yangnor moaned.

"Stop your damned whining," Gangchen growled.

Lizards slithered along the top of the ridge. As they twisted around, rocks and mud rolled down.

It really looked like we wouldn't get back. *Can't get back . . . spend the night in this devil of a place . . . no joke. If only a boat would come! Spent last night in that nice, big hotel in the mountain hollow on the other side. Tonight we're going back across the river to spend the night there again. Milk-white bathtubs, soft beds, that maid with a gray button sticking out the buttonhole of her black blouse. How about a boat!*

All of a sudden my ears vibrated. "Hear that?!" I shouted.

"Hear what?"

"Peng, peng . . ."

They turned their heads and looked around.

"Where's your damned *peng, peng?*" Gangchen demanded.

"Maybe there'll be a boat on the other side of this ridge," Tenphun said.

Gangchen looked around. "Let's go," he ordered and then began climbing. We followed him. Soon the rock face got so smooth you couldn't find a foothold. We stopped, pressed ourselves against the rock face, and glanced down through the crooks of our arms.

"I can't take it," Yangnor wailed. "Gangchen, I can't take it!"

Gangchen cursed, reached up, and felt around on the top of the rock shelf, then leaped, wriggled, and pulled himself up.

"See anything?" Tenphun asked.

"I'm not goddamned standing yet!" Gangchen snapped, still panting.

"Wait a second till you stand up. See a boat?"

"Boat, my ass."

I imitated Gangchen's maneuver and climbed up beside him.

Further downstream, where the river narrowed, I could see a plank bridge to the other side. We could have gotten over, but somebody had pulled the plank to the other side.

"What about me?" Yangnor called, her two hands waving wildly.

Gangchen tested the edge with his toe, but couldn't get a firm foothold. He told me to squat behind him, away from the ledge, and grab him by the belt. "Wait a minute. Let's see if there's any trouble with the belt. Like that . . . But you better back off from me a little. Or your face will be sticking right in my ass." He laughed.

I squatted down as far back as I could, then pulled tight on his belt. He spread his legs, framing my field of vision in an isosceles triangle. The crotch of his trousers, at the apex of the triangle, bit into the crimson sun. Sunset over mountain and river. The surface of the river was empty—not a boat anywhere. On the mountain were a golden-roofed Buddhist temple with an outdoor altar, a cobblestone road, and, further off, rows and rows of green tents: the army camp.

A small path twisted and turned from the far side of the mountain down to a little white courtyard on the shore. A five-color prayer flag fluttered on its roof. The red strip had been torn out of the Chinese flag. I could see the Chinese flag's five little yellow stars.

"Tenphun!" Gangchen yelled.

"Yuh."

"You push her up from down there."

"OK."

As soon as Gangchen gripped Yangnor's hand and started pulling, black dots filled my vision. Gangchen's belt smashed my fingers against his backbone. I wanted to move them, but I couldn't. More and more spots appeared. *Don't get yourself all worked up. Wait till Yangnor's on the ledge.*

But as soon as Yangnor's head appeared over the edge, she stopped as if some demon had gripped her. "You trying to drop me into the river?!" she screamed.

"Tenphun!" Gangchen roared.

"Yuh," he responded.

"What part of her are you pushing against?"

"Her ass."

"Listen, try again." Gangchen's head appeared beneath his crotch, blocking out the setting sun. He stared at me. "Don't you let go."

"I can't let go."

"Good," he said.

We eased Yangnor down, then tried again. *One, two, three*—up she came. Tenphun then climbed up, his forehead and the tip of his nose covered in dirt.

"Take a look at your face," Gangchen said. "You been doing prostrations?"

"If the bodhisattvas sent us a boat, I'd be glad to do a few prostrations."

Far off on the other side of the river, a cowherd waved his sheepskin whip, driving his herd toward the foot of the distant mountain. Now he turned back to give us a wave. Beyond his herd was a little village hemmed in by green trees—a sheet of smoke lingering over their branches. No boat anywhere in sight.

My throat twitched, my eardrums trembled.

"Listen!" I called out. *"Peng, peng!"*

"Hey, hell has a cowhide door," Gangchen said, pointing his finger at me. "You want a *peng, peng*"—he tapped my chest—"go knock there." Grains of sand fell from the greasy waves of his rancid-smelling hair.

He looked around. To the right was a path leading back the way we'd come, down to the water. "Come on," he commanded. Our feet scattered broken rock and sand into the river, creating muddy ripples.

The big rocks were slippery. My foot slid into a crack. Damn it, I was stuck! Gangchen and Tenphun turned around and stood on the rocks with their heads inclined to one side, looking at me. I struggled.

"What game is this?" Gangchen said, grinning.

I spread my legs, sucked in a deep breath to swell my chest (so I wouldn't fall!), and very carefully twisted my body.

"Give me your hand," Gangchen commanded.

I gave him my hand and twisted again. They pulled me out.

"How about me?" Yangnor called. She stood up on the slope, leaning downhill in the middle of the sliding stones, her arms spread like the wings of an unfledged baby eagle.

"Straighten up a little," Gangchen said, waving. "Take a step this way."

She took a step and slid.

"Take a step that way."

She took another step and slid again.

"Damn!" Gangchen stuck his hands in his pockets.

A powerful wind howled, unfurling the prayer flags and driving loose stones into the river. Yangnor's hair blew loose. She cried out and lost her balance, trembling like a bird pulled out of the water.

"I'll save you," Tenphun said, rushing toward her.

Gangchen snatched his arm. "Grabbing each other? This isn't the place." He glanced down. Brown foam swirled in the eddy. "The fish eat your softest part first. Walk," Gangchen commanded Yangnor.

Yangnor remained still.

If only there was a boat!

"Walk!" Gangchen roared.

"Walk!" Yangnor repeated. "Walk!" she repeated again. Then she pulled out of her pocket the clay bodhisattva she'd picked up on the shore that morning, and flung it in the river. "Come all the way here from Lhasa . . . For what? See some damn tourist attraction, collect these things," she mumbled. "Old relics ourselves . . . They put us on show for the blue-eyed tourists . . . ," she yammered, clapping her hands.

"Shut your stinking mouth!" Gangchen yelled.

"Walk this way, walk that way. Walk the way to hell—I can see the cowhide door!"

She took one step toward us and—*poof!*—the sun sank beneath the mountain. A savage gust of wind rushed out of the east, the prayer flags snapped wildly, and sand swirled through the air. Inside the courtyard across the river, the barking of a dog turned into a terrifying howl. Yangnor vanished.

When the sand stopped blowing, a yellow-haired woman stood on the slope below us, six feet from the river, staring blankly into the water.

"Give her a yell," Gangchen ordered.

"Yangnor," Tenphun called softly.

The woman didn't stir.

"Yangnor!" Tenphun yelled.

"Yuh," the woman finally grunted.

"Come here," Gangchen called.

The woman turned and began climbing toward us, her empty eyes staring straight ahead.

"Grab her," Gangchen told Tenphun.

She looked around. Sand fell from her hair like rain. "So this is hell?"

"Near enough!" Gangchen snapped.

The howling stopped. A man, naked from the waist down, walked out of the courtyard. He rested his head on the palm of one hand, laid the other over his crotch, and yawned, then saw us, pulled back his hips, stuck out his tongue in friendly greeting, and dashed jauntily back into the courtyard.

As if eager to be on its way, mist drifted across the river on the gentle evening breeze. The water in the crevices at our feet swelled, ebbed, and swelled, sounding like frothy blood spurting from the neck of a cow.

"*Peng, peng.*" My eardrums shuddered.

"Hmm?" Gangchen said.

"A head!" Yangnor cried.

We looked where she was pointing, but couldn't see anything.

"A head!" Gangchen said, imitating her and twirling his finger by his temple.

"Behind that big, round rock!"

I dashed to the large, round rock at the edge of the river. Its rough, black surface glistened like oil. I reached out with one hand and, with a leap, was on top of it.

"Hey!" Gangchen shouted, "what's the matter with you?!"

"A boat!" I yelled.

The boatman raised himself up from the bow. "It's fifty *yuan*," he informed us.

Fifty yuan—*what do you mean? . . . It was ten to come over and now it's fifty? . . . He brought the boat over here just to get us all worked up . . . We're stuck here, he's extorting us . . . Pay him, damn it, or we'll never get back. If it's fifty, then it's fifty.* Bang! *Right in his hand—ten twenty thirty forty fifty. Pay him!*

"A boat?" Tenphun sneered. "You call that thing a boat?"

With the surge of a wave, the boatman pushed his oars forward. The cowhide boat bumped the rock I was standing on, and I felt a tiny shock. *"Peng, peng."* He jumped ashore with a coiled mooring rope in each hand and tethered the boat to the oblong paving stone that he'd put there this morning. The cowhide boat rocked, spun around in the eddy, then drifted.

The wind had dropped. The mist stuck to the surface of the river like a wet spider web. The village and the restaurant were gone. All that remained were gray land and dark-blue sky. It was all lonely and still. We got in the boat.

The only sound was the splash of oars in the water, clear and sharp, in a rhythm so steady that you forgot it after a while. Silently, Yangnor looked off toward the mountain ridge, gasping heavily, roughly.

A large powerboat shot out from around the bend, the staccato roar of its engine shattering the stillness. Our boatman looked around, cursed, and sped up his rowing. The prow of the powerboat passed us. All the boatman could do was drop his oars and let the waves batter us. An electric light hung from the powerboat's cabin. Its beam, shaped into a cone by the shade, fell on a soldier, asleep with his head on his knees and his rifle cradled against his chest. The black barrel stuck out behind his ear, a red ribbon dangling from its muzzle. A lama came out of the cabin, bumping the light with his head and making it sway. The arc of the light swept abruptly back and forth across the river, making it look as if the earth were shaking.

"Master!" Gangchen shouted, thrusting out his hand with an upturned thumb.

The lama steadied the lightbulb, walked to the rail of the powerboat, gazed at the steep peaks that rose along the riverbank, and chanted in a loud, resonant voice: "*Om ... ma ... ni ... pad ... me ... hum ...*"

The prolonged chanting echoed off the mountain walls. A brown eagle flapped out of the darkness, screeching above the powerboat, wheeled over our heads, and disappeared into the dark.

Yangnor's gasps came faster. She shifted from one foot to the other and burst out crying.

The boatman turned to her, watched her, and shook his head. "Oh, Mamma, *tsk, tsk.*" He groaned, then smashed his forehead against the side of the boat. Its shudder reverberated through me. He pulled the fifty *yuan* out of his pocket, smoothed the bills out, and dropped them one by one into the river.

The moon rose over the mountains. A chill wind came up over the river. The boatman resumed rowing. Yangnor blew out a handful of mucus, washed her hand in the water, took a deep breath, and stopped crying. In the moonlight I could distinguish the crescent-shaped pass on the south bank.

"That's where we're going tomorrow," Gangchen said, pointing. "Up to the hermit's cave."

"It'd be nice if we could find some old relics," Yangnor said.

"Maybe we can even find some jewelry," Tenphun suggested.

"It doesn't matter. Whatever I see, I'll pick up," Yangnor replied. "Just like today."

"Pick it up, throw it away."

"I throw one away, I pick another one up."

The lights came on in the village and the restaurant. From the white courtyard, the dog began howling again. The boatman seemed accustomed to the sound. In a resonant tone like the lama's, he chanted the same six-syllable mantra as he lifted the oblong paving stone from the bow and put it down where the boat had landed. "Tomorrow, get the boat here."

Translation by Herbert J. Batt

The Thief of Tay Ninh

I look at the picture in the newspaper: a man stands on a bunker by a ridge, carrying the flag of the North Vietnamese. The caption says QUANG TRI, 1972. I look at the picture, can almost feel the wind blowing in from the mountains. I know this place well. The man has come to the place four years after we left. His presence here on the page sets me on a journey to another photograph, one found in a book in a small library: a photo of a room full of women standing before a raised altar—one woman bending, dressed in bright, flowing robes. She wears a turban on her head, money sticking out of the folds. She is lost in a spell, the caption says. The two women beside her fan her face. Lilies spike up from the altar behind the swirl of incense smoke. In the front row, a small boy looks quizzically into the camera.

Where do I begin? Like so many, I remain confused about those days. When I look back, I wonder how much of it was real, how much imagined; perhaps I should start with him, the thief, for so much of it, so many memories of that place, remain tied to him.

What struck us all from the start was the craziness of it—a thief in the middle of a war—and the way he appeared so suddenly, only after the move south. It was as if he had been some ghost, waiting for us. Life was to be much better for us there in the south. Much better than up north. Only mountains and rain up there. And cold, the cold that had surprised us all. Nothing to do up there, all day sitting around the bunkers, passing radio traffic, listening to the North Vietnamese trying to jam us. At night, guard duty or maybe sitting up on the berm to watch LZ Jane or Betty down the road get hit, listening to the far sound of the guns, seeing the red flares parachute down in the smoke, wondering if it would be our turn next. Maybe once or twice a week pulling road security, sweeping for mines— the rest of the time digging new bunkers, fighting off the rats. Even the rats we got used to.

But the thief, no. It was as if he had been there waiting for us even as the first planes flew in, waiting there among all the abandoned buildings and bunkers of the base, the scattered old buildings, the wood stripped from their sides, tin roofs caved in, sandbags bleeding back into the earth, the base camp like a great bleached skeleton spread out over a half square mile in the midst of acres of deep-green paddy—the rotting structures sitting like that, maybe since the days of the French.

The thief made his appearance soon after we'd arrived. We were still living above ground then. We were playing cards—Blackburn, Rodriguez, Willy, and myself—sitting in Willy's area in the hootch. Blackburn was winning, Rodriguez was telling the story of LZ Julie again. The rains were falling. Outside, the duck boards swam a few inches above the mud, weaving a maze through the compound. Once or twice we could hear a footstep pass along on them, a door slam shut in another hootch—someone getting back from radio watch. It was when Blackburn got up to go outside that it came to us, the distinctive panicked sound of men running. I can still hear Blackburn's rough voice calling to us through all the years that followed.

"Hey, you. Hey you, hey you, stop—" He yells, his voice choked, half in panic. "Hey, someone, stop him!"

Rodriguez, Willy, and I leap fast, but by the time we are outside the hootch, all we see is a hunched-over figure running off in the darkness. Rodriguez, half in shock, stands, shaking his head, waiting for us back in the hootch. His is the first of the six cots that line the walls of the ten-by-twenty-foot wooden building where we live—each sleeping area walled off by sandbags and short plywood walls scavenged from the base's abandoned buildings. Rodriguez stands, mumbling, talking half to himself, half to whomever is there to listen.

"Jesus, Jesus. I don't believe it. What sorry bastard would want to go and do something like this." He shakes his head again and again. "Man, no one's even got real money here. Look at this shit—he even took my wallet." We stand confused, trying to decipher exactly what has happened, watching Rodriguez's dismay turn to anger and then back to amazement again. We watch as he sits down on the floor, just plops himself down by the cot and drops his head, then turns back to us with that strange, disembodied smile.

It was only a few days later that the thief struck again. That was when they started, the stories. They were always the same: the thief struck only at the most dangerous times, times when people were all around, someone always managed to catch a glimpse of him, he always just missed getting caught. A ghost, some said. Or someone made plain crazy by the war. A death wish for sure.

Maybe it was the strangeness of it that made him seem superhuman, that set against the overwhelming boredom of our work. Every day the same. There are many kinds of work men may do in war. Some carry the weight of heavy packs and weapons through the jungle, every day a slog through sun and mud and rain. Some drop bombs from planes. Some are lifeguards at pools on the white beaches of the coast. Our lot was somewhere in between: all day working the radios, sometimes the small ones down at the landing pad, guiding the Chinooks in and out, sometimes the big VSC-2s, passing traffic back to Battalion and Brigade. Casualty reports, daily stock reports, situation reports. But every day ended the same: the spider flight lifting off from the pad beside us, the Chinook loaded down with the weight of the dead. We looked up as it circled over our heads, kicking up dust, swinging out over the last strands of razor wire. We turned back to our hootches then to drink or walk up the road to stand formation for guard. Life could have been better; life could have been worse. We had learned to be philosophical that way.

Still the seven of us then. Rodriguez, my brother from basic, Rodriguez with his love for the *cao dai*, the strange monks in their white robes, Rodriguez who loved to take the jeep and head straight off through the gate for the temple. It made him feel good to get beyond the wire, he said, to listen to the sounds of the chanting rising from the aisles, to see the lines of believers retreating on their knees from the altar. And Harry, who thought there was a girl. And Willy who agreed. And Kelley and Caspar. And Blackburn, farm boy from Oklahoma who never saw a city until he got drafted, a man whose wife back home was carrying his child, who could never get himself to look at Rodriguez's pictures, the ones he'd brought back after the attack on LZ Julie, the ones with all the bodies in them. The odd angles they took, as if in repose, torsos torn in half. He would look either at the pictures or the letters: the letters with the pages that had what looked like poems and flowers drawn on them, the ones Rodriguez said he'd taken from a man he'd killed, along with what must have been pictures of the man's family back in Hanoi. Rodriguez said he was going to write to them someday.

Seven of us digging in for the dry season, the whole firebase digging in, everyone digging bunkers as deep as they could, scouring the base for timbers, sandbags, metal sheets of PSP. This the first year after Tet Mau Than, the great offensive of the Year of the Monkey that the whole world had watched at home on television sets. A year later, how many were watching? Soon they began: the small probes along the perimeter; the mortar rounds that fell more and more frequently—before long, coming even in daylight; each morning, reveille a cluster of delay fuse rockets slamming into the compound. Replacements arrived. The dead and the wounded were carried off. By the end of January, we were all living underground. And even in the middle of all this, the thief still continued to strike.

So much uncertain, even today, even after studying the history, the maps, even after going back, walking the road to the temple. But I am getting ahead of myself. I did not have the book then, the one with the photograph. Then, there was only the war—and the thief. I did not know then about the mysteries, the legends of the king and queen of the forest, of the princes and princesses who lived in a world just beyond ours—a world happier, sweeter, and more harmonious than ours. I did not know then of the princesses, young girls who carry the names of flowers, Cong-chua Que and Cong-chua Quynh, of their dresses made of deep-red roses, of how, when not in human form, they lived in the Palace of Heavenly Spirits in a region east of Con Lon Mountain or on the moon in a vast and cold forest.

It was a month later that Blackburn and I got our passes to Saigon—a reward for survival. Rodriguez, too, but he chose to stay behind. In the jeep he drove us across the compound to the landing strip, waved as the Caribou took off, lifted us high over the pitted brown landscape, and flew us to company headquarters at Bien Hoa. We slept our first night in the safety of the compound, then at dawn made our way out to the gate, where we climbed up on the back of a tank to catch a ride to the city. To the west, the fields took us by surprise: farmers still working the paddy so close to the heart of the war. Boys in the fields stretched their thin bodies across the brownish gray backs of water buffalo as the paddy turned that shade of blue only paddy water can when the sun is just right, the water reflects the sky, and the rice stalks burn bright green and yellow. No other place to find those colors. Two buffalo boys in the field waved to us; a crane stood up on the back of an old buffalo lumbering along the dike. We passed through the ARVN roadblocks, the MPs checking papers to catch Viet Cong and draft dodgers. I knew I had never before heard noises like the ones we heard along that road or smelled air like that: thick with ash and dung and dust, the heavy smell of petroleum and penoprene. It was as if we were driving into the belly of some dying god. Inside the city, at the intersections and in alleys, garbage burned in open piles. On motor bikes young men in sunglasses zipped in and out of the traffic, beautiful girls in *ao dai* sitting sidesaddle behind them. At every crossing, MPs stood like they were waiting for someone important to drive through.

It was true that it was sex and not love we were seeking back then. I think Blackburn and I had already even lost some of our hunger by the time we arrived at the small stucco house by the airfield the cabdriver took us to. Two girls waited in the courtyard to greet us when we walked in. Blackburn quickly fixed on the prettier one and in a moment disappeared with her to the room above the courtyard. I remained, looking at the girl before me. She seemed so young, not more than seventeen. Quy was her name. I was all of twenty. She asked if I was hungry, then pulled me to the room.

The room was spare, just a bed and a small bureau. It opened onto a dirt alley maybe five feet wide. Across the alley, a family—it must have been hers—sat watching television, the figures on the screen dressed in ancient costumes, looking like Chinese kings and queens. They were singing to each other. The people in the room seemed to ignore me as I fumbled with the weapons, an M-16 and Chicom 44. The girl tried to take them from me and place them in a corner of the room, but I was afraid to have them anywhere but beside me.

"Be calm," she told me. "Be calm." She was not beautiful. She did not have the movie-star looks so many of the women seemed to. Sometimes I think someone made them grow such women just for us. But she had another kind of beauty.

"*Em, co met khong?*" she asked. I looked blankly at her. "You are tired."

"Yes, I am tired," I told her, "very tired." I wished then I could tell her how tired I was, how much I wanted to peel off all the layers of the war from my body, all the clinging fatigue, the nights of not sleeping.

Her eyes rested on my shirt. I was surprised at how gentle she was, how true her actions seemed. Her hands still had the roughness of the fields creased in their lines. Later she brought a bowl of water and a damp towel to the bed. She washed me. Perhaps she was far away then, imagining I was somebody else. But still she made me feel human there in that room, made me feel even more deeply what it was I was doing to her, to her family across the alley, sitting quietly and watching TV, to her country, half on fire.

Again? she asked. I nodded no, wanting to reassure her she was not at fault. She then took me by the hand through the courtyard, up the stairs to where Blackburn and his girl sat, drinking on a small veranda. For a few moments we felt it, felt what was soon to become that savage nostalgia of the war. For a few moments we watched the flares go up around the city and on the other side of the river, the gunships, our guardian protectors, swirling in the distance.

When we returned, we went straight to the Filipino compound at the far edge of the base. Why, I am not exactly sure. The Filipino soldiers were all gathered around the grills, cooking steaks, drinking San Miguel. None of us knew what they were doing there in Viet Nam, in their tight, starched fatigues. Some of them might have even been left over from the Kennedy years, or their time with Lansdale. Some might have even gone out with him into the jungle and kidnapped villagers, drawing their blood in an effort to convince other villagers that we Americans were vampires. We were there because of the Red Cross library—Rodriguez hungry for books on the *cao dai*. It was in this small, strange library that I found the book, the one with large print and expensive binding, lush color prints and photographs, *Les Techniques et Chants des Mediums Vietnamiens*—a strange book that opened to a photograph of a room full of women standing before a raised altar, one of them in a turbaned headdress, moving as if in a spell. In the background, a young boy standing before a mirror, a strange expression on his face. With high-school French as my guide, I began to read the book.

That first night back, the thief was at work again. I woke, unsure at first of what I was hearing. "Get him. Get him!" someone was calling. The call seemed to come from a great distance. Rodriguez stirred slowly beside me, then suddenly bolted upright. I could hear what sounded like the heavy thud of footsteps, someone running.

"Get him, get him!" I heard the words again, and the slap of the footsteps, headed straight in my direction.

It all happened with great speed now, Rodriguez turning, pushing the poncho liner off and reaching for the rifle. The night was clear. I could see the compound three hundred degrees around. I knew where he would come from. He would be coming down the path between the red hats' hootch, he would reach the small clearing and then be running right at us. Rodriguez had turned his body to face him. But the thief must have known that the voices had alerted the compound ahead. At the corner of the red hats' hootch, he made a sharp right. Rodriguez registered the change and drew his weapon up, followed the silhouette along the line of hootches for twenty yards before it suddenly turned right again, then back into the cluster of the burned-out buildings of the artillery compound.

But Rodriguez didn't fire. Neither did I. Something held us back. I still don't know what. Maybe the thought that there were men sleeping and moving all about us. And why should we want to shoot him? Was that the proper punishment for a thief? What had he really done? And what had we really seen? A silhouette, a shadow? A ghost? Later that night, we woke once more—this time to the long, wailing cry of a feral cat. Rodriguez threw a rock. We watched the cat's outline slink down from an old bunker. We tried to fall back to sleep, hollow and shaken.

I was like a bird who seeks shelter beneath a broken bridge from rains. The words keep coming back to me. I don't know how she remembered me or knew how to find me. *Con gai.* Those were the first words that told me she existed. A daughter, the letter said. For days, I slowly let the words sink in. A daughter. My daughter. Our daughter. In the letter, she said she knew it the day I left, felt something change inside her the night I went back to Tay Ninh. She had given birth to the girl in Hue, where she had gone for refuge. A Buddhist, she went home to the city of her mother.

So many years later, this need to find me, to tell me. This need, perhaps the same need I had then. "I knew you would understand," she wrote. "Those difficult days." Her life of sewing names on silk jackets for soldiers. How many hundreds, thousands of jackets until the baby came. An aunt had taken her in. But the fighting grew worse. She knew I would understand. He was a businessman, Chinese. He wanted to marry her, move back to Saigon. But what would she do with the child? She knew I would understand. "I was like a bird who seeks shelter beneath a broken bridge from rains," she wrote. She left the girl with friends. But then came the great battles: Dung Ha falling, Quang Tri. She tried to get back to the girl in the last days, but when she got there, she found the family had packed up and left.

She asked me to come help. What could I say? My life had not taken a straight course. I had wandered from job to job, place to place—always something missing, a hollow place the war had left behind, or maybe filled. And those were the days when men were first going back to Viet Nam. Stories of these kinds of reunions ran in the papers.

I recognized her face right away—the same lonely eyes, the hair frayed and slightly graying—pressed against the glass in the transit area at the airport. Eighteen years gone by, and still I recognized her. Two days later, we watched the mountains rise up in the west as the plane tipped for its descent into Phu Bai. Only grass and rotting tarmac where the airfield had once been. We stood outside the control tower where I had once waited for a chopper to take me to my first home in that place—the firebase north, along route nine—where I had once watched truckloads of prisoners pass, seen the C123s, planes with great mouths swallowing and disgorging arriving and departing soldiers. But now all I could hear was the wind ripping down from the mountains across the empty fields.

Her face seemed not to have changed since that night so many years before. We took a small bus along the bumpy route up Highway One, and there we began our pilgrimage, walking day and night, from house to house, along both banks of the river, asking for her, asking for her aunt, asking for word of what had happened to them. But the stories were always the same. So many families went south, to America, Australia, Canada. Over the weeks, we slowly made our way through the foothills, stopping in the pagodas to light incense.

The book says that in this life we play a brief comedy before a closed curtain, always with the sense that there is something behind the curtain. Some of us go back and forth freely; others always remain on this side, walk past that curtain without ever trying to look through. The book says this is the difference between East and West. On that journey north, I came to believe more and more that I could see through the curtain. At the temples, I saw the young nuns at the pagodas, listened to the stories of the women who, after the war, made their way to distant monasteries. The young nuns, dressed in brown, aged seventeen and eighteen, walked with such ease and grace through the courtyards, their heads shaved, their eyes clear, their faces unlowered in the sun. They would be her age, my daughter's age. Perhaps she had become one of them.

For weeks, we walked or travelled by bus along the mountain roads. Once, we crossed the border over into Laos. By chance we came upon an old village and a familiar-looking temple. Its rooms were empty. Only an old white horse sat, rotting under a back window beside a half-broken, dull glazed mirror. I recognized it then: it was the temple in the photograph in the book. I stood there, staring hard through the mirror, and for a second, I swear, I saw him: the young boy. He seemed to be looking out at me. Maybe she was there with him, she and all the others. I don't know. I only know that in that moment in the temple, I realized how much I had come to hate the war and all the men who had made it.

So we went on, village to village. But after a time, I started to doubt Quy's story, to note the small tic that sometimes ran across her face. Perhaps there was no child at all and she had sought me out as another soul with whom to perform this strange penance. But then I realized it was the war that had done this to her. At the airport, I kissed her one last time.

So much reduced to memory. Those days together searching, hoping.

Sometimes when I think of them, they seem so real, the only real things in the world. Then at other times, like the war itself, they seem to be a dream that I am not sure I ever had. And the thief—he too dissolves into that same dream, even though his end is known. A month after our return from Saigon, Blackburn was just getting back from leave—from seeing his wife and new daughter—waiting at Bien Hoa for the chopper to take him back out to us. I can still hear his voice drawling through the static that travelled to where I stood at the base of the mountain. As if from another world, I told him slowly over the radio about that night: how the mortars and rockets had come; how the sappers had risen up from the tunnels; how Rodriguez had been right beside me, the first to see the figure coming up from the tunnel, he drawing a bead on the figure as I turned to look; and then the flash, the rocket hitting the bunker, throwing me in one direction, Rodriguez in another. Blinded at first, then crawling over to search for him in the darkness, only to feel his mangled body passing through my fingers, his arm and legs shredded. I tried to stop the bleeding, but in the end just cradled his head to my chest like a baby until the others came to take him to die in triage.

But Rodriguez was not the only one to die that night. Toward dawn the medics pulled another body out from a bunker near the green line. By midmorning the news had travelled through the compound. Soon lines of men circled the spot. He was no more than eighteen, a homesick mail clerk from Battalion. I stood there with the others, waiting my turn to see where the rocket had opened a small tunnel leading to a deeper, older bunker, perhaps one left by the French. There they had found his hiding place, the footlocker crammed with wallets, the small box stuffed with money. When my turn came, I crawled down like the others. I stood and stared at those four walls covered with the pictures he must have taken from the wallets: pictures of lovers, fathers and mothers, sons and daughters back home. I tried not to look too closely for I knew if I did, somewhere I would see Rodriguez's pictures. And the pictures of the man he killed and his family. I never learned what they did in the end with all those pictures or the money. Maybe they returned them to the men and their families, or maybe they sent them on with the thief's effects. Something in me believes, though, that they just placed them in a barrel, dragged them out to the green line, and then burned them there at sunset—their smoke rising up like incense to the mountain, to that blue, unforgettable light.

Three Poems

INTERNAL RELATIONS

Christened in whitest snow
A lifestyle the very image of
winter landscape. The horses, blue

crook their necks, sleep
soundly in the snow.
The child peels Chinese bananas

develops very thin life-
long, filled with spirit and good will
Darkness dances in his fine

symmetrical limbs. Riven, like
sex emerging naked in a core
of light. Together with a

pretty woman, kindhearted, moist, the fire
surges up again. Yellow weasels gang up
screaming in a no-man's-land.

Her face is radiant. Black night's
youngest psychic child
dissonant most when alone

Pheasants return in memory before sunset
Wild dogs traipse the snow in the
small town. The child called Xue

utterly lonely, fantasizes all day long
He has seen happiness, translucent, shining, shattered
heaviest snow of the year

Translation by the author with Keith Waldrop

FORGETTING

Six years of drought
Eye on the boats. River grows short

Man lost in a foreign land
speaking some other sort of language

closer to himself
the local scenery

smoke among rocks, dinnertime
through empty walls

Then the guests lift up their bodies
a river in a region without boats

tide rising. It's farther to my hometown
speaking some other sort of language

asking for the road home. A flock of gray birds
carries drought from the mainland

Cold surging from crystals of
oblivion, strange things, transparent

TRANSLATION

Staring at the clouds, I see a single figure
arranging a flower garden. She sets three
streams between her seeds and the dairy cattle

Recalling childhood, I see a collapsed
well, eight full-bellied
pitch-black birds perched

among the ways of thought of
one who has moved into a strip of land
near the ocean. The man lives alone, dreaming

Lifting my gaze toward the sun, I see
a single shining wing, darkness
circling in the air. It is some other city

My loving heart in pain cries, Do love
her elegant, well-made naked body
my lonely unclean imagination

Daydream. Faith
Imaginary life
Love's flower bed beside three streams

Shattered continually by one
act from childhood
Each blackbird on its own

hovering
in the dreams of a believer in luck

Translations by Hil Anderson and Keith Waldrop

SARAH LINDSAY

Three Poems

BOILED MUTTON

Thirst drove us to the poisoned wells,
but habit kept us near them.
The next good water, wherever it lies,
must be too long a journey from this place
now that the horses are gone.
As long as we boil this, it causes only
swollen throats, mild nausea,
a film on the eyes and tongue.
If our sight is blurred,
what is there to see but sheep?
If our tongues are numb,
what is there to taste but mutton?
We save the trouble
of hunting wild onions and mushrooms.

We could walk that way as far as the *obo*
where people leave stones
to honor the glorious warrior
whose name is written there.
But all the stones here have been offered.
You'll never find as much as a pebble
under the feet of our flocks these days.
Sometimes a traveler brings one with him—
pale orange quartz
or porphyry marbled with stony fat—
but when he places it with the rest
as a gesture to what's-his-name, the pile is still gray.
He rides away, blurred long before
he passes the horizon.

ICE FISHING

She shivers, but not with cold,
as she saws out a thick white plug
and lowers her hook and line
through the lidless black stare
in the floor of her hut

Staring back a long time,
she begins to see movements take shapes—
looped and weedy tangles
that might be speech,
upturned paleness that might be a face

She's afraid a two-ton catfish
will bite and haul her down,
she's afraid nothing will rise,
she's afraid before she closes his skull
her father will open his eyes

AMPHISBAENA

On my sleep, where its current runs farthest
from any rooted island, there she floats,
rocked on her folded water-wrinkled legs.

The last few sodden fragments
of her ship have fallen slowly past
the unstartled lamps in the dark beneath her.

Still she floats, combing the water
with mother-of-pearl for mother-of-pearl
or watching the seaweed berries circle.

To the north, one head of the snake
with a head at each end swims steadily west;
the head to the south forges eastward,

and in between a stinging blue jelly goes by her
trailing its poison arms a day's journey behind,
in a sea so full of bottled messages
she could almost walk to shore.

Two Poems

NO MAN'S LAND

You are five OK who cares, who cares your mother
takes you every morning to a lady's house who takes
care of you near the factory where they manufacture
facts and that day across the cold coalyards you've
already figured out how the world works All summer
railcars railcars dump Pennsylvania coal in the yards
you're crossing waiting waiting for winter when
people burn the coal to keep from freezing in the cold
and the eyeglasses your mother makes in the factory
go out to Pennsylvania to help the miners, see? But
as you think of sitting alone at Wilhelmina's all day
watching the sky it's like car sickness, this lump of
fact you are swallowing You beg your mom as you
cross the coalyard Don't leave me at Wilhelmina's
Your mother leans over you, her face is giant, Who
cares Who cares what you think! she yells, I have to
work! Your tongue is frozen in cold black coal dust
your tongue You call up your final courage to ask
how come she says I have to have my own money
or your father . . . you hear her voice die in the useless
why the inconceivable how From then till now, who
cares if you turned out OK at catching on even if
your hands are sewn on backwards The facts are bigger
than your mother, your invisible father, and you

FIRST COMMANDMENT

In the fourth grade
I wondered why after all his *te deums* and *oremuses*
Fr. Smith in white chasuble would chant
"I am the Lord thy God, thou shalt have no other . . ."
pounding the ark against idolatry.
No pagans danced midnight meringues with Moloch in my parish.
Then one day my father showed me *The Racing Form.*
I was to perform the miracle of long division
by seconds into furlongs.
Did I see one number glow like a horseshoe in a forge?
I saw hooves flashing,
wind whistling through jockeys' helmets,
my father shouting *Whip that horse!* in the final stretch.
Later, when he drove me to his place of worship
with its flags and roses, I got his number.
When he hit the Double, the goddess smiled on him.
He lifted me on the geyser of his joy.
Then I watched him play the tote board,
sure the changing odds would show him
where the fix was in, over and over until he was broke.
He wouldn't know who he was
if he came home a winner.
Though I choked
on the eucharist of ripped-up tickets,
I loved him.

The Shard, the Tissue, an Affair

Not that the glass shard had any business with the sole of his foot; nevertheless, it made itself familiar. He teased and squeezed, but it refused his negotiations. Finally, the shard—so small, smaller than the tiniest teardrop—was retrieved, and he, pained still, examined it for a brief moment against the halogen lamp before flicking it out my window.

On my bed he sat, a teary-eyed Shiva, his wounded foot raised in the air, kicking, kicking.

I should have swept carefully. This was no way to welcome a poet. I should have mopped, waxed. Something. Now I watched as he wiped the wound with a tissue paper, and I felt awkward, like a voyeur. But then he looked up and smiled. All is forgiven. Come here, he said.

We had seduced each other over the phone and via modems a year before we met in person. An essay of mine had found its way to his part of the world, and he took the initiative of sending me an e-mail full of compliments. I replied, thanking him for his kind words, discreetly enclosed my number.

He called.

We talked.

Mostly of home, of our tropical Vietnamese childhood. He named for me seasons half-forgotten, our childhood fruits, the fruits eaten in stealth and ecstasy. Remember the green mango? Sweet and sour and crunchy, eaten with salt and red chilli pepper or fish sauce, hidden under students' desks while an old geezer droned on. And the durian, loaves of yellow brain eaten with glee by the entire family after dinner, fingers digging through a split thorny shell the size of a skull. Family brain surgery, that's what it was—a ceremony of shared flesh. And what a smell! Rotting-flesh fragrance, almondine, its pungent aroma remaining for days in your hair, your nostrils, your breath. And the milk apple, green and purple outside, milky white inside, to be eaten after siesta, its cool and smooth texture sliding down your throat like ice. Afterward, washing the milky sap off your lips, scrubbing hard, and seeing how raw they were in the mirror, as if from too much kissing.

I, in turn, recounted for him the flame trees that blossomed in the courtyard of my elementary school: red and green, glowing to the point of blinding under an unforgiving sun, their black fruits hard shells that we used as swords to duel with because they fit perfectly in a child's palm. I recalled a summer villa veiled in a cloud of red bougainvillea and sitting by the ocean in Nha Trang. The way I slept in the afternoon on the second floor, soundly, insulated in my parents' rhapsodic laughter, which echoed like shattered crystals from room to room (and how I loved the roar of waves that poured in through the tall French windows and that made me dream of tigers). My favorite childhood smells: the sea, of course, with its faint suggestion of kelp and dead fish; ripened rice fields at dusk; my grandmother's eucalyptus ointment for warding off evil winds; the sweetness of sandalwood incense burnt by my pious mother nightly.

On the phone late one autumn evening, I whispered, "Read me a poem." Out on the bay the foghorn wailed mournfully. "A poem, please."

"I don't know," he said. "You were supposed to send a photo, remember?"

"I'm sorry. I'll send one tomorrow. I swear. Poem, please."

"Hmm . . ."

"Read."

LEAVING

mother burns pages of albums
wedding day, first child, father's
funeral, Tet
quick, she says, hurry, prepare
we'll sail away
down river
to sea . . .
Saigon in April
a season of smoke

I took a chance: Will you come for a visit?

To your city? he asked.

Of course, I said. By the sea. Out my window you can see sailboats every morning. Hear the cable cars go rumbling and clanging by. Feel the sea breeze on your skin, taste its salt . . .

To fall in love is to have one's sense of geography grafted onto another's, no matter how tenuous, so as to form a new country. I saw Houston in autumn—a city of strip malls, grand old homes, and gleaming glass-and-steel skyscrapers coexisting cheek-by-jowl. He, in turn, imagined San Francisco with its Trans-America pyramid poking the blue sky, windblown hills the color of amber at twilight, sailboats gliding on the bay like playful white butterflies. He imagined—and I could tell this from his voice—that there was freedom somewhere in the next valley.

All right, he said, I'll come. In December, at the beginning of winter.

Then he stepped on the shard. And had trouble walking the next day—his new boots, bought a week before, unyielding, his dye-stained socks sliding down. He walked the city, my city, with the slightest of limps.

We were otherwise happy as doves that first day. At lunch we held hands under the table at Café Claude while I introduced him to friends, and afterwards, walking home, we broke into an old folk song about rice harvesting —a song learned so long before and so meaningless by then that neither of us knew its lyrics entirely.

Under the flapping red awning of a stucco apartment building somewhere on Russian Hill, we kissed and I, impulsively, asked him to move in with me. He stared out to the dark water and contemplated the offer. Then before I could speak, he kissed me again and shut me up.

Day two: I drive to Carmel, my hand resting sporadically in his, Cesoria Evora cooing nostalgic ballads of love. He contemplates the sea, a glittering sheet of silver lamé that stretches back to the past. It must be strange for him to see the Pacific Ocean again, so long hidden from him in Texas—a reminder of that terrible flight on that crowded boat full of refugees from Saigon. He relives it all once more. He sees the small of his mother's back as she huddles her children in a corner of a dark and crowded and stinking hull. He wanted to take her place so that she could rise to the upper deck and smell the fresh air, if only once. But she never did. For the journey, she kept her lioness vigilance over a sickly brood. It was he who begged for water, who gathered bad news. It was he who told them how blue the sky, how vast the sea.

His siblings are grown now, his mother well past middle age and half-crazed, and he, like a benevolent spirit, still needs to watch over her, over them, lest he somehow lose all purpose and meaning, though how he yearns for freedom every evening, God only knows.

He turns to me then, the wind in his hair, the sea a blur in the corner of his eye: *I want to. I really do.*

Day three: Something has changed. A shadow has flown across my window; there's been a movement in the stars. The initial delight of discovery shifts to the fact of too many details; we fall into routine. He sleeps on my favorite side of the bed, my left shoulder hurts from the weight of his handsome head. The way he throws a scarf over his shoulder vaguely bothers me, and I can't say why. Sometimes he has this sad look—a poet's melancholy, I suppose—and is unreachable. He wears it too often, like a geisha her powder. I look at him insulated in sadness and wonder how his books could possibly fit in my apartment when my shelves have no more space for V. S. Naipaul's collected works.

Day four: He discovers an unfinished poem on my desk, an ode to his beauty. He says nothing, but I can tell he doesn't like it. It's not jealousy but the fact that I have moved into his territory, even if to woo him. Something in his sigh I recognize too well: it's claustrophobia.

Day five, or rather night: Rain. A chorus of remembrances. Twenty years and he is tonight as he was then: a moist-eyed boy standing in the refugee camp watching his mother hugging his sickly brother—her youngest pup dying of pneumonia before her eyes. He is drunk, not from the alcohol but from trust and grief. He stares out the window and speaks of leaving, of wanting to leave, leaving his mother, which is impossible, leaving his siblings, who have already left him, leaving Texas, which he didn't care for, leaving everything, his memory, his sadness, what owns him.

We buried Little Binh in Guam. Around the grave we stood and sang his favorite song, then left his plastic dog on the mound until the rain washed it away. My sister went back to look for the grave last year, but she couldn't find it. Some mornings my mother stares out the window and cries as if it had just happened the night before.

Listening to him, I suddenly am also overwhelmed by a memory. It was in summer 1973, a year after the ARVN and Americans recaptured the city of Quang Tri near the DMZ. The city was destroyed in the recapturing, reduced to piles of rubble by B-52 bombs, which left deep holes that, after the monsoon, turned into swimming pools for the children who survived. I visited it with my father via helicopter and walked about—a rather strange excursion. Behind the broken window of a house sat an old woman. She sat as she must have always sat, with an ease of years, but she stared out onto nothing now, the old neighborhood gone. The wall that held her window was the only part of the old house left standing. I remember waving to her. She did not wave back.

Day six: I want to tell him, my angel sleeping on my shoulder, that it's strange how love between two exiles can be thwarted by the hunger of memories, that Viet Nam remains, in many ways, an unfinished country between us—even now, body to body, lips to lips.

Day seven: She needs me, he says. You're lucky, he says. You're free.

And therefore, I thought, utterly alone.

On the way back from the airport, it suddenly occurs to me how the tiny shard came to be there on my floor. A thin crystal vase that held a dozen white tulips toppled over one windy evening last spring. I remember holding the flowers upside down, a lake of sharp crystals lapping my feet, water dripping from the grieving bulbs like melted snow.

A month later: Still no news. His phone has long been disconnected. This morning I found under my bed the wrinkled tissue dotted with dry blood—my own shroud of Turin. He is so far away now, hidden across time zones, cocooned in requiems; I walk barefoot in my apartment, hoping a shard will pierce me too. But I'm not made for such a thing, alas, and must resort to keeping under my cool, blue satin pillow the bloodstained tissue—remnant of an uneasy dream of communion whose yearning is long.

Facing the Village

> To leave home very young and to return very old,
> With accent unchanged, but hair grown thin,
> They see but know me not,
>   the smiling children who inquire:
> "And from where do you come, Honored Guest?"
>   He Zhi-zhang (T'ang poet, A.D. 659?–744?)

On the morning of Tuesday, February 3, 1998, during the first hours of the Year of the Tiger, my father abruptly stopped our chauffeur-driven mini-van just short of his childhood village in China. It was the end of an anxiety-ridden journey for him, one that he felt he had been dragged into by my mother and me: I was on a search for my roots, and Mother was fulfilling a lifelong dream of returning home. In the stubborn, juvenile way that he resorts to whenever the women in his life get their way and he is all but flailing helplessly, my father was making one last desperate attempt to abort our trip, thwart our schemes, and show us that he was in charge. We had come halfway around the world—my husband and I from New Jersey, and they from Seattle—to the threshold of reunion and discovery, and my father was still determined to turn us back.

"See," Father said in his what-did-I-tell-you tone, "nobody's home."

Father was impatient. He had been irritated by a mob of drivers at Guanghai, the Taishan port on the South China Sea, where we arrived after a four-hour hydrofoil ride from Hong Kong. Each desperate for our fare, the dozen or so drivers had singled out my father as the tribal chief of our party, swarmed him in the dusty parking lot after we had gone through Customs, and fallen into an angry shouting match and tug-of-war over the day's catch of overseas Chinese.

"I'll take you for one hundred *renmingbii!*" one man screamed upon seeing us. His shirt, shiny from wear and moist with perspiration, opened between the buttons as he pushed himself against my father.

"No, ninety here!" another man yelled, spitting white foam from between his brown teeth. A million droplets landed on my father's face. He grabbed the suitcase my father was holding and started to pull. Already, our journey to the village was worse than Father had predicted. He had feared that our presence as overseas Chinese in this area of deep poverty and lawlessness might tempt even an otherwise honest driver to take us into a remote field and rob us, but his darkest scenarios did not include stepping into an ambush at the start. It was a terrible omen.

"Don't listen to him!" seethed another, pulling my father's other arm in the opposite direction. "Eighty will do."

"Eighty!" Four or five others joined in, waving arms and fists at my father, who looked like a condemned man facing his executioners.

"Seventy!" another spat, anger pulsing through a blue, hose-sized vein in his neck. A round of "Seventy!" rose up, quick and vengeful.

Crushed on all sides, Father looked frantically for help from the two armed guards standing on the edge of the parking lot. Catching my father's eye, the guards, who had been watching with unguarded amusement, turned as though they were being summoned from their favorite TV program and retreated into the Customs building. Left to divide their spoil, the drivers began to tear at the suitcases in our hands and to pull each of us in a different direction.

Then my father spoke. He demanded to see their cars. The man tugging at my bag let go. Suddenly game-show hosts, the men made exaggerated sweeping gestures toward their prizes. To no one's surprise, these were of the booby variety: heaps of rusting scrap metal that might be mistaken for cars in working condition if one were heavily drugged or intoxicated. But there was one exception: a white, late-model Toyota minivan. The driver, with his combed hair and tweed sports jacket, emerged like a shining redeemer. He quickly settled for sixty *renmingbii* (about $7.50) for the hour-long ride to Tai Cheng, the provincial capital of Taishan County, where we expected to find hotel accommodations.

We rode nervously to Tai Cheng. My mother kept trying to make small talk with the driver, a thin, laconic man who had large, bloodshot eyes and protruding cheekbones and who seemed uncomfortable with her prying questions. She extracted from him his surname, Moy, and told him that her mother was a Moy. They must be from the same village, she said, meaning, You wouldn't rob your relations, would you? It turned out they were from the same place. The driver then speculated on our *ho sai gai* (good fortune) at being North American Chinese, by which he meant, I hit the jackpot! My father quickly responded with a tale of hardship, indicating to the driver that we were not worth robbing. Father explained that he had toiled most of his life in the hot kitchens of Chinese restaurants, where there was no money to be made. We are *ho kuung* (very poor), he added. It was true. My mother had recently confided to me that she earned no more than ten thousand dollars last year, sewing at the same garment factory she joined nearly thirty years ago. My father, still a cook at age sixty-eight, has reduced his hours to three days a week, undoubtedly earning much less.

For all of my parents' working lives, their income has hovered around the u.s. poverty line, tethered there by their lack of education and language skills and perhaps their self-imposed isolation in a foreign, and often racist, environment. But how do you explain this to someone whose income is even lower than theirs?

While watching the driver's eyes in the rearview mirror, I discreetly removed my jewelry and lipstick, both signs of affluence, and prayed he did not know the cost of airfare. What I thought was Father's paranoia was now a sickening possibility. We were driving through nothing but remote fields on a two-lane highway that held no other traffic. In an area where a family earning the equivalent of fifty dollars a month is considered affluent, we were probably the only ones with cash in our pockets, coveted American passports, and who knows what other items that might enable a poor family to cover medical costs and other basic needs. If the driver were to rob us, there was no better place than right there. Thick and thicker cataracts of suspicion clouded our eyes, and I began to see us as a truckload of fat chickens about to be plucked. We drove on and on into nowhere.

To our inestimable relief, we finally arrived at the Taishan Garden Hotel. Our driver promptly asked if we were intending to *fan heang haa* (return to the village). He was practiced in this. Only overseas Chinese directed him to the town's fanciest hotel, which cost the equivalent of thirty dollars a night. My parents, unnerved by this stranger's foreknowledge of our itinerary, began to say that we had other plans. Sightseeing, they said. The driver was not convinced. Tai Cheng has no tourist attractions, no shopping —nothing. The only visitors are pilgrims. Miserly with conversation earlier, Mr. Moy was now mouthy, even aggressive. He pressed further, offering to drive us to the villages of our choice for another pittance: three hundred *renmingbii*—nearly forty dollars—for the entire day. There were no other cars to hire unless we were to return to the knot of drivers at Guanghai. Reluctantly, my father negotiated again with the man all of us now suspected would eventually rob us.

The Taishan countryside, birthplace of Chinese immigration and the ancestral home of most North American Chinese, is flat as a frying pan. Meaning "elevated mountain" and known locally as "Hoisan," Taishan refers to a small mountain range that appears in the distance. Located just south of the Tropic of Cancer, in southern China's Guangdong Province, it is covered with a patchwork of rice paddies and taro fields, which benefit from the sun's high elevation, even in winter. Elevated dirt roads flanked by ditches four feet deep run between the paddies. These roads are wide enough for one car and one water buffalo. Lone houses, some large and ornately decorated with Victorian gingerbread or Greek Revival motifs, such as Corinthian columns, stand in an area uncharacterized by excess of any sort.

Located in the western part of the Pearl River delta region, Taishan is on the margin of the highly commercialized zone centering around Hong Kong and Guangzhou. Too remote to have benefited from the trade with European merchants that began in the early nineteenth century, Taishan continues to sleep on the fringe of commerce, subsisting on a farming economy. But unlike any other part of China, it receives remittances from its native sons and daughters who have left and, with these, has built homes, schools, and roads.

My father's village was not what I had expected. Children's-book illustrations, movie scenes of walled Chinese courtyards decorated with swinging red lanterns, fish ponds, and filigree balustrades were what had filled my mind. Perhaps I was also expecting to hear the airy notes of a bamboo flute and the cries of children clad in silk pajamas and playing in leafy bamboo groves. Instead, in front of us was a cluster of low, two-story concrete buildings, gray and darkened by age. Looking like tree branches, cracks ran merciless fingers all over the walls. Windows were boarded. Not a stalk of bamboo anywhere.

The last of Father's immediate family and close relatives had immigrated to the United States in the 1960s, leaving Gnin On, the Look family village, mostly uninhabited. My great-grandfather, Look Ah Lung (Ah Lung, meaning "Big Dragon," was a name he took for himself), was the first of the Look clan to leave his centuries-old village for America. In 1889, seven years after the first Chinese Exclusion Act was passed in the States, thirteen-year-old Ah Lung, fearing starvation, became a stowaway on a ship leaving Hong Kong Harbor for Port Townsend, Washington. A waiflike youth who had a queue when he landed on American soil, he grew into a handsome and affable man who displayed a Western panache in subsequent passport photographs. He made friends quickly in the Seattle laundry where he worked and by 1903 had obtained sworn testimony from white friends that he was a native-born United States citizen, thus assuring himself and those he claimed as children a place in the Land of the Flowery Flag. His remittances and those of kinsmen whom he subsequently brought to the States were what built the concrete-block homes that stood before us. A wealthy man by village standards, Ah Lung died in the village in 1951, two years after he helped his first grandson, my father, make his way to Seattle. His widow, my great-grandmother, was the last to emigrate, doing so in 1968, at the tender age of ninety.

Father expected no reception at the village. He'd sent no advance word of our visit, certain that those who had had no means of leaving several decades ago surely would have found their way by now to Guangzhou, about two hundred miles east. There they would have found work. This remote village was quiet except for our idling car and the song of thrushes in early spring.

Father directed us to stay in the car. He opened his door and stepped out, his shoes crunching the gravel and dirt that he had not touched in fifty years. The last time he had walked that path, he was nineteen. It was a hot, tropical day in monsoon season, and he was leaving his village with an older cousin to seek his fortune in America. He had one hundred Hong Kong dollars hidden in small sums throughout the pockets of his thin cotton shirt and pants and tucked into his socks. A short time later, gun-brandishing thugs would hold up their bus, and Father would lose one-tenth of his wealth—having been told by his cousin, who had traveled before, to have the sum ready in a convenient pocket. Father wore cotton shoes on his feet, and on one shoulder had a drawstring bag that contained the rest of his wardrobe and worldly possessions: two extra shirts. His mother had not even packed him a lunch because, as he remembered it, "there was nothing left to eat."

It was 1949. There were rumors that Mao Tse-tung and his army were coming their way. Father's village was familiar with armies, having dodged Japanese soldiers for years: they hid in caves in the nearby mountains during the day and went back to their homes at night, when the enemy would return to camp. Then there was the advancement of Chiang Kai-shek's Nationalist troops, who forced out the Japanese but demanded rice, pigs, and chickens from the villagers. Another army would mean further trouble, so it was arranged for Father, the eldest son, to join his father in America. From this tiny dirt path, the two young men walked out to the larger road, where they hitched a ride on an ox cart that took them into Tai Cheng. Father had attended boarding school there, a privilege reserved for boys from families who received foreign remittances. From Tai Cheng, they took a bus to the seaport of Guanghai, where they squeezed into a jam-packed boat to begin a sixteen-hour tow by dinghy to Hong Kong. In Hong Kong, my father and his cousin boarded a plane for Seattle, where my grandfather resided and where they would resume their lives of toil and hardship, but in a new place.

Father ground his right foot in the dirt as though putting out a cigarette, a habit he had picked up in the village but long since given up. Then I saw him stop, as though caught by something long forgotten. There was an almost imperceptible change in his breathing. Perhaps his toes curled around the shape of a stone, or something about the road felt familiar, or his feet found something he didn't know he was looking for.

"I'll see if anyone's home," he continued in Taishanese, the rural area's patois that I grew up speaking. His tone softened slightly as his curiosity increased.

My father had good reason for resisting a return to his birthplace. As meaningful as such a visit might be, he felt the health risks were too great. As he entered his sixties, he was diagnosed with hepatitis B, a common and sometimes deadly malady among Southeast Asians born under unclean village conditions. For two years, he fought back with the aid of experimental drugs, but these left his body wasted and his spirit despondent. Finally he regained normal liver functions and had enough energy to do more than sleep away his golden years. He was afraid that any contact with the village would trigger a relapse. He fussed about this incessantly. And I bought into it, failing to see until now that it concealed a deeper resistance that he had no words for. He spoke of this only once, many years ago, almost unwittingly, letting it slip out in a conversation about something that has long since run out of memory's sieve. A few years after Father's departure, the Communist Red Guards marched into his village and paraded his mother and grandmother into the grassy area near the common well. The crazed teenagers accused them of being bourgeois pigs, for having built three houses with foreign remittances and sending husbands and sons abroad, and then they whipped them until the women fainted. No one in the village dared come forward in their defense. My grandmother, to her dying day, vowed never to return to the village and admonished each of her children and grandchildren against ever stepping foot in China. She hated her native country with a rancorous vehemence that left no room for further betrayal. But my mother would not return to China without my father; as for myself, I had every confidence that I would have found their ancestral homes on my own, though I now know I was wrong. Without my parents' childhood memory of where things were in the landscape and of the shape of their village rooftops against the sky, it would have been a futile search through a countryside of unmarked dirt roads and people so provincial that no one was certain of the names of neighboring villages.

In my mind, I have written several dozen essays, a book of poems, a jaunty travel narrative, and a voluminous family biography—all based on what happened next: the moment my father turned to walk toward his village, and the few steps that followed. But in reality, I have created these large things only in my head. None of the many pieces that I've begun have I been able to finish, and each abandoned project has taken me further from the place I need to be in order to begin. As the Year of the Rabbit commenced, marking the first anniversary of our trip, most of my other writing projects stalled or failed as well. Now—strangely and to my chagrin—my inability to tell the tale has become part of the tale.

How hard could it be to write about a simple trip to a poor village? How long should it take to describe the house where my father was born—its wooden door secured with a twist of dried grass for more than thirty years? How is it that I have not been able to describe a place so spare that it did not have electricity or running water?

Setting my own foot in the place that has been my source of myth was supposed to give me a sense of reality and purpose with which to better understand myself and my life. This enlightenment would, of course, cause me to write marvelous things. But, instead, this place has extracted from me more than I could take from it. I've come away with what I could not even dare admit I feared: an overwhelmingly unproductive year and a terrible knowledge of my limitations as a writer. The task, I've taken this long to realize, is not an accounting of details, but the cherishing of events; not the rendering of exactitudes that I have so long mistaken for truth, but a need for remembering the striking and poetic side of things—and accepting that I will never be able to fit the contents of my heart onto a page.

"*Ai yaaaaahhh!*" a man's voice cried deeply across the stubbled fields. The cry startled those of us in the minivan. Birds scattered into the chalky sky. I was transfixed by what happened next. A man had emerged from the village and was striding quickly toward my father, who froze in his tracks as if he were an actor who had stepped into the wrong play. From a distance, the man looked as old as tree bark, his skin tanned and leathery. He wore Western clothes: a striped knit shirt under a thin polyester jacket; belted trousers; and black cotton shoes. His shoulders were slightly stooped, sloping gently like melted snow toward the earth, but his thick, dark hair was windswept in a youthful way. I needed to get out of the car, and fast. I knew with an insect's certainty that something big was about to pour out of the sky—the signs were everywhere—and this was what I'd come for. Yet I could not anticipate it, did not know I was looking for it. With one hand I struggled to unfasten my seat belt and with the other to hold on to my camera.

"*Hoiiii Lauuuuu!*" the man cried, unfurling my father's milk name like a banner across the sky and calling the birds back from their flight. His voice filled the earth, coating every brown blade of grass and stubble, every stone and pebble between us and the distant blue mountains. It was a name, as ancient and powerful as the newborn, that I had heard only my grandparents use for him.

Now it was the sound of remembering.

The thunder of resurrection.

The sound of the earth rearranging herself for his steps.

My father stumbled forward as though pushed abruptly from a long dream and immediately extended his arms in a way I'd never seen him do, like a child who wants to be picked up, held, and loved. The long decades of Father's life merged into a few brief hours, and I knew he had not really been gone from there for fifty years but only a short afternoon. Hadn't he simply gone up the path to investigate a rumor of frogs, or into the fields to tie praying mantises onto his fingers as pets, and wasn't he just now returning home after a euphoric afternoon? And wasn't his mother about to put *chaai* (kindling sticks) into the oven and begin preparing the evening rice?

I felt it: joy filling my father all at once, complete and overflowing. In a slow, peaceful moment, like the one preceding a car crash, Father floated above his difficult world, looking unfamiliar, like a stranger. Then I realized I'd never before seen him happy. He was proud, maybe, when I graduated from Princeton and approving, perhaps, when I got married, but even on those occasions, the realities of his difficult life were still reflected in his tired eyes. But here in this village, he was happy—so happy I cannot describe it. *Resplendent* perhaps comes closest. My father was *resplendent*. I had never in my life seen anything more wonderful.

Suddenly, I felt this place was familiar to me, as familiar as my own house. I was the baby being pushed into the world, I was the bride being carried down the path, I was the dead entering the earth. I was the departing emigrant seeking a future and the foreign-born daughter searching for her history. This is heritage, and the many layers of mine unfolded and embraced me in a single cry.

By the time I finally escaped from the car, the men had pulled away from their embrace. However, Father's fingertips kept touching—no, kept bouncing lightly on—the back of the man's hand, and up and down the sleeve of the man's thin jacket, as though he could not trust his eyes to believe what was before him.

The man was Father's fourth cousin, Yik Fu, who was either two years older or two years younger—neither man able to remember which. They had been constant companions in their boyhood, but had not seen or heard from each other in the half century since Father's departure.

"How did you know it was me?" Father finally stuttered when he found his voice, looking dazed yet seeming more wide awake than he'd ever been. His eyes darted wildly. In the photographs that I took of him, Father's lips are folded in at this moment, as though he is making a Herculean effort not to cry. In fact, he is wearing the same expression in each photograph I took of him on this visit.

"What do you mean how did I know?" Yik Fu replied, sounding insulted. "How can I remember? Tell me, how can I forget?"

Father folded in his lips even more, looking like a dried-apple granny. Standing next to his cousin, who was lean from a lifetime of farm work and eating only the fruit of his labor, Father looked well fed, even overfed. Father's hair was much grayer than his cousin's, but due to a life lived indoors, his face was as pale and smooth and oiled as a wealthy man's. By then, an old woman and a few children were standing nearby, watching us with curiosity. Father held on to his cousin's hand; they were again boys about to go out to play.

"Is my house still here?" Father asked tentatively, his face lit with wonder.

"Of course," his cousin said, surprised at the question.

The old woman came close to me and slipped her arm in mine. Gaunt and sun-browned, she resembled a mummy. I patted her leathery hand and smiled uneasily.

"You his daughter?" she asked through her toothless grin.

"*Haaile,*" I nodded.

"You come from far?" she asked.

"The Beautiful Country," I said, using a vernacular I thought she'd understand. But she didn't at first. Her eyes drew a blank.

"*Aiyaah,*" she said and then exclaimed, "you speak our language!" Her eyes flashed with knowledge. She understood that my father had been gone an afternoon and that I'd come back with him, a daughter he'd found among the grasses, among the frogs, among the happy times clinging to the cool underside of leaves in the nearby fields. Someone from any further away would not speak her dialect.

Taishanese closely resembles Cantonese, but suggests that the speaker is so ill bred that whenever I used it in Hong Kong and Guangzhou, I would always get the same reaction: laughter. Then feigned horror. Using the dialect made me an instant outcast, a vagrant baring a mouth of diseased teeth. Even in the United States, the dialect's associations with peasantry have not disappeared. Although Chinese dialects vary only in spoken form, not in the written, Chinese-language programs are almost always in Mandarin, the dialect of the northern scholars and now the PRC's official language. While I was growing up in Seattle, where nearly every Chinese family was of Taishan origin and spoke Taishanese at home, Chinese school offered only Cantonese, the urban and urbane dialect. But here, on the soil of my parents' home, my uneducated southern accent, deep from the muddy river delta, gushed pearls. The old woman clutched my arm tighter and looked so earnestly into my eyes that I knew she saw clearly to the bottom of them.

"Come inside for tea," she said as though we had strolled arm-in-arm every day for centuries. The children, barefoot or in plastic slippers and dressed in varying vintages of sweatshirts and sweat pants and sagging sweaters, shuffled a little closer. A woman about my age who had been gnawing on a sugar cane the size of a broom handle suddenly appeared at my side and offered me a similar treat. Instantly, I felt ashamed. I was ashamed of possessing so many sugar canes in a world so far from hers and not bringing a single one. I had come without gifts and had even talked my mother out of bringing hers.

"They'll laugh you out of the village," I had replied when Mother told me she had packed three, sixty-pound bags of her old clothing to take to the villages. She had secretly squirreled away nearly every piece of clothing she had worn since her arrival in the States in 1960, hoping someday to distribute them in her village. For weeks prior to our departure, we argued about her intended offering. Once, I pointed to a *National Geographic* article on the fashion conscious in Shanghai and then recounted numerous newspaper reports on China's new middle class. She insisted that her carefully curated collection was an appropriate gift. In the end, I triumphed.

She left her used clothing at home. It sounded plausible to her, too, that there had been some changes in China in the forty years that had elapsed since she left.

But how naive could I be? Where there are no jobs, there is no money, no modernization, not even toilets. Except for the many boarded-up houses, Father's village, which now consists of only four or five families, was the same as when he left it a half century before. The Looks eat what they grow. Without refrigeration, they line up their cauliflower heads and the other *tyoi* that they've harvested from their fields along their cool kitchen floors. Their homes are swept and neat. Each house has the same floor plan, the central area being an atrium that holds the family altar, the main piece of furniture. Every day they wear the same clothes. The youngest children go around barefoot and bottomless. The oldest children were fourteen-year-old girls, who had completed middle school two years before and come to the end of their education. When asked what they'd do next, they shyly replied that they didn't know about "next."

Growing up, I knew my parents sent money to their villages. It was another one of those terrible arguments my parents had over how little money they had. But always the check would be cut, the envelope sealed and mailed. And still we ate, never missing a meal, and heated our home, though not too warmly, and marked the beginning of the school year with new clothes that Mother had sewn from inexpensive remnants. My parents never spoke to me or my brothers about the remittances, so it never occurred to me that there were beneficiaries like myself, whom they helped feed and clothe despite their own meager means. Now those children had grown, and we were meeting their children.

Speaking to me now are the faces and voices of these young women, who share my name, and others whom I met later in my mother's village. The young women are mirrors of whom I could have been, and I am a mirror of whom they could become and yet should not hope to be. I am a grown woman, the mother of two daughters, a wife, the owner of two automobiles and a house filled with as much comfort as my heart desires. I have never known hunger or cold. I collect things I do not need; I discard things that are still good. I have to exercise to stay slender. I am college educated. I read for pleasure, I attend the opera, I visit museums, I vacation in Europe. I enjoy the benefits of modern medicine. I have all my teeth. I belong to the first generation of my parents' families born outside the village. Growing up, I erased as much of my Chineseness as I could. When my parents spoke to me in Taishanese, I'd reply in English. I refused to attend Chinese school, eat with chopsticks, wear red for luck, refrain from washing my hair on holidays and birthdays. Although I made a concession to my parents to study Chinese (Mandarin) in college and found myself loving the language, I was in complete denial of any deeper links to China. In a society where remaking oneself is nearly a national religion, I was well on my way to being what I wanted to be: white. China was a disembodied foreign entity somewhere far away—interesting to study and analyze and form opinions about, as white people do, but not to be taken too seriously. I belong to the first generation to not send remittances.

Father quietly pressed two hundred *renmingbii* into his cousin's hand before we left. "Spread it around," he instructed. His cousin nodded, teary and quiet, closing his fist around a poor substitute for my father. The next day, Father repeated the gesture, pressing a fold of bills into our driver's hand, who, instead of robbing us as we had suspected he would, insisted on taking us, without charge, to where we could catch the bus to Guangzhou. The giving of money is very Chinese, and for the first time I saw the usefulness of it—and the uselessness of what I had become.

Ironically, it was my arrogance that had brought me to the village: I came looking for what I could take from it. Details for a novel in progress. But somewhere between my desire and the fulfillment of it, I fell into an abyss. Like my father, I heard my name called in that place—audible only to my ears perhaps, but maybe not—and I tumbled headlong after him into that strong morning light, undeserving. In that place full of beginnings and endings and everything in between, I knew that I, too, had come home. Here was the home that I sought. I cannot turn from it—it is more than I deserve, and it is enough.

VIRGIL SUÁREZ

Two Essays

The Day the Police Took My Father Away

That morning a heavy downpour flooded the sidewalks on our street. I heard its rushing down to the corner gutter. My father, as was his habit, got up early with my mother, dressed in his khaki pants and work shirt, drank her *cafecito,* and took off to work at the Hatuey Brewery, where he sat by a conveyor belt and inspected clean bottles in front of bright fluorescent light before the beer was poured into them. Even though school had been canceled because of the bad weather, my mother was dressing me and combing my hair when the knock at the door startled my grandmother, asleep in her room at the front of the house. She came in her pajamas and slippers to my parents' room and told my mother there was someone at the door, and my mother clasped her robe tight around her neck and chest. I snuck up behind her when she opened the door, and the sound of rain stormed like horses inside the house. Two men in uniform said good morning and asked if a certain civilian—they spoke my father's full name—lived there, and my mother said yes, then asked who wanted to know, and they told her they were there to arrest my father for plotting against the state, and I didn't know, being seven, what they were talking about, but when the men turned around and walked back into the rain, my mother flew about the house, getting dressed and putting on her shoes, because she knew they were going to get him at work, and she wanted to be there, to go with him wherever they were taking him, and when she left, I stayed with my grandmother in her room, where she kept her dentures in a glass of water, and she sat with me on her rocking chair, by the open window for the light (there had been a blackout the night before, and the power had not been restored), reading to me my favorite story out of her Harvard edition of *The Thousand and One Arabian Nights,* trying her best to disguise her worries and nervousness as she read about Ali Baba and the forty thieves, about the cave that would open only if you said, "Open, Sesame!" while the rain fell hard on the roof, relentless against the plantain fronds that knocked against the window, my father about to get arrested and my grandmother and me sitting in the half light of her room, where we had countless times before, she reading to me as best and as convincingly as she could in hopes that we would get lost in the fantasy of my favorite story: how rock can be coaxed into something soft, malleable, like a child's hope that his father not be killed.

Tin Can & Fruit-Crate Art, or How My Grandmother Spent Her Days

My grandmother spent hours cutting out the labels, scissoring around the shapes of plums, pears, grapes, and she'd make these beautiful collages of fruit or horns-of-plenty and give them away as gifts. She had cigar boxes full of the labels, and I helped her pick and choose the ones we both liked. The fruit I had never eaten off a tree, only tropical ones like mangoes, mameyes, guanabana, pomegranate, but not apples, pears, plums—those she said I'd get to eat when we went to live in the United States, and when I asked when that would be, she'd say, "*No se . . . No se.*" She'd mention a visa, which was needed for us to leave the island, and when I said that I didn't want to leave, she'd say that neither did she, but she was worried about what would happen to my father if we didn't. My father had already been arrested twice for counterrevolutionary activities. She said he had been a beat cop in old Havana, and a lot of people knew him, people who wanted to cause him ill, and I sat on her bed and helped her arrange these cut-out fruit on the pieces of cardboard she cut from boxes. Her room filled up with these collages. One of my father's friends worked at a print shop and brought my grandmother several hundred sheets of Chinese prints of carp, tigers, egrets, flowers, hummingbirds. When my grandmother saw those prints, her eyes watered because she knew that her collages would be even more beautiful. I was lost in the intricacies of the inked lines, the colors, the drama in each setting. For months, when I came home from school, I sat with my grandmother in the afternoons until it was dinnertime, lost in how she cut and pasted. My mother filled old mason jars with glue from the rice and yucca starch she cooked. While my grandmother cut and pasted, she told me the story of how the Chinese families had come to Cuba to flee their fates in Communist China and how they had gotten stuck in Cuba. When I asked what Communism was, she pointed to a rendering of a tiger stalking a pair of royal egrets wading on the banks of a river. She was worried only about my father, our family—not about what happened to governments, to politicians. Most days we put together maybe a single collage. I liked the prints of the emperors, the Buddha, the warriors, the red and yellow carp under the arched bridge of a garden pond. My grandmother rearranged them so that they told a stronger story. She added more people, trees that produced lots of fruit delicious in color and arrangement—the way, she said, things were going to be, so much better, in the United States, where she had visited as a young girl. She called out the names of the large cities—*New York, New Orleans, Chicago*—and these sounded as tantric to me as the names of the fruits I had never tasted.

Tashi Angmo Sabo, October 26, 1986
I walked across the fields and asked her for some water.
She invited me in for butter tea and bean curd.
Photograph by Karl-Einar Löfqvist

Black Hat, Tiktse, October 20, 1986
*Black-hat dance during the annual
festival at Tiktse* gompa.
Photograph by Karl-Einar Löfqvist

An Old Nun Tells Her Story

The month I was born, my mother dreamed that there was a gold buddha as long as her arm inside our stove. As she carefully lifted it out, the buddha's head fell off. Several days later, I was born. My father had wanted a boy. My mother told me that if I'd been a boy, I wouldn't have lived because, as her dream showed, it wasn't her fate to have a boy. Except for my father, everyone in the family was happy about my arrival, especially my sister. Before I was born, she was lonesome. My five brothers, by my father's other wife, spurned her company. The afternoon Mother was giving birth to me, my sister was in the sutra room, praying for a girl. When, years later, she told me this, I was quite moved.

My father was an able merchant. By the time I was born, he owned a silk-goods shop, a tea and porcelain shop, and an estate in Toelung that he had bought from an impoverished aristocrat. However, the estate was not completely ours: we still had to pay annual rent to the Kashag government. There were thick groves of willows on the banks of a little brook gurgling past the back of the house, and a garden that overflowed with the scent of roses. But we stayed on the estate only for short periods, every now and then. It was only after I was grown that I realized the soil on the estate was so poor, and its irrigation system so inadequate, that the harvest sometimes wasn't enough to cover our rent.

Father was of pure Khampa ancestry. When he was fourteen, he left the tiny temple where he'd been a lama and came to Lhasa to seek his fortune. He had realized that the powerful ambition surging within him would be a kind of desecration in the monastery. The wealth and influence he acquired proved the wisdom of his decision.

Father had two wives, so I had two mothers. They lived peaceably, like sisters, and together bore my father five sons and two daughters.

Old Mother was a devout Buddhist. She passed the greatest part of her day in our sutra room. As far back as I can remember, she ate vegetarian food—rarely having her meals with the rest of us—and sometimes she fasted. Despite this, she was fat; so I think whether one is fat or thin is probably fated by heaven. She wasn't my natural mother, but it was from her that I received most of my childhood education, just as my brothers and sister did.

Without any doubt, my natural mother was a beauty. She was fond of dressing up and gave herself a fresh, new look every day. It was she who managed all the affairs in our home, and under her direction, everything in the household was kept orderly and neat as a pin. She liked to sing and play the *dramnyen* and knew all the street singers' popular songs. The trouble was that she was so busy she never had time for us children, who needed her care and attention.

My only companion was my older sister. I always gave in to her whims, and she always discovered fascinating things for us to see and do.

The year I was five, Father and my eldest brother set out on a long business journey. They were gone almost two years. When they finally returned home, I thought, Why are these strangers hugging and kissing us? I didn't dare approach them.

Barely three years older than I, my sister had the opposite reaction. She threw her arms around Father the moment he entered the room. I found this strange because she'd told me that she hated him so much she hoped he'd never come back. Pretense isn't always a bad thing; on the contrary, sometimes it makes us lovable.

When I was eight, my natural mother told me I would be taken to a convent in Gyantse to become a nun. She dressed me in a reddish-brown skirt and robe and told me I looked lovely in them. I stood a long time looking at myself in the mirror, worrying that I wouldn't be beautiful after my hair was cut off. As I look back now, I realize how ridiculously vain I was. Fortunately, reddish-brown becomes me.

Who decided to send me away to be a nun—my father or my mother? I hadn't the understanding to consider the matter then. I only hoped the place I was going to would be as beautiful as our manor. So, bewildered and confused, I left my family and home.

It was a fine temple: the solemn, magnificent sutra hall, the glistening snow-white stupa, the great, heavy gate painted with elaborate designs, the narrow, stone stairway up the hillside, the green trees, the bright, many-colored flowers, the little birds whose names I didn't know. I couldn't help immediately falling in love with it. It was so much more wonderful than I had imagined.

There were seventy or eighty nuns. When I looked in their placid faces, I hadn't the least doubt that I would become one of them. We were so tiny, so insignificant. We could only kneel before our master, the incomparable Lord Buddha, and pray—not only for liberation from our misdeeds, but also for the liberation of all sentient beings.

Convent life was austere, but once I had grown accustomed to it, it didn't seem so. It was monotonous, but once I accepted it, it no longer seemed monotonous.

The convent had a dozen yaks and a few dozen sheep. Winters, the nuns took turns tending these animals in the fields. Summers, the temple turned the animals over to herdsmen who took them to distant mountain pastures. All this followed an ancient unwritten practice: when summer comes, the herdsmen pack up their tents and take the animals up to the mountains to graze, leaving the lowland grass to grow for the herds in winter.

The winter pasture was quite a distance from our little temple. More often than not, we were completely exhausted by the time we reached it. Still, I liked being sent there, liked the boundless grasslands, lying on the grass and looking up at the sky, and the feeling I got watching the smoke rise into the heavens as the tea brewed over the fire. Sometimes the nomad herdsmen teased us with brazen jokes so that we blushed until our ears turned red.

We went to the pasture in pairs. I was usually paired with Nechung, who was four years older than I. From the time she was little, she had neither father nor mother and was brought up by her brother and his wife, and so she knew how to do many things I didn't, but she was understanding and sympathetic and didn't mind my mistakes. She was not beautiful, but in my eyes she was lovable. The year she turned fourteen, a young herdsman fell in love with her and was always thinking up ways to get near her.

One beautiful sunny afternoon, Nechung and I built a fire, made our tea, ate the *tsampa* we'd brought with us, and then lay down on the grass. A light breeze was blowing, and the sun was so dazzling that we couldn't keep our eyes open. Gradually, we fell asleep.

I'm not sure how much time had passed. A cry awoke me. The young herdsman was clutching Nechung in his arms and kissing her. Presently, he stood up and walked off a few steps. He'd put his arms around her before to tease her. I felt it was all silly, lay down again, closed my eyes, and fell asleep. When I woke up, Nechung was sitting at my side with a blank stare on her face. She looked at me. Something in her expression made me uneasy.

"He made me sleep with him," she said calmly. "He was so strong I couldn't stop him."

I knew she was upset, but I didn't know what to do for her. We went back to our temple, returned the livestock to their pens, filled the water jars, ate our supper, chanted the sutras, and went to bed. I woke up in the middle of the night and heard Nechung crying. We sat with our arms around each other until dawn, terrified.

Looking after the livestock was no longer something beautiful for us now. The moment we set foot on the pasture, fear was at our side. Fortunately, the weather turned warm early that year: the herdsmen soon took the herds off to the mountains, and we no longer had to look after the livestock.

I was only ten at the time, too young to understand what had happened to Nechung. I couldn't comprehend her anguish, and she was afraid to express it; neither could I console her. I realize now that she didn't expect a ten-year-old girl to help her solve her problem. She just needed me at her side.

Before this happened, she had been a happy girl, though no one ever came to visit her. Her faith told her that everything that happened to her was determined by her actions in her previous life, so she wasn't worried about this life. She believed that if she just tried hard, her next life would be one of good fortune. And so she chanted more sutras than other nuns, worked harder, and bore the misunderstandings and burdens that others created for her. But with this calamity, her purpose in life was snatched away: she believed she had defiled herself in the eyes of Lord Buddha.

Worst of all, she was pregnant. We realized this months later, when her stomach was so swollen it was impossible to hide. If we hadn't been so naive, perhaps we might have realized it earlier and thought of something to do about it—perhaps . . . But until our teacher explained it to her, we were paralyzed by anxiety and didn't know that inside her slender body a tiny life was stirring.

She told her teacher everything. But it wasn't a story that everyone could believe. Probably everyone but me doubted her story to some degree. I was disgusted with the nuns around me, but I realize now that I ought not to have blamed them. Anyone with common sense would have had some misgiving.

One morning our teacher came to tell Nechung that the abbess would permit her to have the baby in the convent, but Nechung would have to leave after that. She was devastated. She told me that she didn't want to go on living. To leave the temple, she thought, was to forsake all hope for a good life in her next reincarnation.

In the convent barn, among the piles of hay, Nechung gave birth to a sturdy, healthy boy. The sight of the baby dissolved the nuns' misgivings and moved the abbess's heart to compassion: if Nechung and her child were to leave the temple now, how would they survive? The abbess said she would allow Nechung to remain a year.

And so she should have enjoyed a year of peace and security, during which her wounded soul might have healed. But this was not to be.

Another nun got pregnant, and the abbess's rage fell like lightning on Nechung. The abbess felt that the second nun had gotten pregnant because she hadn't punished Nechung severely enough. Our convent's reputation for purity and upright conduct had been blackened. The abbess announced that both Nechung and the other nun were to leave in ten days—never to return.

For two days Nechung spoke to no one. There was no resentment in her eyes, no blame. She accepted her expulsion as her fate. She gave no thought to how she would live after she left the temple, or where her path in the world might lead. She was waiting for death.

When punishment for someone else's misdeed crushes us, may we put an end to our life? May we ignore the teaching that, by choosing to die, we terminate the cycle of our reincarnations and suffer in hell for eternity?

It was my turn to take out the herds. Out of breath and panting, I reached the pasture with my new companion, a girl of infectious merry spirits. Our laughter attracted a crowd of other children watching their livestock. Someone began singing, and we danced around in a circle until we were worn out. I lay down on the grass.

Suddenly, my thoughts returned to Nechung. When I got back that evening, would I find her dead by her own hand? The boy who'd violated her was nearby, cheerfully drinking his tea. An irresistible impulse brought me to my feet.

His eyes shifted nervously as I stood before him. I discovered that I was frightened too. How should I begin talking? He had made love a pretext for doing what he wanted and had no idea of the suffering he'd caused. I wanted to chastise him, curse him, beat him, stab him, kill him. I didn't dare. I couldn't even scold him.

Stammering, I blurted out everything—what I should have told him and what I shouldn't have—as if I was just telling a touching little story. When the story was finished, I had nothing more to say.

There was an awkward silence. He sat silently, and I walked away.

Had I run all this way just to tell him he had a son?

When I got back to the temple, I was relieved to find Nechung still alive. She rushed up to me and said, "He's here."

"Who?"

"The boy who . . ."

"What for?"

"I don't know."

"Where?"

"With our teacher."

Like criminals awaiting sentence, we mutely sat side by side, gripping each other by the hand as if we would never see each other again once we let go. Nechung clutched her baby to her breast. Presently, the sound of approaching steps jolted us out of our daze. Then he was standing there before us. "I confessed everything to your teacher," he said. "If the abbess won't let you stay, there's a place for you in my tent." He looked at the baby, reached out, stroked it, and said, "A child without a father . . ."

The abbess changed her mind about Nechung staying at the convent, but now Nechung insisted on leaving—with the man she'd feared and hated. "It isn't my fate to serve Lord Buddha in this life," she declared. "Heaven sent that man for me to take care of. I'll keep in my heart everything I've learned here in the temple."

I was so young I didn't understand what it meant to part with someone.

I thought she'd remain in the pasturelands nearby, but though I later searched and searched, I never found her. She and her man had disappeared forever.

My only good friend was gone. I grew lonely again. Luckily, people from home came to visit me. They brought alms for the temple, as well as things that I needed.

Sometimes I left the convent in the company of other nuns to go begging in distant cities. Often we'd stop several days in towns along the way, and so I saw something of the varied, colorful life of the world. But it did not make me want to change where I was.

When Old Mother died, the family sent a servant to bring me back home. As I again stood at the gate of the courtyard where I was born, my heart grew anxious. How much had changed in four years? How much had I forgotten?

The face of my own mother seemed strange to me. Watching me from my mother's side, dressed in violet satin *pume* and matching yellow *puyod*, was my sister. Could this beauty be the girl I'd slept with in the same bed when I was little? Her skin was so fair, so lovely! Suddenly I thought of my own face. How long had it been since I'd looked in a mirror? Did I look like her? I must look like her—we had the same mother! But maybe I didn't—maybe I didn't look like her at all . . . As my imagination was running away with me, my father walked into the room as solemn and majestic as ever. He was genial, even smiled at me, but I was still afraid of him.

Several of my brothers were there, but I couldn't tell them apart. Only my second brother, who was lame, told me which one he was.

I must have been a stranger in their eyes as well.

Though Old Mother had already died when I arrived, she is the only distinct person in my recollection of that time. She had visited me once a year at the convent. The donations she had brought made me proud. Her words, her tone, the expression on her face had given me such courage.

The whole house was grief stricken. Father had lost a good wife. My mother had lost a friend and sister. My brothers and sisters had lost a compassionate mother. The servants had lost a benevolent mistress. She had treated everybody kindly, done whatever she could to help people, and never caused trouble for anyone. She considered everyone's mistakes forgivable. A person like her was sure to be reborn into a beautiful next life and to enter the way of future reincarnations in peace. If we were grief stricken merely because we would not see her again and benefit from her kindness, wasn't there some selfishness in our sorrow?

I stayed on at home for four months, gradually becoming reacquainted with my family. They were especially attentive to me; still, I spent most of my time in the sutra room.

I didn't know what I would have felt in a truly rich house, but the luxury of our home shocked me. I recalled our little temple, where we considered radishes a treat, where we had our tea with just a tiny lump of yak butter or nothing at all, where we never thought of cake or candy. We worked so hard, got up with the stars still hanging in the sky and recited so many sutras. Yet it all made sense. Watching the life of my family after Old Mother died helped me to understand how impossible it is to set out on the path that leads to self-liberation and peace without deep faith and prayer in our hearts.

My sister turned sixteen that year. Beauty is always something good— her loveliness delighted me. My brothers were frequently away from home, absorbed in their own affairs. I never bothered to discover what they did. My mother was still the same: elegant and graceful. The daily round of life in the house went on beneath her watchful eye, as before. She had two more helpers now: my two new sisters-in-law. My sister took no trouble to conceal her strife with them.

A merchant friend of my father gave him a piece of beautiful White Russian cloth. To this day, I can't say what kind of material it was. Its texture, its sheen, its pattern—everything about it mesmerized my sister and my two sisters-in-law, but it was only big enough to make two skirts. I knew that dividing this piece of cloth would create a problem. Without the least hesitation, my father gave it to my two sisters-in-law, and my sister was heartbroken for an entire week.

Finally, I returned to the remote little temple, where there were always tribulations but nothing of the sort to make me think there was anything wrong with convent life.

I next returned home three years later. What a difference between one person's death and another's! Till then I had naively associated death with the elderly. My sister's death hurled me into depression.

If only she had lived, she would have been a bride and then a mistress of an aristocratic home. She would have borne beautiful children, devoted her life to her husband, and become a radiant star in society. Her fatal illness had snatched away a vibrant, lovely girl with such magnificent hopes . . . Death was truly omnipotent.

My companion was gone, and our home seemed alien to me.

My sister's death aged my mother. The first wrinkles appeared on her face. She was my mother, but we had never been close, never confided in one another. Still, I loved her, and her anguish troubled me.

I'd been home half a year, and still there was no sign of any preparations to send me back to the convent. Early one morning, when I was chanting my sutras, my mother came to me carrying a light-blue robe and matching skirt and a pair of black leather shoes. She told me to put them on.

"Why?" I asked, surprised.

"Your father wants you to wear these. Guests are coming."

She looked over my hair and seemed quite satisfied. Though it was only an inch long, it had a natural curl and probably didn't look too unattractive.

She left. Bewildered, silent, I changed my clothes. In the past when guests had come for dinner, nobody had called me to join them. I ate alone in the sutra room. I thought solitude was the lot of a nun. After I changed into the new clothes, I felt ashamed. I didn't return to the sutra room. To sit on the cushion dressed like that, reciting my sutras, would somehow be improper.

When Mother came to call me, she had recaptured the radiance she'd lost after my sister's death. There was only one guest, a man thirty or forty years old, not very tall or robust, a very ordinary-looking person. As I sat at the table and started to eat, I found myself doing such ridiculous things that I regretted having come. I dropped my food in my lap. My spoon rang against my bowl. The noise I made as I began to eat my soup was so loud that I couldn't bear to take another mouthful. It had been so long since I'd eaten in the company of other people! My hands were shaking. I must have blushed to the roots of my hair. For the first time in my life, I felt like an ugly little buffoon.

I was weak with the realization that I was embarrassing my father and mother. Thank heaven, dinner finally ended. Alone again in the sutra room, I realized that the life I'd led in the convent had been so remote from anything my family had experienced that I could probably never be like them again.

Another month went by, and still there was no sign of preparations to send me back. My mother now insisted that I begin wearing bright, colorful clothes and taught me how to match the colors. She made me put on showy rings and bracelets. Was this how she thought a nun should dress? She gave me jars of fragrant facial creams, a box of face powder, and a makeup kit and taught me how to use them. In the convent, we just rubbed our faces with a bit of yak butter and never gave it a thought. I would sit like a variety storekeeper's daughter, perplexed by this dazzling display of glittering objects.

When Mother went out to play mahjong with her friends, she insisted I accompany her, and along the way, she would explain how to walk, smile, eat, and talk in public. She taught me how to use a phonograph. She even wanted me to learn to sing. Everything she said made me feel uneasy. I began to have a premonition.

I had always been a good daughter and believed it would be wrong to defy my parents. At the same time, I gradually began to understand my position in the family and in society. I sat and reckoned to myself—it had been a whole year since I'd left the convent.

"Mama, I think I should go back."

"You don't like it here at home?"

"No, no. But my teacher won't like it if I stay here longer."

"If your teacher says it's all right, will you stay?"

"I'm a nun. I should live in the convent."

"No, you're not. You've left the convent. We arranged it all for you six months ago. You don't belong to the convent anymore. You're our only daughter now, you belong here at home, and your father and I have decided to arrange a much better life for you." Mother gave me a little hug. "We know you probably haven't gotten used to it yet, but you will in a while. Remember, from now on you're not a nun, you're the young lady of our family. We're not aristocrats, but we don't lack for money, and the day will come when you'll become a true noblewoman."

To become a noblewoman was probably my mother's greatest dream, but such a notion had never entered my head. Her words startled me.

Half a year later, I was married. My husband was the man who had come to our house for dinner—the only man outside our family with whom I'd eaten at the same table. Though his family was far from prosperous, he had pure aristocratic blood. By my marriage to him, I'd become a true noble-woman, and my mother rejoiced.

My father had originally picked him out for my sister. If she had lived, she would have made him a fine wife. Her beauty, warmth, and charm would have assured his happiness. Stupid and clumsy as I was, I made up my mind to please him. I had to do this for my sister.

And so another phase of my life began. I was nineteen, he thirty-nine. Our life was uneventful, even dull. Time passed, we had four children, and I discovered the joys of being a mother. I had learned many things at the convent, and I realized that I was a knowledgeable mother. Of this I was proud.

He never shouted at me or hit me—unlike in my own family, where my father had struck my mother brutally. And he was a good father. I still recall the tears that came to his eyes when our son fell down the stairs.

His father had died when he was young and his mother had gone blind, so his only sister, who was older than he, had left her convent and come home to manage the household. She had never married. I was terribly frightened of her. Through the disgust and contempt in her eyes, I came to know the arrogance and prejudice of aristocrats. To her I was just a little beggar-devil; and she took every opportunity to create trouble for me.

The family took its meals in a dark-red room. I could see in the walnut table and elaborately carved chairs the luxury of bygone days. Although the family's financial circumstances were nothing like in the past, their lifestyle had barely changed. My husband's sister obviously believed I was not worthy of sharing this lifestyle. Her hostile, overbearing glare so spoiled my appetite that I always left the table half hungry. My husband simply thought I couldn't eat any more. As a nun, I had learned to make an effort to look on the good side of things; I had my sister-in-law to thank for my slender figure.

In my new home, I undertook many things that I'd never attempted before, and discovered that I learned quickly. The convent had taught me that life takes hard work. Gradually, I became accustomed to my sister-in-law's slights and provocations. I did my best to ignore them, and when I had to cry, I went off to cry alone. From the first I gave in to her. After a time I found that her troublemaking left me unmoved, and I wasted fewer tears, until I eventually became indifferent to it all.

I assumed she could never like me, never cease trying to provoke me, but one day she started being nicer. I didn't know what to make of it, but in fact it made me happy. As we began to get to know and understand each other, I discovered that she was really a most sincere person, a woman who expressed all of her feelings and held nothing back. If she hated you, she hated you to the marrow of your bones; if she liked you, you never needed to keep up your guard. My arrival had caused turbulence in their family; as it subsided, everything became quiet again.

My husband had two younger brothers. One had left the family and become a monk. The other lived at home. He and his wife were mild, gentle people who never bothered anyone. Ten years after I joined the family, he fell ill of some disease that baffled the physicians, and he died. Their uncle asked my husband to take his brother's widow as his second wife, for the sake of stability in the family.

I didn't mind. Hadn't my own father had two wives? My sister-in-law was a good woman, and my husband a good man. Why shouldn't two good people come together?

But my husband refused.

He said to me, "I don't see any need for it. She's still part of the family. I can fulfill my responsibility to my brother by taking care of his widow and children. Besides, you and I have a good life together. Why should someone come between us?"

In the ten years of our marriage, my husband had treated me well, he'd looked after my health, but he'd never revealed anything of a man's feeling for his wife. I had always thought his concern for me was nothing more than a father's for a daughter. But the emotion I saw in his eyes now could only be love!

To accept the love of a man nearing fifty and try to love him in return . . . Although it might have been called late love, there was nothing late, nothing incomplete about it. For the first time, I knew the incomparable joy of being a woman, a wife. Ten years I had remained aloof. I thought that as long as I looked after him and bore his children, I would be fulfilling my duty. Deep in my heart, I had always thought of him as my sister's husband. It took me ten years to begin to understand him, to let him into my soul. What a difference when a man and woman rely on each other . . . how much the heart can accomplish!

Our children were growing up now, and several years later, his sister-in-law remarried and left the household. Then his sister died, and I had to manage the household finances and oversee our expenses. When I realized our situation, I persuaded my husband to sell our unprofitable manor in far-off Kham, dismissed some of our servants, and cut our expenses. Things were easier for a time, but after a few years we were again short of money.

My husband had little understanding of financial matters, and his health had begun to deteriorate. If I'd explained our situation to him, he never would have stopped blaming himself, so I kept my lips sealed. My one consolation was that our eldest son was now a grown man, and my chief support.

Now I faced the greatest calamity of my life: my husband was ill, and the family's finances were collapsing. I had nothing but prayer to keep me from despair. One evening my husband died . . . at dusk, in my arms. Fortunately, by then I had become indifferent to death.

He was gone; I remained. I called my children together and told them that from then on we had to be tough, learn to bear hardships, live by our skills. They hardly grasped the full significance of what I told them. We had no choice but to sell our home, and now, aside from our aristocratic blood and noble name, we had nothing. When, half a year later, my children found themselves penniless, trudging along the streets of Lhasa, my one hope was that they might keep their courage.

I'd brought them into this world. They were the tender spot in my heart. When they came in the door dejected over some opportunity lost through their own mistake or stolen because someone had cheated them, I tried to bolster their self-confidence by reminding them of past successes. I hoped they wouldn't dwell on defeat. I witnessed their vulnerability, their frustration, their suffering, and their toil . . . Most often, hard work leads to defeat, of course, but I saw that they had begun to understand how to face defeat. Reversals and disappointments, bumps and bruises are unavoidable out in the world. From what I endured in those days, I learned that the most beautiful thing in life is not splendor and luxury, or wealth and rank, or occupying a position of power wherever you go, but the self-assurance that comes from having overcome obstacles, step by step, through your own perseverance.

It is a beautiful thing to raise children. So many things you do not experience directly, you experience through your children. Children represent hope for the future. But what do old people represent? My braids are silver-white, but I still have hope.

My children were busy with their own affairs, and at last my spirit was free to find itself a home. I'm a common, ordinary person, and like most old people, I've chosen an ordinary way to spend my remaining years. I left my family and became a nun again. I've returned to the little convent where I lived as a girl. At sixty, I've shaved my head and put on a reddish-brown robe again.

Many of my convent sisters of bygone years are still alive. We tell each other the stories of our lives, and everything we've suffered becomes something beautiful. We discuss our hopes for the future, after this life is over. The pasture where I tended livestock as a child is as vast as before, the sky as blue. The white stupa, the red walls, the green leaves . . . Nothing has changed. And I realize now that the tumultuous life of a human being is no more than a passing flash of light against the timelessness of nature.

Translation by Herbert J. Batt

Lamayuru, January 22, 1988
The gompa is situated on the mountaintop, high above the village.
Photograph by Karl-Einar Löfqvist

The Glory of the Wind Horse

Ugyen walked into the camp: forty or fifty tents squeezed together on a stretch of ground that looked like a garbage dump. It had just rained. The blazing sunlight heated the steaming odors inside the tents and drew them out: human piss and shit; dog piss and shit; damp, moldy leather; horse dung; the musty stench of damp sheepskin; the sour smells of fermenting beer and human sweat; gasoline and plastic; dog carcasses; the rotten breath of death from old people's bodies; cheap perfume; rotting leftovers. The camp made Ugyen feel sad.

Something flashed above him and he looked up. An airplane soared over the city, leaving behind it a gigantic roar. Then, as if the roar of the plane had sucked up every other sound, the entire earth was marvelously still. There was not a soul's breath. On the ground lay the body of a dog covered thickly with flies. The empty, lifeless, dirty, ramshackle camp was no ideal hiding place. At this very moment, someone could be watching him, peering out through a slit or hole in a tent. He paused beside a water-logged hollow. In the back of his mind, something rang like a bell. It was a premonition. A boy scurried out from someplace and walked up to him. The boy's head was wrapped in a filthy towel. Over his shoulders he had draped a grown-man's coat, which fell past his knees. Ugyen could see the boy's stomach was covered in mud. The boy had a cigarette in his mouth and a red firecracker in his hand, which he raised to the cigarette. He walked up to Ugyen. Ugyen saw the hissing, smoking firecracker fly toward his face. With a sweep of his hand, he snatched it as if he were catching a fly. The twisting, burning fuse prickled his palm like a fly beating its wings. Before he had time to open his fingers, the firecracker exploded and Ugyen ran in circles, waving his hand like crazy. He felt something wet in his palm. He thought it was blood. A clear yellow liquid smeared his fingers. He sniffed it. It was urine. He pressed his burning hand to his trouser leg and ran after the boy, searching here and there, but the kid must have ducked into one of the tents.

Holding up the tents were vast networks of criss-crossed cords fastened to wooden stakes and metal pegs driven into the ground. It had just rained, so the ground was a quagmire and some of the pegs and stakes had been loosened, cords had gone slack, and sides of tents had collapsed. Ugyen began pushing stakes back into the ground with his foot, but this was futile. Still damp and slack, the cords couldn't hold up the tents. He raised the door flap of one tent after another, but found no one inside. Finally, he found an old woman sitting cross-legged, her back bent. She leaned over some ancient coins. When she heard Ugyen at the door, she plunged her head between her knees and froze as if she'd been caught doing something shameful. In another tent, someone lay with head covered, asleep. In another, a girl lay on a cowhide rug playing with a dirty, ragged pack of cards.

"Hey there, kind man," he heard a voice say from inside a tent. Ugyen went over and raised the burlap bag that was its door flap.

An emaciated woman lay on a bed cushion, her hair in disarray. Her sunken eye sockets created dark rings around her eyes. Her body was covered in various scraps of old clothes. A swaddled child lay beside her. A strange, powerful odor—like the stench of some weird, monstrous beast—suffocated Ugyen.

"Brother, I'm thirsty," said the woman, pointing. Outside the door a pot stood propped on three rocks—some tea at the bottom of it.

"It's cold," he said.

"Doesn't matter. Here's a bowl."

He dipped out some tea and gave it to her. "A boy or a girl?"

The woman didn't reply.

"The smell's unbearable. You haven't changed the baby."

The woman didn't reply.

Ugyen held his nose as he talked. "I, the hero, didn't come in here to give you tea, ma'am. I'm looking for someone."

"My man left a long time ago!"

"I'm not looking for your man. I'm looking for somebody named Pock-face Sonam Rigzin from Gonjo."

"What do you want with him?"

"It's nothing to do with you, woman." He let go his nose, took a breath, and held it again.

"The one you're after—he's my man. Left a month ago!"

Ugyen knew she was lying. He saw beside the woman a square black tray with a black-tasselled awl. He realized that it was for black-magic rituals and that the woman was a witch. If he made a false move, she could make thick black blood gush from his nose. He saw the child stir and a head appear from the swaddling clothes. Between its eyes was a tiny green horn, and its face was covered with wrinkles, horribly ugly. The sickening odor must have been coming from this little monster. Ugyen covered his nose, terror stricken, and backed out of the tent.

Three men stood by the waterlogged hollow where Ugyen had been standing a moment before, every one of them tall—well over six feet—and stalwart. The tallest had black tassels coiled around his head. A younger man had a fierce, savage face. The third man played with a ring on his finger. They were looking at him.

"Say, brother, can you tell me . . . ," Ugyen called to them.

They stood motionless as statues, looking him up and down with narrowed eyes.

"If you're not going to open your mouths, just forget it," he said. Ugyen sensed the three were bored, looking for a reason to start a fight. He didn't want to stir up any more trouble.

"The doors of our ears are not closed," said the one with the black tassels.

"Where's Pockface Sonam Rigzin from Gonjo live?"

"He died," the savage-looking one said after a while.

Ugyen was confused. In the back of his head a dog barked. He gave himself a knock. The sound disappeared. "How long's he been dead?" he asked.

"Oh, four or five months . . . so I heard," said the one playing with his ring.

Ugyen didn't ask any more questions, just kept blinking his eyes as if a bug had flown into one of them. He turned to go.

"You're his relative?" the one playing with the ring asked.

"No. You saw him?"

"It's what I heard. Everybody wants to find out something about him— isn't that right?"

"There's nothing worth finding out about him."

The youngest one growled malevolently, yawned languidly, and started walking off. Ugyen felt there was something wicked about him: he'd said Pockface Sonam Rigzin from Gonjo was dead.

"You're Ugyen?" the one with the tassels asked in a somber voice.

He didn't know how to reply, so he just nodded.

"Evening the day before last, the police were back again, searching the place. With your photograph."

"Three days ago, Ngawang Melong," corrected the one playing with the ring.

"It doesn't matter," said the one with the tassels. "Where were you that night?"

"Robbers' Forest," Ugyen replied.

"That's what I guessed," Ngawang Melong said, nodding. "My grandpa hid out there in the old days. Did nothing big. Ran off with some Nepalese peddler's radio. Never seen a radio before. Tore the thing to bits. Never found the little guy inside who did the talking."

"The police won't come tonight," said the one playing with the ring.

"I don't care." Ugyen stared off.

"Find someplace for him to hide, Dhargye," tall Ngawang Melong told the one playing with the ring.

Dhargye gave Ugyen a look. Dhargye seemed to like this murderer, standing out in the open while the police were running around hunting for him. "You're not going to be carrying your victim's head back into my tent in the middle of the night, are you?"

"Listen, I don't like that kind of joke."

"Right!" Dhargye said with a grin.

"Hey there, time to go," the youngest one said, waving from a distance.

"Find tent fifty-three," Dhargye said. "Fix yourself something to eat. If you're tired, sleep on the bed by the telephone."

"You've got a telephone? Where's it hooked up?"

"Up my asshole. I picked it up and put it there for looks."

"Remember, don't let the gatekeeper get a look at you," Ngawang Melong warned. "He's the eyes of the police."

"Yeah, yeah." Ugyen waved impatiently. "I didn't come here for orders."

"Right, you came here for Pockface Sonam Rigzin from Gonjo, murderer, but he's dead. So I hear." Dhargye winked. He was an optimistic, uninhibited young guy.

When the girl in blue jeans and a low-cut blouse heard he was looking for Pockface Sonam Rigzin from Gonjo, she shook her head and said she'd never heard of him. There was a guy named Sonam Rigzin, but he didn't have a pockmarked face and he didn't look like somebody from Gonjo. She pointed to a young man in a suit sitting over by the wall. Ugyen rushed into the crowd, his mind blank. Just inside the entrance, red neon lights swirled in dazzling, incomprehensible letters. They seemed to soak everyone in fresh blood. On a wall by the door hung a sign embossed with regulations in a foreign language. Somehow or other those few lines of foreign words and those neon letters burned themselves into Ugyen's mind so that he'd remember them for the rest of his life. During the subsequent investigation, he recalled them exactly, reproducing every last detail—to the bewilderment of the police—and triggering the fatal denouement.

The people coming into the bar were dressed in flashy clothes. Their walk was rough, their laugh crude. All of them looked like foreigners. The bar had an unusual odor, a disgusting atmosphere. Red and green lights flashed to the beat of the music and made people look like they were swaying back and forth. Ugyen stood in the aisle, staring all around. A couple of grim-faced, hefty guys in motorcycle jackets walked towards him, helmets in hand. Ugyen was a tough Khampa with a knife stuck in his belt, but they shouldered him aside. Everybody here acted like a fearless desperado. Nobody paid him any attention.

Sonam Rigzin was sitting alone at a table with a cup of strong black coffee in front of him, looking bored, as if his friends hadn't shown up. He certainly seemed to be a regular. Ugyen sat down opposite him and coldly stared him in the face. He wasn't sure this was Pockface Sonam Rigzin from Gonjo. The fellow was dressed immaculately, like a real city gent. Ugyen couldn't make out the color of his suit in the pulsating light. All he could see was that the material had fine, almost invisible stripes. The tailoring was exquisite, a perfect fit. His tie was embroidered with golden thread, in a pattern suggesting the eyes of wild beasts glaring in the dark. His jet-black hair was combed neatly and elegantly. He was probably the only other Tibetan here. Ugyen never thought it would be like this. He'd always thought he'd be facing a Khampa who looked like himself. He didn't like facing this clean, tidy, stylish guy.

"Mister," Ugyen said, leaning closer and striking up a conversation. Perhaps from his work, Sonam Rigzin was used to meeting all kinds of people. In a very friendly way, and even with interest, he replied to Ugyen's questions one by one.

"Right, I'm the one you're looking for." He stroked his face, laughing with embarrassment. "So, after all these years, there's somebody who still remembers my nickname. Only somebody from my hometown could remember it." How could people have given him that nickname? There wasn't a single pockmark on his face. "Maybe I had pockmarks when I was little—I don't remember. Right, I'm from Gonjo County. Like something to drink? You don't like coffee? How about a beer? Sure."

Ugyen phrased his questions carefully, and Sonam Rigzin verified his identity as Pockface Sonam Rigzin from Gonjo.

"Tell you something about my father and mother? *Ha, ha,* you're a funny one all right. You must be one of those relatives of mine who're always creeping out of the woodwork, eh? Every damn one I run into, just as poor as you. What's your name? Ugyen, is it? What do you want to know about my father and mother for? Dad's name was Abo Delang, right. Mama's was Drachang Chodon. Yes, they were minstrels. You seem to know all about us. You know, I'm thinking of writing something about them. The old days are vanishing!"

Sonam Rigzin propped his cheek with his hand, shut his eyes, and, carried off by a sudden impulse, recalled the trials and feats of his father. Abo Delang was a wandering acrobat, famous everywhere. Stirring up thick clouds of dust, the minstrel troupe's wagons would come into town and children would race out to meet them, shouting with joy. Dogs ran behind the wagons, barking. Young girls stood shyly on the roofs, watching the merry minstrel troupe singing and dancing. Then would come Abo Delang's elegant performance: the one-legged whirlwind. Seventy-two coins formed a circle on the ground. The whole clan beat drums and rang bells as his father balanced on one leg and sprang faceup at the sky like a great eagle, a giant writhing dragon. Seventy-two times he would soar and whirl, snatching one coin after another till not a single one was left in the dirt. Cries of praise and wonder poured from the villagers.

But these endless roving performances made for a dangerous life. In the loneliness of a desolate mountain valley, a gunshot reverberated glorious and eternal, shattering the dream of little Sonam Rigzin there against his mother's bosom. Opening his eyes after the gunshot, he saw the white clouds in the blue sky, the yellow valley, the minstrel-troupe horsemen in single file along the little winding path on the valley floor. When the sound of the gunshot died away, it was deathly silent all around, just as before. Then came the urgent rocking of the horse that set the tiny bells on its neck to jingling—and another gunshot, glorious, interminable, resonating throughout the valley. His mother screamed and held him close. As her powerful hand thrust him back under her robe into the drowsy moistness of her bosom, he saw a man in front of her fall softly off his horse. Only many years later did he learn that this was his uncle. In the excitement, he got pushed so far down his mother's bosom that he couldn't breathe. A roar filled the silent valley, the horse neighed in fear, people whispered curses, bullets whistled by. Oblivious to danger, he forced his head out of his mother's robe and stared wide-eyed at the gun battle. He saw tiny figures of men moving high up on the hills. From all around him in the valley burst a cry full of wild power: *"Ah-hei-hei!"*

His father, Abo Delang, was not only a master acrobat but also a crack shot. He saw his father calmly roll over behind a rock, coolly raise his rifle, aim at a black figure on the hill, and pull the trigger. The tiny figure swayed and toppled to the ground just as his mother's hand shoved him down into her bosom again, this time so tight he couldn't wriggle out to watch more of the battle. It was only much later, after years of seeing his father bent over as if looking for cow dung, that he realized his father had been injured in the gun battle with the bandits. The wound in his father's back got worse and worse. The man who'd always braved the itinerant life died regretting that he'd never pass his skills on to his son.

Ugyen knew that all Sonam Rigzin had said was true. What he'd felt during the battle was more or less the same. He too had witnessed an unforgettable scene from his mother's bosom high up on the valley rim. Ugyen walked around the table. Sonam Rigzin stood up, watching him in helpless panic. Maybe if this son of the minstrel clan sitting before him had learned his father's unique trick, he could have dodged the mortal knife that Ugyen calmly, coolly, effortlessly thrust into him now. The long knife in Ugyen's hand plunged through the layers of Sonam Rigzin's clothing and into his stomach with as little effort as if they had been sheets of paper. Ugyen thrust upward with all his might, probing for the heart. He heard bone crack, saw the bloody tip of the blade come out through Sonam Rigzin's clothing, behind his shoulder blade. Ugyen had thought it would be difficult to plunge a knife through flesh. Now he knew he had strength enough to drive his knife through two bodies at once. Half of Sonam Rigzin's face twitched to the left, half to the right. He groaned a cold laugh, his head dropped, his body collapsed. The bar went quiet. The patrons were either used to this sort of business or frightened out of their wits. In silence they stared at Ugyen. No one moved. At last, one man tossed down a card with a practiced hand, jabbed his neighbor with an elbow, and tapped the table, meaning by this gesture, Your play. The man's neighbor looked at his own hand and pulled out an ace of spades. When Ugyen wiped his knife on the dead man's suit, it left no bloodstain. He thought the suit must have been blood-red. He'd never seen anyone wear a suit that color. He walked out of the bar, knife in hand. Nobody stopped him. Maybe the girl wearing the blue jeans and low-cut blouse and leaning in the doorway hadn't seen what happened. She paid no attention to his knife, just stood with a cigarette in the corner of her mouth, arms crossed, glancing indifferently out of the corner of her eye. It made him think of a girl he'd seen in a movie. "Dirty whore," he muttered.

There were no streetlights. No one ran after him, and no one tried to stop him. All around him it was dark. He heard a roar. He thought a crowd of people must be applauding in a big square nearby. As he walked aimlessly, his head rang with the awesome undulating melody of a gunshot in a lonely mountain valley. Nobody in the future would ever hear such a stirring sound. Now he was finished with all that. He felt light and easy. He'd searched painfully all these years, worn out so many pairs of shoes, worn himself out, gone without sleep. Now that was all finished. In the future, whenever they mentioned his name, people would give an admiring thumbs up in tribute to him. He didn't care if he never saw them do it. Suddenly, he sensed a vast crowd of shadows following him. He turned to look. An expanse filled with green stars glimmered behind him, flashing like the stitching on the dead man's tie. A pack of stray dogs lurked close behind, ready to pounce and tear him to pieces. Could his victim's soul have turned into a stray dog and come after him so soon? He hefted his knife, ready for a fight to the death, then looked down in confusion. The knife he'd clutched since he killed his victim had turned into a shank of dried mutton. He raised it to his nose and sniffed: it stank of bloody human flesh. He threw it away in disgust. In a flash, the pack of dogs pounced on it. A warm, putrid stench swept past him on the breeze. From where he'd thrown the shank came the yapping of dogs fighting over food. Ugyen heaved a sigh of relief. The knife he'd carried all these years was no good to him now. He sure didn't want to kill a second man.

Hey! Those dazzling magic letters—what country could they be from? Coiling and twisting together, they made you feel like dancing, like getting it on with a woman. When Thome Sambhota created writing, he sure wasn't thinking of those letters. And that writing on the sign—what was it, anyway? If he had the chance, he'd go back to that bar. Just for a drink. The beer wasn't bad. And if the stinking whore at the door . . . He started reckoning how long it had been since he'd slept with a woman.

Early in the morning, the Khampa vagrants came out of their low, cramped tents and greedily sucked in the fresh, clean air. Men and women with swollen faces and dishevelled hair stood at their door flaps, pulling on their clothes, doing up their belts. Puffs of blue smoke rose, laden with the pungent smells of rubber, oil, and chemicals. The old people had gotten up early and already finished circumambulating the Potala Temple. The old Khampa vagrants always tried to be friendly and chat with the old Lhasa people they met as they walked together around the city, spinning their prayer wheels. But for centuries there had been bad blood between Lhasa residents and the people from eastern Kham. The old Lhasa people led on leashes cute little Pekinese dogs and fat, tame sheep they'd rescued from the butcher. They wanted nothing to do with the grizzled old vagrants, who had nothing in their travelling bags and who once might have been robbers, swindlers, bandits, or horsethieves. Feeble now and shaking like candles in the wind, the old vagrants didn't care what the Lhasa residents thought. They worshipped the same Buddha as the city folks, they walked the same road, they prayed the same. And as for the bliss of the life to come, well, they thought, we'll just walk along, spin our prayer wheels, and see. At every turn, they prayed for blessings on the holy Potala Temple. Then, still spinning their prayer wheels and murmuring prayers from dry throats with parched tongues, they turned back toward the campground.

Around breakfast time, a blue police car with a flashing red light on its roof entered the campground gate. Five policemen jumped out. The vagrants who'd lived in the campground awhile were used to the gentlemen of the police force bursting in at any time. Whenever anything happened in the city, the manhunt would always start here. The police usually carried out their raids at night. Piercing sirens would wail. Policemen with urgent, hectoring voices would flush naked men and women out of their tents. The police would gape in amazement at the stolen items they found: automobile engines; tires; all kinds of auto parts; brand-new motorcycles; new and old bicycles; a dark-green safe, still unopened, full of cash; rolls and rolls of cloth; countless boxes of canned food. They found a maternity-ward birthing chair and a high-tech flush toilet from a hotel's restroom. They even recovered a golden-haired, green-eyed European baby that people say was stolen from some foreign tourists—who knows what for? The police nicknamed the vagrant camp The Launch Pad. In a cold, majestic voice, a policeman in dark glasses announced through a loudspeaker their reason for coming. He commanded each family to leave one person behind to watch its tent. Everyone else was to line up and go to Cultural Palace Square to witness a mass public trial.

Many people wondered what the trial had to do with them.

"It's to scare us so that we'll behave here in Lhasa," Ngawang Melong said. He was tying on his boots. "They're going to kill somebody!" he cried out with a swipe of his hand across his neck.

"It's a shame," Shega said. She poured Ngawang Melong and their savage-faced brother, Dorje, bowls of tea, put a little leather bag of *tsampa* between them, and set a spoon on top of it.

Dhargye hadn't arrived yet. He lived in tent number fifty-three, the one with the telephone.

"How come you didn't put butter in this tea?" Dorje grumbled to his sister.

"I had to save some for Buddha Tsuklakhang's lamp."

"Don't give me that."

"Where's Dhargye—doesn't he want his tea?" Shega asked.

"Kill somebody—hunh!" Dorje said.

"Shut your mouth!" she spat. A couple of policemen walked up to the tent, bent over, and looked in. One of them pointed to his watch. "Hurry up. You leave at eight thirty."

"Dog!" Dorje said.

The policeman didn't hear.

"Who'll stay behind?" Ngawang Melong asked.

"Shega, you."

"No. I'm going with you," she snapped.

"Listen, you," Ngawang Melong growled, "my fist's just aching to let you have it."

"And who's going to beg for your lunch then, huh?"

"You stay here," Ngawang Melong conceded. "We'll come back. Just make *tsampa* for lunch and some tea."

Dhargye was at the door. He bent over, looked in, and said, "Hey, we might see Ugyen on the platform today."

The others didn't make a sound.

"The guy's going to die today," Dhargye said, entering.

"Don't talk like that," Shega said.

Dhargye gave Shega a nod in greeting. She returned his surreptitious smile, passing him a bowl of tea. With no butter in it, the tea was clear. When Dhargye drank the first mouthful, he discovered phantom images appearing and disappearing in the bowl. First he saw a pile of white rocks with a prayer flag thrust in it and then a *mani* cairn wrapped in wool. Next he saw strange, twisted, luminous letters drifting up out of a still, green lake, then the mark of a human body left on the sand of a pure-white beach.

Trembling, with the bowl in his hand, he rushed off to old Longna's tent. In her youth, she'd been a village soothsayer. Now her toothless mouth uttered curses against the times. "It's an age," she said, "when hoards of demons arise and stir up trouble, when the bodhisattvas fall silent and even the awesome heavenly guardians can't hold back the demons' power. Oh yes, the glittering golden temples around Lhasa still celebrate solemn festivals, and the deep resonance of the lamas' long copper horns pulsates back and forth over the city, and fierce, scarlet-robed lamas in yellow cockscomb hats, their shoulders padded so they look like sparrow hawks, strike rhombus-shaped clubs of bronze-inlaid iron against the earth over and over, terrorizing pious pilgrims from the countryside till they don't dare look up from the ground"—old Longna closed her eyes—"but they don't vanquish the evil spirits! It's just for foreigners to take pictures now." Then she would cover her nose with her sleeve and mutter about the sinister dust polluting the air of the holy Tibetan plateau. Or she'd throw dust that she'd combed out of her graying braids into the fire, where it crackled and sparked. "That's a few more demons dead," she'd say, laughing in delight. Folks said all she'd killed were a few of her lice.

She stretched out a long fingernail now and stroked Dhargye's face in a sign of welcome, then listened, eyes shut, as he told her why he'd come. The two crouched shoulder to shoulder: two pairs of eyes gazing into the tea like people staring at a goldfish in a bowl. There were definitely some strange images in that tea, but Dhargye couldn't decipher them. Longna took a crystal lens out of her bosom, spat on it three times, wiped it on her sleeve, and began a vague incantation. The images in the bowl gradually became more distinct. She gave Dhargye a little pat on the back and pushed him into the bowl. A hot breeze swept the desolate pastureland. Foul, moss-like grass knit the dusty yellow soil in place. An indistinct trail stretched away among the slopes that rose and fell off to the horizon. Traces of the moist odor of horse dung drifted on the air. Dhargye listened. He could hear the faint tinkling of a bell like celestial music, swinging from the saddle of some distant, lonesome traveller. He set off into the wilderness, searching for this ephemeral ringing.

The wilderness vanished—or had he reached the end of it? A dizzying abyss yawned at his feet. Out of the canyon blew gusts of cold air. Far below, a river churned and swirled. Looking over the precipice, Dhargye saw Dorje and a woman walking to the temple, followed by Pockface Sonam Rigzin from Gonjo. Dhargye looked carefully. The woman was Shega! Around her neck she wore a sacred jade unicorn. Dhargye recognized it as the one the Chinese emperor had presented to the Fifth Dalai Lama, who had preserved it in the Potala until somehow it had found its way onto Shega's neck. And Pockface Sonam Rigzin from Gonjo had spotted it! As Dhargye watched in impotent rage, Sonam Rigzin slid his lust-crazed eyes from the jade unicorn hanging from Shega's white neck and down over her breasts, down to . . . But her brother Dorje was right there watching, and when he saw Sonam Rigzin slip his hand around Shega's waist, he reached for the sheath at his belt. Dorje and Sonam Rigzin danced back and forth, waving their knives. One quick slash of Dorje's blade, and Pockface Sonam Rigzin from Gonjo lay dying in a pool of blood. Shega ran to the dying man, embraced him, raised him up! As Dhargye looked on from afar, Shega took off the precious jade unicorn and hung it round Pockface Sonam Rigzin's neck, then touched her forehead to his.

Dhargye couldn't get near them. Dhargye wanted to run to Shega, but it was as if a glass door stood in his way.

Brother and sister didn't even glance at Dhargye, but floated off, propelled by some invisible power. In a flash they were gone. Now Dhargye was standing next to the body of Pockface Sonam Rigzin, lying on the sand. A shepherd and some peasant girls passed, spotted the body, then eyed Dhargye suspiciously. Dhargye got flustered. He didn't know how to explain that he had nothing to do with the murder.

And right then who should burst in but Ugyen! In the corner of his tent Dhargye was gazing at Shega's white neck, sliding his arms down lower, slipping his hand around her waist—and Ugyen didn't pay attention to what the two of them were doing, just walked in and pulled away a pile of worn felt carpets and a sheet of plastic, then lifted some wooden planks to reveal an enormous hole, big enough to hide a yak, filled with stolen goods, mostly scrap metal. Ugyen was rummaging for something. Dhargye heaved a sigh and let go of Shega. She straightened up her hair, did up her buttons, spat out, "He's just a jinx, damn him!" and walked out of the tent.

"What the hell are you looking for?"

Ugyen didn't reply.

Who did Ugyen think he was, Dhargye shouted, a pillar of the community? The police were looking for him all over, and here he was, swaggering around in broad daylight where anybody could spot him. Dhargye muttered something about reporting him to the police if he kept spoiling his fun with Shega like this.

"Where's that camera I left here?" Ugyen asked him.

"Sold."

Ugyen put the planks back down over the hole and sat on them. "How much did you get for it?"

"Three hundred."

"Is that all?!" Ugyen scratched his head, dejected. "You saw how I almost got caught grabbing it off that foreigner."

"You told me to sell it."

"You think it was junk, worth just three hundred?"

"The guy said one of the parts was broken."

"He robbed you."

"What did you want with it?"

"I made a deal: I give this guy the camera, he'll tell me where to find Pockface Sonam Rigzin from Gonjo."

Dhargye pushed him away from the hole, pulled the carpets back into place, picked up the telephone from where Ugyen had knocked it to the ground, and solemnly replaced it on the empty soapbox by the bed. "He's dead," Dhargye said.

"He's not. I know."

"I saw him die myself," Dhargye said, "I think."

"Maybe . . . ," Ugyen said, lost in thought, "there's nobody named Pockface Sonam Rigzin from Gonjo."

"Can you see him clear?"

"Seems like the third one on the right."

"No, it's not. You can't see that far."

"I don't like this. What a crowd! My head's bursting."

"The bodhisattvas aren't happy about this."

"The wind will come up in the afternoon."

Tall and robust, Ngawang Melong, Dorje, and Dhargye stood outside the meeting ground, their hands on each other's shoulder. They looked as if they were standing around Tromsikhang Market to barter jewels. A policeman came over and told them in a low voice to get inside with the rest of the crowd. They paid no attention to him. Police began to surround them. People near them became nervous. Ngawang Melong could tell from their green uniforms that these were military police. Usually when the three of them stood around, they rested their hands on the handles of their knives, but the police made them check their knives with the officers who stayed back at the camp. Now that they didn't have anyplace to put their hands, they just swung them idly back and forth.

The police herded the two hundred Khampas into the square. Fond of a joke no matter what the occasion, the native Lhasa people saw this confused gang straggling in, staring at everything, and immediately cheered and applauded as if the Khampas were the honored guests. The Khampa men appreciated the joke and started laughing too. One of them complained that his seat was so far from the platform that he couldn't see anything. "Hey, mister! What's the show?"

"The Last Judgment."

"Never heard of it. Something about a goddess?"

This silly question started the Lhasa people laughing again.

A row of criminals stood on the platform. Three of them had already been sentenced to death. When the public sentencing ended, they would be taken to the execution ground outside of town. One was a Lhasa teenager who had shot and killed a policeman; the second was a peasant who'd stolen three hundred thousand *yuan* from a bank; the third was the murderer and escaped convict Ugyen. In a valley outside of town, the police had found a body. From the testimony of a shepherd and a couple of peasant girls who identified Ugyen and from evidence discovered at the scene —fingerprints on the handle of an English-style bayonet, the accused's hair under the victim's fingernails (which indicated that there had been a struggle before the murder occurred), and footprints found near the scene—as well as from the relationship of the victim with the accused before the crime, it was conclusively established that Ugyen was guilty of premeditated murder. The victim was Sonam Rigzin, also known as Pockface Sonam Rigzin from Gonjo. The motive: a revenge feud that originated with the murder of Ugyen's father by the father of Sonam Rigzin.

Ugyen knew nothing of legal procedure. As soon as he was captured, he admitted committing a murder, but the time of the crime, the location of the crime, and the victim were different from those in the case under investigation. He simply and straightforwardly confessed all the details. The time—one evening. The place—a certain bar in the city. The victim—a man wearing a suit and called Pockface Sonam Rigzin from Gonjo. In addition to describing the bar, Ugyen recounted in precise detail—and even drew—each stroke of the letters in neon lights inside the bar's entrance and on the sign. The police didn't recognize the place. They felt the case was getting complicated. They began to wonder if he'd committed a second murder. In a police car they drove Ugyen up and down every street and byway of Lhasa without finding the bar. He said the incident happened at night and he couldn't remember what part of town he had been in.

The police concluded that the crime Ugyen was describing was nothing but a fiction invented to confuse the investigation. First, they reasoned, no other murder had been reported. A murder before so many witnesses, such as Ugyen had described, would surely have been reported. Second, the letters Ugyen was talking about . . . the devil knew what they meant. Maybe just some nonsense he dreamed up. And as for neon signs . . . never mind shady, low-life bars jammed with mobs of people—even the luxurious, modern Lhasa Hotel didn't have neon lights. There wasn't a single neon light glittering in all Lhasa.

Ugyen was confused. He admitted committing one murder, but the police said that it was all a hoax and that he had committed a different one, which he didn't know anything about. He didn't understand law, he didn't understand science. All he knew was what he had seen and what he remembered. So he broke out of jail to try to find the bar and prove it existed. He lived underground. But before he could find it, they caught him and put him back in jail. Maybe he could have avoided the death sentence, but everything he'd done had only added to the weight of his crime. At last his name was put on the execution list.

"They've got it all wrong." Dhargye shook his head.

The three men had been herded to their seats among a sea of spectators. The sun shone straight down. People held newspapers, books, and handkerchiefs over their heads to block its rays.

"It wasn't *Ugyen* who killed Sonam Rigzin. I know," Dhargye said, giving Dorje a significant look.

"I suppose that crazy old Longna put all these ideas in your head."

"She pushed me into the tea bowl, and I saw it all clearly. What I still can't figure out is why they've never mentioned the jade unicorn. But I know who killed Pockface Sonam Rigzin from Gonjo. It was *you!*"

Dorje gave him a strange look up and down. "You've got a problem in your head."

"You knifed him, then Shega threw her arms around him, and hung that jade unicorn around his neck as he died," Dhargye said in a low, tense voice.

"Damn! I'll knock the shit out of you."

"Go ahead, knock the shit out of me." All of a sudden Dhargye pointed stealthily at Ngawang Melong. "What's he up to?"

Ngawang Melong had squeezed himself up against old, white-haired Longna. The two of them had their heads together. It looked like they were hatching some secret plot.

"He knows Ugyen killed somebody," Dorje said, "but that Ugyen is innocent of the crime they're accusing him of, and he wants to save him."

"How?"

"There's always a way," Dorje said mysteriously.

Ngawang Melong left the crowd and walked up to the magistrates' platform. In about fifteen minutes, he returned. He had told the police he was Ugyen's friend and asked them to give him a ride to the execution ground so that he could take care of the body when it was all over. A couple of friends, he added, would come along later to help him. The police knew Ugyen didn't have any relatives in Lhasa, so a policeman agreed to save Ngawang Melong a seat in one of the vans.

Soon the assembly ground grew noisy. The sentencing was over. Crowds of people walked around on the sun-baked mud, stretching their aching backs. They mobbed the platform, trying to get a good look at the three criminals bound for execution. Ngawang Melong said he was going with the motorcade straight to the execution ground and told Dhargye and Dorje to follow on foot.

Police and soldiers were everywhere. Guards escorted the condemned men onto an open truck. The motorcycle police started their engines and pulled into formation, ready to clear the road. Pious men and women thronged the truck, pleading with the soldiers not to sin by taking the condemned men's lives. Guards lined the perimeter of the truck bed, their rifles at the ready. People in the crowd spat at the soldiers and military police on the truck, clapped their hands in derision, cursed them. A few rocks came flying, thrown by stealthy hands. The soldiers stood motionless, stiff as ramrods. The police kept order along the road, pushing back the crowd. Up ahead, the formation of motorcycles was cutting through the crowd like the prow of a ship slicing through the sea. The long motorcade followed behind. In its wake came a dozen motorcycles—the fellow gang members of the policeman's murderer, his funeral procession. At the execution ground, the peasant bankrobber's family already had a tractor waiting for his body outside the police cordon. Dhargye and Dorje had no transportation, so they had to walk as fast as they could.

Dark, rolling clouds blocked the sun and covered the mountains. Soon the wind would rise. The two men talked on the way to ease their sorrow.

"I'm moving back home in a few days," Dorje said. "How about you?"

"I want to stay. If I settle down here, my children will be Lhasa people."

"I'm taking Shega, but she doesn't really want to go. She likes you. Everybody sees it. Someday, if you really want, come to our town—we'll have a wedding."

Dhargye stared fixedly at the road ahead, pondering. "Maybe some incarnate lama used that bowl Shega gave me my tea in, and it was his power that made me see all that stuff."

"Holy treasures of heaven!" Dorje said. "Maybe I really did kill somebody. Maybe I did it in a past life."

"Maybe everything I saw is going to happen in the future. Who knows?"

"We don't know anything. We're stupid as donkeys."

"Ugyen! That guy owed me three hundred *yuan*."

"It's not fair!" Dorje shouted angrily. "He's unarmed. His hands and feet are tied. He's a man, not a sheep!"

"We're all just sheep. I heard an incarnate lama say that Compassionate Bodhisattva Chenresig is shepherd of the Tibetan people. He came to earth to gather us into the safety of his sheepfold, and as long as there's a single sheep outside the fold, he won't leave us and go back to heaven."

"Hail, Three Jewels, present everywhere." Dorje turned back to the Potala Temple, rising far off in the distance. He joined his hands and closed his eyes, murmuring, "Holy ground, supreme wisdom, protect us travellers far from home."

They walked a couple of hours before they reached the execution ground, a bare, sandy slope at the foot of the mountain—empty, silent, lonely. It was all over: only hawks remained, circling in the sky. Far off they saw Ngawang Melong sitting next to Ugyen's body, which lay on the hillside in a pool of blood. He waved his broad-brimmed hat over Ugyen's face to drive away the flies. Dhargye and Dorje came up and stood silently behind him. The setting sun cast their three shadows far out across the desolate hillside. In their shadow, the pool of Ugyen's congealed blood looked like a patch of oil on the ground.

Ngawang Melong's face was without expression—no grief, no suffering. His outstretched hand continued to fan Ugyen's face. He looked like a *shashlik* vendor fanning the flames beneath his skewers of meat. He murmured, "It's OK . . . it's OK . . . one bullet and it was over . . . didn't say a thing . . . just looked at me as if he never expected me . . . sure I came . . . these filthy flies . . . "

The wind rose. Swirls of sand blew past their feet, rushing at Ugyen's body as if to hurry it off the face of the earth.

Far off, amid the swirling sand, riding toward them on horseback came a vague, terrifying figure. He looked like a wandering hero: the brim of his hat was pulled down over his eyes, and he wore an indomitable, haughty expression on his pockmarked face. His jaw worked as if he was chewing a piece of dried meat. He glanced at the three men, then at the body of Ugyen, hands tied behind his back, lying in the pool of blood, and smiled faintly. "Don't even think of trying to kill me," he drawled.

"Hey! Are you Pockface Sonam Rigzin from Gonjo?" Dhargye called out boldly. This wasn't the man Dorje had killed!

Pockface Sonam Rigzin from Gonjo gave a contemptuous laugh, jerked the reins, and kicked his horse. The chestnut stallion neighed shrilly, and the man raced off into the depths of the hazy, windswept desert.

The medical examiner who checked the corpses found a piece of paper inside Ugyen's shirt. On it the dead man had printed some foreign letters and, below them, a couple of lines of foreign writing. At the bottom, Ugyen had written LOOK EVERYWHERE. THIS PLACE EXISTS. The examiner immediately passed on the piece of paper to the detective who'd been in charge of Ugyen's case. The detective's wife worked as a translator in a travel bureau. She took one look and knew the foreign writing wasn't English or French. An interpreter from Beijing who happened to be in her travel bureau immediately recognized it as Spanish and translated it for her. The flashy letters read BLUE STAR, and the script underneath, 57 AVENIDA DE LA PLAYA, CALLE. It looked like an address. With the help of his son, a high-school student, the detective pored over countless maps of the Spanish-speaking world until they discovered that Calle was the name of a port on the Peruvian coast. Blue Star was probably the name of a bar. The words underneath must have been the bar's address. What mysterious connection could there be between this Peruvian address and a routine Tibetan revenge murder? Unless Ugyen had gone to this seaport bar in Peru and killed somebody there . . . But that was absurd, preposterous, impossible. The riddle continued to trouble the detective. He knew he would never solve it. "But even if Ugyen went to his death denying that he committed the murder in the valley, this bizarre address doesn't prove his innocence," the detective reassured himself.

The gunshot in the valley long ago determined the vagrant road Ugyen was to travel as a man, the holy mission out of ancient myth that he would take upon himself, solemn, tragic, a road stretching on and on over the endless Tibetan plateau, following the spirit of ancient ancestors, pointed and hardened into the tip of a steel knife blade . . . lonely, self-reliant, resolute, throwing down the gauntlet to this modern society catering to foreign tourists. At the pulsating sound of that melodious gunshot, he saw the rifle fall from his father's hands. His father turned. A strange light glittered on his twisted face. With an enormous effort his father seemed to twist himself into an iron rod. A froth of yellow snuff smeared his sparse beard. A rope of saliva hung like a muscle from the corner of his pale lips, stretching, contracting, dropping onto his chest. He staggered, collapsed on the ground, rolled over, then miraculously stood up, raised his slackening feet, and, with his dying strength, walked, then fell to the ground again. He fixed his eyes on his wife, standing before him with their child at her bosom, motionless as a stone. He'd been beaten, struck down by the shot of that wandering acrobat down in the valley. He should never have set out to rob those wandering minstrels. He never imagined the famous Abo Delang was such a crack shot. He had fought his last battle with his robber clan. He would never train his son to be a famous bandit. His young wife shook her head in pity for her dying husband. He crawled to her side and marked a bloody cross on their son's pure-white forehead. With a laugh, he spoke his last words: "Damn. Killing everywhere. With knives. With guns. That's life." Ugyen watched his mother pull his father's knife from his belt and solemnly lay it on him there inside her robe, passing on the legacy to him. The icy blade on his face made him shudder as if he'd gotten an electric shock. The cold steel of the knife pressed against his chest so heavy he couldn't breathe. His father stroked his face, laughed contentedly, and then died.

Twenty years later, on a hazy afternoon, in the final seconds of his life, as the executioner took aim at his heart, Ugyen felt that of all the sorrows of living in this world the greatest was not defeat, not death, but his entanglement in an enormous unfathomable riddle: why had he set out to kill Pockface Sonam Rigzin from Gonjo when he'd never even met him? Whether he really killed him or not . . . whether he killed anybody . . . whether or not the bar with the neon lights really existed . . . what he really desired . . . All at once he understood—a man's greatest desire in this world is to have a son. The overpowering desire to survive and reproduce exploded through his body, tied hand and foot. With a tremendous howl, he leaped like a lion. His every nerve, artery, bone, muscle struggled to free himself.

The gun roared.

With his last ounce of strength, Ugyen sprang forward violently, his wide-open mouth panting. Then everything went dim before his eyes.

Sssst. Someone struck a match and raised it to a half-burned candle. Between him and Dhargye, the telephone without a cord was ringing loudly, shuddering on the soapbox. The two of them gazed at it suspiciously. Dhargye picked up the receiver, trembling. "Hello?" He passed it to Ugyen. "It's for you."

Apprehensively, Ugyen took the receiver. "Who's there?"

He could hear the sound of someone's peaceful breathing. Instinctively,

Ugyen knew who it was. After a moment, a voice said, "Still searching for me?"

"No. Not anymore." Ugyen shook his head.

"Then what do you want now?"

He thought a moment. "A son." When he'd spoken, he hung up.

"Pockface Sonam Rigzin from Gonjo?" Dhargye asked.

Ugyen didn't reply.

"We met him. At noon, on the execution ground."

"I'm not dead?" Ugyen asked, at a loss for an explanation.

"Go ask Ngawang Melong and old granny Longna. They'll explain." Dhargye cradled the telephone in his arms, checking all around it. He gave it a pat and said, "Funny telephone. No cord, still rings."

Ugyen folded his hands behind his head and looked up through the narrow slit in the tent roof at the crystal-blue stars. The execution ground appeared vividly before his eyes. He didn't know if he was alive or dead, but he knew he could still think. And he had one idea. He wanted a son. He felt this was a good thought.

Translation by Herbert J. Batt

Cleaning the Statues, Leh, July 2, 1988
Lama Iche Wangchuk dusts the statues.
Photograph by Karl-Einar Löfqvist

Two Poems

TIBET, MOTHER, *MANI*

Deep is the mantra essence of Tibet—
the Six Syllables.
Pure white is the snow flower of Tibet—
the Six-Petalled One.
Profound is the dharma of Tibet—
our mothers' precepts.

With smiles, Tibetan mothers
bestow our earliest good wishes.
With smiles, Tibetan mothers
relay our first words of reason.
These flow from our mothers' hearts with
sincerity and warmth. And in that same moment of nascent
wonder when we come to know both mother and *mani,*
we utter the words together, *"mani"* and *"Ama."*
Hearing the croon of our mothers' *mani,*
we fall asleep without fear.
Listening to the croon of our mothers' *mani,*
we grow up unharmed.
Fierce Protector of Life,
which burns with the force of our mothers' blessings—
the prayers for our karma
which suffuse our mothers' earnest breath.

With these words by the mothers of Tibet,
mani is chanted by the people of Tibet,
mani falls on the mountains of Tibet,
mani is carried in the waters of Tibet,
and the winds and fires of Tibet roar *mani.*
Mani grows with the flowers of Tibet.
Mani falls with the snows of Tibet.
The *mani* of Tibet emanates from our mothers,
and is thus imbued with the *ama* of Tibet.

The pure goodwill and prayer
offered her descendants by the mothers of Tibet—
the great happiness and peace
offered all people by the mothers of Tibet—
Om mani padme hum!

Translation by Lauran R. Hartley

THE WORLD SEEN FROM ANOTHER ANGLE

Riding the wave of history the wrong way
I am left here.

When the accusing finger presses
The belly of the sky demoness
Hard and very deep
It makes just a murmuring sound.

The friend who sells you
A poison concoction
Extends a tongue of honey.

While pouring milk in your mouth
He reaches inside of your heart.
While stroking your head with his hand
He kicks your foot.
Although you meet with opportunities,
The higher you climb the steps
The more your hands are bound by fear.
Habit dictates you sit cross-legged on the grass,
Experience makes you smile for the Lord of Death.
Although your mouth laughs,
Is it possible that you do not suffer inside?
I think there are tears in the corners of your smiling eyes.

Sometimes even—
At night I hear the gods devouring corpses
And I see ghosts meditating in the day.
When I listen closely to the melody of a pleasant song
The notes sever my tongue at its root.
When I see clearly the surface of a beautiful drawing
My eyeball is pierced by a line.

Sometimes even—
When the red part returns to the heart
And the white part sinks down
Oh, God—there are no footprints in the soul.
A knife tears the heart
And the body shakes with fear.

Hey—Go back, go back!
Here your feelings will be transformed.
Instead,
Look at those in deep sleep,
Their heads cushioned on the old myths.
How happy those dreams are,
How contented those bodies and minds.

Translation by Ronald D. Schwartz

Two Poems

Turquoise among clouds
Gold in waves of light
Crystal-headed spirits seated among silver firs,
Their flash is their song,
The chant of the grassland:

Deer graze under heaven, drink
The waters of ancient earth.
Antelope bolt through the fragrance of flowers all year round.
O God, how fair is the noon you bestow!
Our eyes brim with oceans of animals,
Elegant-horned, sturdy-coated.

Flames of hotsprings tremble in bright air,
Red-robed lamas cover the hills.
At the words of their prayers, yaks nod their enormous heads.
Swans emerge from the lotus-filled hearts of round lakes.

Grassland, silent under your black cloak,
Chanting yourself with unceasing song
In the coolness of each smooth round stone,
Every passing bird's shadow,
Since long before flowers were given their names!

THE WOLF

Eyes
Deeper than darkness
And more silent

Fangs
Sharper than grief
And more bright

When the sun shines on the earth
The wolf has nothing to do with us
Hidden deep in mountain wilderness.
But when twilight dims the peaks
    And my gaze vaguely follows the river into the dusk
Suddenly I'm alone
Musing on grassland, cliffs, wind

And the wolf floats up before me
Loping out of deep mountain folds.

Its stride more fluid than wind
And more fierce

Its howl
Longer than any knife
And more keen.

Translations by Herbert J. Batt

Breakfast Tea, January 2, 1998
Breakfast at the home of the schoolmaster.
Photograph by Karl-Einar Löfqvist

Your Birth Day

1

I know you, I know everything about you because I am always with you. You are an ordinary man, you have five senses like other men. But you are very clever, knowledgeable, honest, patient, and brave—in those ways you are much better than other men.

However, you are an unlucky man. When you came into this world, there were no special signs, such as earthquakes or rainbows. I am sure that you came into this world with a loud cry. Your father was overjoyed when he learned you were a boy. He went on the roof with a conch shell and, as is our tradition, blew it three times in order to announce that you had been born on this earth. Moreover, having been blessed with a son, he pressed his hands together in front of his chest and prayed that all your wishes would be fulfilled.

As soon as you were born, your mother, although in the grip of unimaginable pain, raised her head to see if you were a boy or girl and had all five senses. However, only your parents heard your cry, only a few neighbors heard your father blowing the conch shell. When your father prayed for you, nobody knew; even the local gods and protectors didn't hear. Only your mother knows how painful it was for her.

You are an unlucky child. When you were born, both your father and mother were beside you, but your father disappeared two hours later. Since then, you have been an orphan.

Your parents' life story is a long one, sometimes sad and sometimes humorous. If you want to know their story, please ask your mother. She will tell you about her life with your father.

2

However, I have to tell you something that is not clear in your mind and that you could never remember—your birthday.

You are really an unlucky child. You are one of the children born during the Cultural Revolution. You were born in 1968 and don't know your birthday. Even your mother doesn't know it. You were raised during the movement to destroy the Four Olds—old thoughts, old customs, old culture, and old habits—and among people shouting, "Revolution is no crime. It is reasonable to rebel." Your father's crime was that he believed it is indeed reasonable.

Two hours after you were born, five or six Red Guards came to your home holding sticks in their hands. One of them was your father's best friend, Samten. All your father's crimes can be traced to your birth. His crime was blowing the conch shell three times to announce you were born on this earth—that was your father's crime.

The Red Guards tied your father's hands behind his back and led him away by a string around his neck. At that moment, your father called out, "My son, my sweetheart!" and turned back to look at you with tears falling to the ground. It is impossible for you to know how your father felt at that time. Even I cannot describe it with pen and paper. Since then, your father has not returned home.

I don't need to tell you about your mother's feelings, the situation of you and her at that time, because your mother knows this and she will tell you. You don't know your father's story after he left you; even your mother doesn't know. So I have to tell you the story of what happened to your father after he left you. Please listen to me.

3

Your father is a brave man, a really brave man. He was twenty-nine years old at the time the Red Guards led him by a string around his neck into the heavy rain and the strong wind. There was a clap of loud thunder. For your birth, this could not have been a good sign. It was a sign that you would be an orphan.

Your ancestors had something they could rely on for protection: the Triple Gem. That is why your village has something precious, something to which everything is offered generation after generation. It is the monastery located above your village.

The Red Guards took your father, beating him all the way to the monastery. The gate of the monastery has a picture of Mao Tse-tung. Not long before, DGA DHE ZIL NEON LING (the place of subduing enemies) was written above the gate. Now, there is written MIMANG CHIKHANG (the common house of the people).

A few years ago, monks recited prayers in soft voices: "I take refuge in the Buddha. I take refuge in the Dharma. I take refuge in the Sangha. I take refuge in the Triple Gem." Now, people shout, "Defeat the Triple Gem! Long live Chairman Mao!"

Not long ago, many young people in your village gathered together and burned incense. With the smoke spreading across the sky, they shouted,

"Lhagyallo, protector Amny Nyanchen, . . . Kiki soso Lhagyallo!" Now, the cry "Religion, gods, and protectors are superstitions; annihilate the Four Olds" fills the air.

That day was not just your birthday. It was also the day of the meeting to refute counterrevolution. Communist Party secretary Zheng and other staff were on the stage, proud of their meeting. All the people of your village were heroes and heroines because of the counterrevolutionaries, which included your father. All the people were enraged. How did they get this angry? I should ask a god, if there is a reliable one. But it was a time for not believing in each other or anything.

Opening the meeting to refute counterrevolution, Party secretary Zheng announced the crimes of the counterrevolutionaries:

> Damchoe, for drinking human blood and eating human flesh.
> Lhagyal, for believing in religion, gods, and protectors.
> Sonam, for being connected with the Dalai Lama clique.
> Geden, for deceiving people to get goods from them.

These were the counterrevolutionaries. Each man was wearing a tall hat made from paper, and a square plank hung on his chest from the neck. On the plank were each man's crime and a red cross. One of the men was your father. I am going to tell you what your father's name is. Your father's name is Lhagyal. Lhagyal believed in religion, gods, and protectors. He is your father. All this happened on your birthday. That is why you are an unlucky child.

Not only that happened. The people of your village beat the counterrevolutionaries, beat them to make them confess their crimes. Actually, the people who beat the counterrevolutionaries didn't know what the crime of counterrevolution is—they didn't even know why they were beating the counterrevolutionaries. The people, including your father, who had been accused of counterrevolution by the Communists didn't know what their crimes were, so what were they going to confess to? All the people getting mad had no idea what they were doing.

Your father's best friend, Samten, became a hero. He slapped your father on the face and said, "Lhagyal, the counterrevolutionary, if you have gods, you bring them here."

Your father clenched his teeth and raised his head.

"Raising your head to challenge the Communist Party," said Samten and stuck his finger in your father's eye.

4

I am going to continue telling your father's story. The Red Guards took the criminals, including your father, to Rebkong town. There were many counterrevolutionaries who had been brought there from different areas of

Rebkong: Shar Kalden Gyatso, Alak Dzangkar, the chief of Gyolpo Lingt-shang, and Rongwo Nangso, among others. All of them were accused of counterrevolution and were surrounded by soldiers with guns and by hundreds of Red Guards holding the red book called *Selected Works of Chairman Mao* and shouting, "Refute the counterrevolution! Long live Chairman Mao!"

The day of your birth was nearly over. The sun was going down behind the western mountain. The busy town of Rebkong was slowly becoming dark and quiet. The counterrevolutionaries were divided into two groups, put into two trucks, and taken somewhere—nobody knows where.

However, the tracks taking the counterrevolutionaries north of Rebkong broke into the quiet night. I am so sorry. I don't know anything about your father after that. I don't know whether he is alive or dead. I can tell you only that your father has not yet returned home.

Room 218, Hurrah!

1

The night breeze scattered yellow leaves across the long, silent path, wafting the scent of autumn foliage over the campus. From the goose-necked streetlamp poured an inexhaustible milk-white glow. In its radiance, Sanga was immersing himself in the study of *Human Anatomy*. His eyes were hooded with fatigue. For two years he had sat there every night, the streetlamp his only companion. *Isn't that enough now?* The question echoed in his mind. *So tired . . . No! Remember your vow!* His ardor rekindled, all these distractions were swept from his mind.

Finally he reached into the pocket of his cotton trousers and pulled out a wristwatch with a broken strap: 1 A.M. He raised his head and looked up at the sky, crowded with silent, tranquil stars winking at him. In praise? Admiration? Mockery? Envy? He shook his head. The enigmatic expression of the stars baffled him. He shook his head and slowly began to gather the notebooks and mimeographed handouts spread on the ground before him. How many fifteen-hour days of intense study and heavy physical training had ended this way? Did he regret them? No, he must not! On the day he'd gotten back his first test, he'd made a vow to catch up to Zhang Cheng in two years . . .

"How much did you get, Gaga?" Zhang Cheng asked Sanga, using his nickname. He displayed his own test paper, marked "93," across his chest.

"Thirty," Sanga replied in an almost inaudible voice, his head bowed as if he was meekly apologizing.

"Thirty! Not so bad—after all, you can't compare with the rest of us. You're from Tibet."

"Can't compare with you . . . ?" He looked up in surprise at Zhang Cheng.

"Hmm . . . What I mean is: Tibet has leaped from a primitive slaveholding society to a socialist one. But what's in here"—he crooked his forefinger and tapped his forehead—"can't change as fast as social conditions. I was . . . Now Sanga, don't get mad . . . I went to the southwest for my job, and I saw Tibetans. Your faces and bodies are all covered with hair, right? So you haven't completely evolved into modern humans."

Sanga had not heard the last of Zhang Cheng's goading. Ready to explode, he could feel rage rising in his throat. He stared balefully at Zhang Cheng, but held his anger. Instead he sublimated it, poring over the notebooks and handouts lying on the ground before him . . .

Sanga slowly walked down the empty, pitch-black dormitory corridor, trying to muffle his steps. The metal cleats on the soles of his shoes rang against the cement floor.

He stopped in front of room 218, quietly pushed open the door, and heard the familiar sound of even breathing and snoring. These sounds always gave him a warm feeling, and he couldn't help a smile, knowing his roommates were off in dreamland.

Crash! Sanga banged his foot against someone's tin washbasin. Immediately the four beds creaked. "Doesn't sleep himself," Zhang Cheng muttered through his teeth, "doesn't let anybody else sleep."

Zhang Cheng enjoyed his status as dorm-room monitor. He liked calling out in a commanding voice, "Gaga, go get some more boiled water," "Gaga, mop the floor." But he wasn't as good at discharging his responsibility as a study-group leader and assisting Sanga with his studies. When Sanga came to him with *Human Anatomy* in hand, Zhang Cheng would explain that the sympathetic nerve system regulates the skeletal muscle system, but not bother to explain that it also regulates the function of the inner organs.

Sanga forgave him for this. What he couldn't forgive Zhang Cheng for was killing animals—a sacrilege to Buddhists. Whenever he had a chance, Zhang Cheng enjoyed catching and killing birds, frogs, little turtles. That one time . . . Suddenly Sanga remembered that he hadn't fed the birds. He took a few grains of rice from the bowl on the table and scattered them into the little cardboard box on the ledge outside the window. At once he heard their chirping. He smiled . . . They were still alive! The only thing he'd ever asked Zhang Cheng for was these two little sparrows. Zhang Cheng had climbed up to a nest under the gymnasium eaves and taken these newly fledged sparrows to fry for a snack. Sanga hadn't wanted the little creatures to perish, so he'd swallowed his dignity and said, "Zhang Cheng, please give me the little birds. I . . . " When Zhang Cheng saw Sanga's sincere expression, he couldn't refuse.

Sanga lay down. A comfortable feeling of well being spread through his whole body. The end of another fifteen-hour day.

He dropped off to sleep, but Zhang Cheng lay awake. As Sanga worked later and later into the night, Zhang Cheng felt more and more pressure. What if this low-IQ guy beat his grades? Sanga couldn't match him in brains or educational background, and it was he, Zhang Cheng, who belonged in first place. If one day Sanga should . . . Zhang Cheng didn't even want to think about it.

Zhang Cheng enjoyed prestige not only as dorm-room monitor and study-group leader. He was also skilled at debating. And before enrolling in the college, he'd worked for the research institute of a municipal physical-education bureau. As his first choice on the registration form for the university entrance exam he'd written MEDICAL SCHOOL. He knew Mendeleev's periodic chart of the elements by heart, so he thought he was sure to qualify. Then fate had plunged him into this place for people with well-developed bodies and simple minds—a physical-education college. Whenever he went downtown, he always carefully placed the flap of his breast pocket over the part of his college badge that read PHYSICAL EDUCATION. All that people he met on the street could see was BEIJING . . . COLLEGE.

2

"Professor Lu, what did I get?"

After a test, Sanga never asked the teacher his grade. But today he couldn't help himself. He'd started to study a month before the others, beginning with cell structure and going all the way to the lever action of the limbs. He was certain that he had finally caught up with his classmates.

"Come on up, come on," Mr. Lu beckoned to him with a pleased smile. Then he lay a test paper before Sanga on the desk. Sanga looked at it: 93! He stared at the sheet, then glanced up at Mr. Lu.

"Powerful as a yak!" said Mr. Lu. "Third in the class!"

"Third in the class?" Sanga felt his body tremble.

"Yes—and the champion of dorm room 218."

"Ah!" He held the precious test paper. It felt heavy—like the college's acceptance letter of three years before. But this was more thrilling! He dashed from the anatomy building out onto the athletic field, sprinted around the track, turned ridiculous somersaults, did laughable backflips.

"Victory!"

The four hundred meters of the track couldn't contain his mad joy. After two years of suffering, agitation, confusion, he'd beaten forty-nine of the fifty-two people in the class, including his own study-group leader, Zhang Cheng.

Like a wild colt let free, he gamboled from the athletic field to the dormitory. "Tang Wei! Tang Wei!" He wanted to share his joy with the roommate whom the department had assigned to tutor him. For two years, Tang Wei had sat at Sanga's side, showing him where each muscle attaches to the skeleton, explaining in detail the function of the myelin sheath as an electric insulator for nerve endings. When Sanga didn't understand what an insulator was, Tang Wei patiently took the plastic insulation on an electric cord and demonstrated that an insulator is a substance that doesn't conduct electricity.

"Tang Wei! Listen! Wait till I tell you! . . ."

Tang Wei lay on his bed, using a rolled-up blanket as a pillow. Sanga threw his arms around him and his blanket too. Over the past two years, lively, rough, spontaneous Sanga had gradually become solitary, taciturn, restrained. Now his pent-up feelings burst forth like a mighty torrent.

How he wished, as he hugged Tang Wei, that his classmates were like the hometown pals that he used to wrestle with: reeking of sweat, grasping each other's waists until their two bodies became one.

"What's the matter with you? You've got my blanket all dirty!" Tang Wei shoved Sanga away and began to brush the dust off his bed.

Sanga's boiling heart was plunged into an icy river. He looked at Tang Wei. No, Tang Wei couldn't take such primitive, hot emotion.

The class monitor opened the weekly youth-league meeting that night by saying, "On behalf of the entire class, I want to congratulate Sanga on the great advances he's made in his studies. If he goes on working like this, he'll get 150 on his next test and we'll have to award him a pair of glasses."

As soon as the class monitor's voice fell silent, Sanga heard someone say, "Nice going! He ought to explain his method."

"Method?" somebody else sniffed. "He just memorized the whole stinking book."

Torn between the congratulations and the sarcasm, Sanga didn't know what kind of expression to wear. He rejoiced silently. Not only had he fulfilled the vow he'd made to himself, but he'd also erased the ignominious reputation that Tibetan students had acquired at the college. His teachers mentioned former students from Tibet who always ranked at the bottom of their class. Now, perhaps, these teachers would no longer tell him "You special students from Tibet aren't required to take English . . . aren't required to take accounting . . . aren't required to take organic chemistry. . ."

"Sanga, you got 93? Great!"

"Sanga, I missed question number five—can I see your answer?"

He'd never imagined it. Even students in the other classes had heard about him. Sanga's grade became the news of the whole department. He recalled the only other time he'd been the center of attention . . .

3

"How come you're not wearing a leather robe?"

"Can you understand what I'm saying?"

"Where's your Tibetan knife? Hey, how many men have you . . . "

Curious freshmen encircled Sanga, staring at him as if he were a space alien. The blood rushed to his head. His face, copper-colored from the powerful ultraviolet rays of the Tibetan sun, grew dark as a thundercloud.

"Know what this is?" One pointed to the rice in his bowl.

"If you don't all get the hell out of here, I'll . . . !" he roared, sounding like an angry lion. His words resounded up and down the corridor. The curiosity seekers ran for their lives.

A few diehards still gazed at him through half-open doors when monitor Li Xiang came along carrying a thermos of boiled water. "What do you guys think you're staring at? Sylvester Stallone? . . . Don't get mad," Li Xiang said, turning to Sanga. "They've just never seen a Tibetan before."

"If they bother me again, I'll knock them flat!" Sanga responded firmly.

Li Xiang stood with the thermos in his hand, resting his gaze on Sanga's face. "You're a real Tibetan!"

Li Xiang had grown up in the far-western province of Xinjiang, among children of different minorities. He felt nostalgic for his primitive homeland and its straightforward, rugged people. Their bold, free ways had made a strong impression on Li Xiang and inclined his own character toward independence.

Though his marks couldn't compare with Zhang Cheng's, Li Xiang was a responsible, capable class monitor. When it was Zhang Cheng's turn to get the dorm room's hot water, Li Xiang roused him, saying, "Hey, Zhang Cheng, the bell is ringing down at the water hole!" This line never failed: without a word, Zhang Cheng laid down *Nine Hundred Sentences in Modern English*, picked up the thermos bottles, and set off for the hot-water tank.

Li Xiang felt ashamed that he wasn't able to help Sanga with his studies. He had to write more than one supplemental examination himself. But he spent a good deal of time helping Sanga improve his hip-thrust technique in the shot put.

Most diligent in helping Sanga was Zhou Da, who slept in the far corner of the dorm room. This taciturn young man hardly ever spoke a word to Sanga, and when he did, it was no more than a toneless "Have anything to wash? Just put it with my things there." If ninety percent of athletes are the outgoing type, Zhou Da certainly belonged to the introspective ten percent. It took only a few days at the college for his classmates to nickname him Silent. But those who understood his character realized that, once roused, quiet, well-behaved Zhou Da would explode like a volcano.

In the shot-put test at the end of the previous year, Zhou Da had been manning the measuring tape while Zhang Cheng called out the results. Sanga's first two tosses went the same distance: 6.5 meters. Zhou Da watched uneasily. Sanga would fail if he didn't make 7 meters on his last try.

As Sanga prepared for his last attempt, Li Xiang walked up to him, demonstrated the stride-and-hip-thrust technique they'd worked on together, said something in Sanga's ear, and patted him on the shoulder. Zhou Da saw Sanga instantly look more confident, pick up the shot, pause a moment, stride, thrust out his hip, and give the shot a mighty heave.

Splendid! The shot cut a rainbow arc through the air. Eight meters at least, Zhou Da reckoned.

"Six point nine," Zhang Cheng called out.

What? Six point nine? How could Zhang Cheng make a mistake like that? Or . . . could he be trying to . . . "Check that!" Zhou Da commanded Zhang Cheng.

"If you don't believe me, come check it yourself!" Zhang Cheng snapped back and in a tone so rude he thought Zhou Da would not dare take him up on it.

But Silent stood up. And as he did, Zhang Cheng slid the measuring tape with a move so subtle that no one on the sidelines, including the burly shot-put instructor, noticed it. But this move didn't escape Zhou Da, who in spite of his languid appearance was as keen-eyed as Sherlock Holmes.

"You rotten . . . Give him the right distance!" Zhou Da gave Zhang Cheng a surreptitious poke.

"Oh, uh . . . no—8.3!" Zhang Cheng called out in a shaky voice.

Neither Zhang Cheng nor Zhou Da ever mentioned this incident to anyone.

4

In the perpetual round of college life, the one thing a student looks forward to is a package from home. Every day after class, the students of room 218 peered in the mailbox, asked the mailman . . .

"Sanga, you've got a parcel slip!" Tang Wei shouted from down the corridor.

"A parcel slip? Give it here!"

Sanga snatched it and raced to the post-office counter.

His four roommates flocked around him for a look at this exotic present from the roof of the world. As they pressed closer, he laid his package on the table and carefully cut the strings one by one.

"Packed in a mess tin?"

Sanga opened it. "Yak butter!" he shouted excitedly.

"Yak butter?" Tang Wei echoed uncertainly.

His roommates had heard of yak butter, but they'd never seen it. In their minds, yak butter was something sweet and crispy.

There before Sanga, the golden-yellow butter glistened with the love of his family far away. He smiled.

Instinctively, his roommates drew back. The yak butter gave off a strange and unpleasant odor. "That yak butter's rancid, isn't it?" Tang Wei couldn't help asking.

"Uh . . . it has a strong smell, like . . . hmmm . . . "

Zhang Cheng took out his handkerchief as if he was going to blow his nose and pinched his nostrils. They looked at one another, embarrassed and silent.

Li Xiang spoke up. "In fact . . . you know . . . yak butter is really nutritious." From the table, he took half a steamed bun left over from his lunch and spread some of the butter on it. "In Xinjiang we often eat—" He chewed the buttered roll. His face twisted into an awkward expression. With a struggle, he managed to swallow.

"Good?" Tang Wei teased.

"Not . . . bad." Li Xiang reached for the thermos and poured a cup of water.

After the last class that afternoon, Sanga remained to ask the teacher a question. His four roommates went back to their room.

Tang Wei sniffed. "Hmm . . . That yak-butter smell is stronger all the time."

"It stinks," Zhang Cheng responded caustically.

Zhou Da opened the window, walked back silently, and sat down on his bed.

"Let's wait," Li Xiang put in. "Maybe we'll get used to the smell. I'll have a talk with—"

Sanga rushed in excitedly. Though there wasn't much, he was going to share the yak butter with his roommates. "Nobody buy anything at the cafeteria today. You can all have a treat. We'll bring back some steamed rolls and have yak butter with them," he said, taking the tin out of his drawer. Since he loved yak butter, he assumed everybody else would too.

"Why don't you throw that stuff away?"

Sanga couldn't figure out if Tang Wei was joking. "Throw it away?" Surely he must be teasing.

"Listen. Thanks, Sanga," Li Xiang said in a conciliatory voice, "but we're not used to yak butter. Besides, it's warm in here, and it could spoil. Why don't you put it out on the window ledge? It'll keep cool there."

What was this? Sanga sized up the expressions on their faces. And then it struck him . . . They despised him . . . They even despised what he ate . . . He felt violated, as if his heart had been plunged in ice-cold water. "OK. Go ahead and eat," he said. "I'll take care of this."

When they left, he pulled out the kerosene stove from under his bed. The flame of the stove surged like the rage inside him. In a moment, the smell of the melting yak butter filled the whole room, pouring out into the corridor. When he'd finished melting the butter, he picked up his bowl and went to the cafeteria for some steamed rolls.

Standing in the cafeteria line, he couldn't take his mind off the yak butter . . . He was going to soak his rolls in the melted butter and feast.

With his bowl full of steamed rolls, Sanga walked into his dorm room. "Where's my butter?"

Tang Wei gave him a glance and snorted, "Hunh!"

"You—where'd you put it?!" Sanga grabbed Tang Wei by the shirtfront and made a fist.

"I . . . What're you gonna do?" Tang Wei didn't dare look in Sanga's daggerlike eyes.

"I'm going to . . . " As he raised his hand, Sanga saw Tang Wei's faint-hearted look. He felt the pity of the strong for the weak. Unconsciously, he lowered his fist.

At the class meeting next evening, Sanga and Tang Wei were each called upon to give a self-critical speech. Tang Wei gabbed on and on. It was supposed to be a self-criticism, but it turned into a self-defense.

"It was my fault yesterday," Sanga said when it was his turn. "I deserve to be punished—I won't eat yak butter in the dormitory again. But I want to ask my roommates not to eat garlic there either. That's all."

Everybody thought Sanga's short, simple self-criticism was sincere, but asking his roommates to give up garlic—well, that was a bit too much.

5

The last day of their last semester had arrived. Winter vacation would begin the next day. When they returned to campus next semester, they would immediately set out to their internships at various schools and institutes all over northern China. Students were busy buying delicacies and treats to take home with them for the New Year celebrations.

Every year when his classmates left for winter vacation, Sanga remained alone for three weeks in the dormitory. The tiny cluttered room became empty, vast, bleak. Late at night, all human sounds ceased. Another vacation alone on the campus . . .

Soft, downy flakes of snow fell thickly all that night.

Next morning, he stood at the window, taking in the first winter scene of the year. The snow-covered campus gleamed in the early light, bringing memories of his homeland teeming into his mind. Quietly, his roommates came to the window, lost in contemplation of the white universe.

"Listen," said Li Xiang, "this is our last time together in this room. When we come back next semester, we'll be going right out to our internships. The trains will be packed today with all the students going home. Let's stay here and clean up the mess in this room. Tomorrow the trains won't be nearly so crowded. What do you say?"

Everyone agreed. With Li Xiang taking the lead, they began cleaning the litter out from all the corners of the room.

From under one bed, Sanga pulled out a bone that Zhou Da had sneaked from the anatomy room when he was studying for an exam. "Silent, what are you doing, running around without your tibia?"

"Gaga, you're even worse"—Li Xiang called, pulling a skull out from under Sanga's bed—"losing your head like this." Sanga chuckled and everyone joined in, the room filling with laughter.

When they'd finished cleaning up, the others began packing their suitcases. Afternoon sun poured through the window. The room was clean, the suitcases were packed, and everyone was sitting around bored.

Li Xiang stood up. "Listen, to celebrate the end of our three years' study and the new look we've given room 218, let's have a little party. I'll contribute something for toasts!"

The campus lay deep beneath the winter snow. The dormitory rooms were dark and deserted. Only the window of room 218 shone, and its laughter echoed up and down the empty corridor. Tang Wei brought out a huge cake he'd packed to take home. Silent fried up some eggs. Zhang Cheng brought out some milk chocolate, some peanuts, and an almost empty bag of malted milk powder.

Li Xiang poured everyone a glass of strong, clear liquor. They all stood up, tossed back their heads, and emptied their glasses. Li Xiang poured another round.

Amid the happiness of the moment, Sanga felt a twinge of sadness. He was the only one with nothing to give the others. He felt in his pockets, then looked in his trunk, but all he found was a little plastic bag. "I'm sorry . . . I don't have anything, just this dried yak meat. My family sent it to me. Do you want to try it? It doesn't smell," he said softly. "Really."

"Sure. Come on," Li Xiang said, then took a piece and nibbled at it with evident gusto.

Zhou Da took a slice of the yak meat and gave Tang Wei a look. Tang Wei reached for a piece. As he put it to his mouth, he smelled something sour.

Zhang Cheng did not fail to grasp the import of all this. He reached for the last piece of yak meat, raised his glass, turned to Sanga, and said, "Sanga, I want to make a toast to you. My toast is not just to congratulate you. I want to ask you to forgive me. I didn't help you with your studies as I should have." Perhaps it was the enthusiasm of the moment—for Sanga failed to notice the cool, calculating look in Zhang Cheng's eye.

They emptied their glasses.

"Last round," Li Xiang said, grinning as he poured again.

Tomorrow, Sanga thought, his roommates would be leaving, and he . . .

Taciturn Zhou Da stood watching the expression on Sanga's face. Suddenly he exclaimed, "Gaga! Come home with me for the holidays. My family would love to meet you."

Sanga stood dumbstruck, gazing at his roommates. He threw his arm around Silent, raised his glass, and shouted, "Room 218, hurrah!"

Translation by Herbert J. Batt

A God without Gender

She gazed around. Everywhere were lustrous purple willows and houses. She didn't understand what the steward shouted to her. She turned, looked back, saw the dome of a gigantic white stupa towering between lofty twin mountains. At its base, human figures were stirring. A sparkling scarlet ring crowned its pinnacle. She shut her eyes against its burning light. "Second Little Miss, wake up. Look!" She opened her eyes again, perplexed, and stared up where the steward pointed: a shining precipice cut by brown fissures. Its crest blazed.

"The Potala Palace, Second Little Miss! You remember?" No, it was no dream; it was her nanny's hoarse voice that called to her. "The dwelling of Bodhisattva Chenresig, *ah mo mo!*"

A fresh, cool breeze swept her face. She awoke from her stupor. From the foot of the mountain, a steep stairway wound up through a cluster of tall trees. On the trees' branches hung wisps of greenish smoke from burning juniper boughs. The ringing of bells and the drone of prayers poured from the windows of the red-walled palace. Trembling smoke scattered down through the forest.

She joined her hands and recited the mantra *"Om mani padme hum,"* merging body and soul in this holy sublimation of the powers of apprehension.

Gaslights blazed in the courtyard. The steward helped me down off my horse.

"Second Little Miss has arrived."

The glaring, hissing lights hurt my eyes. I couldn't see the people around me, but only heard the voice of the steward, the sharp, broken cries of servants, the pleasant sound of the Lhasa accent. I walked into a broad corridor.

Three women in splendid satin gowns stood before me like painted ladies on a vase. Thin and covered with jewels, they smiled at me. One woman a little older than the others took my hand and said, "Little girl, who's your mama?"

I looked behind me. My nanny bowed, beaming. I pointed at her. She had accompanied me into my new home.

The older lady turned to the two women behind her. "*Ha, ha!* Doesn't even know her own mother!" The three ladies laughed gracefully.

A second lady walked up to me and stroked my face. On her long hand was a diamond ring. "Just like a peasant girl."

"Hair all matted with dirt!" exclaimed the third.

"When you've had some tea, Governess," said the tall, older lady, "please take her for a bath." This lady was the most senior of the master's three wives.

"Yes, Mistress." A tall, thin woman with sunken eyes—the manageress of the household—stared at me, then approached.

My nanny touched her forehead to mine and blew out the candle. "In the holy land of Lord Buddha, you can sleep soundly. Good night, Miss."

There was a fragrance in the quilt that made my head ache. I felt sick to my stomach. I'd ridden on horseback for eight days; now I couldn't sleep. It was terribly muggy. I sat up. Moonlight streamed in the window. The sickening fragrance congealed in the moonlight—gray-white, gray-white. I heard the hiss of gaslights, the clack of mahjong tiles, voices, laughter, but I didn't know where they were coming from. I'd lost my sense of direction. A dark light flashed in the corner.

That person in the mirror: maroon silk robe, smooth-shaven head . . . Was it me? How had I changed . . . into a nun?!

"You don't like it?" Governess asked me. I noticed that she knit her eyebrows.

Her teacher told her a story . . .

Smoke spiraled upward all year long. A crisscross of gullies, an ominous mountain, weeds scattered everywhere. The smoke from the brazier of burning juniper branches drifted out over the valley, marvelously forming an auspicious hooked cross. Villagers from beyond the mountains realized that an incarnate lama deeply compassionate, clairvoyant, and possessed of awesome powers dwelt in this valley. In search of spiritual growth and mystic teaching, the people climbed up along the little brook, through the tiny pass.

Tashi, the lama's disciple, watched all this in consternation. At first he thought the stream of people would ebb when autumn had passed, but every day more and more pious believers flooded into the valley, prostrated themselves, touched their foreheads to the incarnate lama's feet in deeper and deeper veneration. Their ever-growing numbers dismayed Tashi.

Besides diligently serving the incarnate lama, Tashi assiduously studied a variety of sutras. Observing this, the lama led Tashi up to the top of the mountain, pointed to a little cave barely visible among the lofty cliffs, and told him to meditate there for a month . . .

Tashi emerged from the mountain cave with his head down. His pale, sunken face was distraught. He had meditated a month, enduring hunger and cold, but no sign had appeared to him. He had had no vision, heard no miraculous voice. He reeled down the slope, then suddenly smelled a terrible stench. Covering his nose with his hands, he searched for its source. A swarm of flies buzzed around a sick, ugly bitch lying flat on the ground, and countless maggots wriggled in her dark-red anus. "Ai!" Compassion welled up in his heart. He took off his robe, tore off its bottom half, and spread the cloth on the ground. Squatting down, he gently picked off the maggots one by one with a pair of twigs and placed them on the cloth. He drove away the flies, carried off the maggots in the cloth and buried them, then covered the dog with the other half of his robe. Continuing on his way down the mountain, he shivered in his sleeveless shirt.

He knelt in shame before the incarnate lama. "Teacher, I failed. I meditated a month in vain."

"You did not fail. Stand up."

"What?" He raised his head and gazed in bewilderment at the lama.

"On your way back, you saw a sick dog. And what did you think? A live dog covered in maggots—how pitiful!" The lama nodded. "Your month-long meditation was barren because your heart was impure. You thought of the prestige and status that success would bring you. But your meditation has borne fruit. The root of the dharma *is compassion." Tashi reached out and received his robe from the lama. It was whole, bearing no mark of repair.*

"How did the lama get Tashi's robe, Teacher?"

"It is only a story. A story can say anything."

With her teacher, she stood on the slope of green grass and trees. A tiny path wound down from their feet to the bottom of the mountain. Quietly, wild goats meandered by a murmuring brook on the side of the valley. Beside the path grew wild pomegranates, dazzlingly bright. "What the incarnate lama taught Tashi was not secret magic arts or profound Mahayana doctrine, but the importance of a pure heart and love." Teacher tossed away a stone and walked down the slope.

The light, delicate scent of the wild pomegranates filled the air. The drifting fragrance seemed to merge with the brook and the bright, clear calls of the birds. Today, for the first time, the convent was sending her to the city to beg for alms. She wanted the little path to continue forever, but she also wanted to go home to see her mother and her nanny.

"Don't hurry." Teacher bent over again with difficulty, picked up another stone from the road, and tossed it away. "Throw away the one under your foot too."

She threw away the stone, gazing down at the pass at the foot of the mountain. "When I get to the city, won't it be dark?"

"To clear the obstacle of sin from the spirit, making travel easy for all those on the way is also compassion."

Their red robes wafted in the leisurely wind like prayer flags.

"Is that a way to accumulate virtue?"

"Of course." Teacher caught up from behind, panting slightly. "Why are you wearing those funny gloves? To clear away obstacles and plant good *karma,* you cannot avoid filth. Please take them off." Obediently, she pulled off the gloves. They were exquisitely knitted and of fine white wool. Embroidered on the back in yellow thread was a tiny hooked cross. The gloves didn't cover her hands entirely, but left the fingers bare.

Funny gloves.

As soon as I awoke, I couldn't resist the impulse to leave the bedroom.

"I've brought breakfast to your room, Second Little Miss." A maidservant caught up with me in the corridor and blocked my way. "You can wash your face."

"I want to go out," I said, waving her away.

Governess walked straight in the door. "What's this noise? The mistress has just fallen asleep."

"I have to get out of that room. I don't like that smell. I want to use my own woolen quilt tonight."

"Second Little Miss, it is only servants who do not use satin. I sprinkled it for you with French perfume. Of course, if you have better, please tell me." When she said this, she raised her eyebrows and left, her face devoid of expression.

The lawn gave off the clean, plain smell of grass and earth. It gave me a cozy feeling, like being on the meadow back at the manor. But here they fussily trimmed the grass, so it wasn't uneven as at the manor. A furry little dog came running up to me with its tongue hanging out, plopped down at my side, and licked its belly. Bees came buzzing around my head. I sat down on the grass, indolent as a bee, dreadfully bored. Through the light-blue smoke drifting through the grove came a slow, leisurely song that made me uneasy.

I went to look for the source of the song. At the back of the grove was a dark row of servants' cottages, small and dreary beneath the high walls. The melody was coming from the open door of a cottage with windows covered in cheap white cloth.

With head down, someone was sitting on a straw cushion and knitting. Black cotton shoes, a Tibetan robe of black cloth, close-cropped hair, a white, white face on a slender neck. Suddenly the furry little dog appeared in front of him, and the man's voice abruptly ceased. He looked up and stared at me in alarm. After a pause, he set down his bamboo knitting needles, gestured to me, and said something I couldn't understand. I asked a passing maidservant who this was.

"Chinese Lobsang." She explained that the lord of the house had brought him back from Chamdo and replaced his Chinese name with a Tibetan one.

He raised his head and smiled at me, his two eyes squinting into one long crease. The wrinkles covering his forehead looked out of place on so smooth a face.

Whenever she heard it, she felt uncomfortable. Though Governess forbade it, she often ran off to the servants' quarters to gaze at him as he knit with his bamboo needles and to listen to him sing his peculiar, desolate song. In broken Tibetan, he told her that it was an ancient song from his hometown, but what it was about, he didn't know.

"Are you afraid of demons?" she asked him.

"In Tibet, Miss?" His needles froze. "Demons?"

"Yes! They come out as soon as it's dark!" She thrust her head in the window, opened her eyes wide, grinned, put her fingers against the sides of her head and extended them so they looked like horns, and then swayed back and forth, howling.

"Me . . . scared?" His two eyes squinted into a single seam, and he burst out laughing. "You not be afraid. I come catch."

That night a sheet of low black clouds covered the moon and stars, stirring a wild wind. The prayer flags on the courtyard wall fluttered in the wind with a peculiar, cracking sound. The bewildered dogs barked madly. People went to bed early to escape the frenzied gusts. After the last courtyard lamp went out, the wind fell silent. The dogs' barking ceased and their eyes shone dimly in the blackness.

A piercing scream rang out: "Mistress!" A dark shadow rushed through the servants' entrance and into the courtyard, then scurried up to the main door.

Instantly, lamps and candles were lit in every room. People dashed out, terrified. All they could see was Chinese Lobsang standing barefoot on the steps in a pair of floppy underpants, waving his arms. "Demon! Mistress! Demon! In quilt!"

Supported by her maidservants, the mistress came out trembling, her robe draped over her shoulders and her hair in disarray. She shouted to Governess to light the gaslights and ordered the steward to take every manservant to Chinese Lobsang's cottage.

The maidservants cowered together, their robes pulled on in haste, their hands over their bosoms as they screamed.

Two manservants dragged a great black shape into the courtyard and threw it on the steps. *Whack!*

"*Ah mo mo!*" the household cried, shrinking back.

Before them was a great, bulging cowhide sack, its top knotted with a leather cord, its smooth, round bottom painted with a terrifying red face that had a huge, bloody mouth full of long, sharp teeth. "The soul-sucking sack!" the people cried in panic. Such a sack took the last breaths of dying people.

"From the Hall of Heavenly Guardian Tsimare in Tengyeling Temple!" the steward shrieked, approaching the sack with a look no one had ever seen on his face. "Stolen from the temple! Who could have put it in Chinese Lobsang's bed? Heavenly Guardian Tsimare will be enraged! Light up boughs, purify the house with juniper smoke, or there will be disaster!"

The mistress gasped. Her hair stood on end. Her long robe dragged on the ground.

"Give it here, give it here," the steward said as he snatched a smoking brazier from a maidservant who had approached the sack with it.

"A woman mustn't touch that sack!" Governess hissed at the maidservant. "It would suck the soul out of you!" A cloud of thick smoke merged with the cries of Chinese Lobsang and the susurration of the maidservants' prayers.

She sat beside her teacher, looking out over the valley . . .

A flock of yellow ducks flapped their wings and quacked contentedly in the grass. The wandering monk sat by the stream, scrubbing his clothes with deft, practiced hands. He then spread his clothes on the grass to dry, took out some baby yams from his bag, and scattered them for the ducks to eat. When he had finished feeding them, he rang his ritual bell and began a hymn. A fierce male eagle swooped down, calmly snatched up the bell in its beak, and flew back into the sky. Watching the eagle, the monk saw it circle gracefully, set the bell down on a cliff on a distant peak, and then fly away.

The wandering monk built a hut at the top of that peak and lived there as a hermit, continually meditating. The mountain people brought him offerings of food. One day a rainbow appeared over the peak, and the air overflowed with the delicate fragrance of wild pomegranates. The monk paused in his meditation, then felt a sudden burning, like a flame pouring into his stomach. An uneasy feeling gradually filled his body.

The people who were there with their offerings saw the monk changing. His voice became delicate and high-pitched, his face acquired a womanly beauty, his bosom swelled. Long, long ago, some old people had seen the sky mother goddess appear on this precipice. The people watching the monk realized that the sky mother had taken possession of his body and that the place was sacred. Crowds from all around and, later, from the holy city beyond the mountains came to help build the sky mother's temple, and many women offered themselves at the temple as nuns.

The mandala turns, age succeeds age. Over and over, people rebuild the wooden steps of this temple, over and over the chant leader appoints a successor, and still the fragrant smoke of the holy fire rises—vigorous, clear, and pure.

"I pray for the blessing of the Buddha, I pray for the blessing of the *dharma*, I pray for the blessing of the lamas . . . " At her teacher's side, she knelt on a thin cushion in front of the tiny, gentle lamp burning before the simple Buddha image in the ancient shrine and softly chanted "Sutra of the Refuge of the Dharma."

After they finished evening prayer, they left the little hall and were walking down the narrow stairs when that marvelous, sorrowful song ran through her mind. In an instant, her mind's peacefulness was shattered.

Chinese Lobsang entered the room behind the steward, wearing a pointed, black, Tibetan-style hat that he'd knitted himself. Around his long, slender neck, he had knotted a red silk cord into protective Buddhist talismans. When had he begun accompanying the steward as he spun prayer wheels at nightfall on the Barkhor? As soon as Chinese Lobsang saw me, he joined his hands and bowed deeply, saying, "Honored Jetsun!"—a term meaning "spiritual guide." The prayer beads between his fingers swayed slowly in the setting sun's rays. His black clothing made his face seem paler, more emaciated.

Since I entered the convent, everyone in the household except my mother had been calling me Jetsun, and was respectful and reserved in my presence. This courtesy reminded me of life at the old countryside manor —its big kitchen, its grain pile, and the clean scent of earth and rain.

I was sitting out in the sunlight and peeling the scabs off the back of little maidservant Tsomu. When my oldest cousin had gotten angry at her, he'd poured burning coals down the back of her neck. Tittering as I touched her, she blew the white sheets of skin into the sky.

The warm, dimly lit kitchen was full of the scent of burning yak dung. Little Tsomu and I ate roasted potatoes as we listened to the caravan drivers' loud, crude talk about sly female shopkeepers and the color of Nepalese women's skin.

The beating wings of the wild pigeons swept over the roof, bearing away their mellow cooing. The five-colored prayer flags were motionless against the background of evening clouds. All around there was a solemn stillness. In the rose-colored evening, the slow, bleak song came drifting from beyond the grove like a dream. My body seemed to dissolve and float into the evening fog. An inexplicable, overwhelming desire rose up in me.

His hands knitted with practiced ease as he leaned against the door frame. Lost in reverie, he gazed at the setting sun and sang. His usual expression had vanished as if the hand of some demon had wiped it from his pure-white face, leaving an expressionless mask in its place.

I walked up to him and said, "Tomorrow is the Day of Universal Peace, when we celebrate Buddha's birthday and his enlightenment. Won't you come worship Lord Buddha with us?"

He turned to me and said, "Honored Jetsun!" Apprehensively, he folded his hands and bowed.

I repeated my invitation.

"How I dare? How I dare? Mistress not allow me go. I am servant." He rocked his head oddly.

"Tomorrow is the Day of Universal Peace. The mistress will let you go."

He continued rapidly bowing to me, hands clasped. "Day of Peace, Day of Peace. My breath stinks. Blasphemy."

"But didn't the mistress give you a box of tooth powder?"

"But . . . it does not wash out garlic stink." Knowing the smell was offensive to Tibetans, he clutched his head, his whole face red.

"As long as you sincerely want to worship and you practice good deeds, Lord Buddha doesn't care about that." The setting sun was a disk of red. Gratitude welled up in my heart. Thank you, Compassionate One, I thought.

"Thank you for paradise fruit you gave me, Jetsun."

"Thank you for the beautiful gloves you made me."

> May all follow the way of bliss.
> May all sources of bliss increase.
> May all beings extricate themselves from suffering,
> And from the sources of suffering.
> May all sentient beings cast off enmity and vain desire,
> And be of one heart, one mind.

She set down the book, still open, on her knee. The sky was clear azure. The mountain ridge blocked the sun. The valley was dark, translucent. The white stupa was suffused with a cold, clear, lonely light. A little calf kept close to the mother *pian* cow that roved back and forth by the bank of the stream among a herd of wild goats.

"You're doing well, doing well, my disciple."

Her heart shrank suddenly at this voice, and her thoughts were thrown into turmoil. Angrily she shut her book. "Who is it?"

"It's me, your honored teacher!" Behind her the strange, mannish voice spoke again.

"It's you, Chungchung! You frightened me!"

She turned, took the pail from Chungchung's hand, and plunged it into the stream. The two of them then sat down on the bank.

"Look!" Chungchung shouted, pointing to the distant slope, where a figure quickly disappeared behind the rocks.

"It's Norlha, isn't it? Where is she going?"

"Down the mountain maybe," answered Chungchung. "Her teacher gave her a scolding this morning."

"She didn't remember her sutra again?"

"No, her teacher said her shape had changed."

"Her shape had changed?" All Norlha had done wrong was to eat a lot of wild pomegranates. Her nose had turned black, and she was often sick to her stomach, had gotten fat, and often vomited. Why had Norlha's teacher been so harsh with her? The scent of wild pomegranates burst over her with the ring of bells on the necks of goats in the weeds. Fear consumed her . . . Hadn't she secretly filled her own pockets with wild pomegranates whenever she went to collect firewood?

"What a shame . . . such a pleasing beauty." Chungchung leaned and stared at the distant slope.

"Don't say that. Her teacher got angry when she heard someone call Norlha a beauty, and she said that was the reason Norlha hadn't memorized her sutra."

"The old biddy."

"There you go again! My teacher is going to have tea. I have to leave." Agitated, she wrapped her book in its yellow silk cloth and hastened away . . .

Slowly she walked up the stairs with the sand-ware teapot. The yak-butter lamp shone on the little, low table. A book with a threadbare, brown-wool cover lay open on her teacher's knees. Teacher sat under a cloak, legs crossed, head swaying continuously from side to side as she whispered the praise of Lord and Protector Jampeyang Bodhisattva.

She shook the teapot and poured tea into her teacher's little wooden bowl. "Why don't you eat some *tsampa?*" she asked.

"Tea will be enough. I can eat at noon and in the evening."

"There's plenty of *tsampa.*"

"No need to waste food. Many are hungry," Teacher said, then blew lightly on the butter that floated on the tea. "Why don't you eat something yourself?" She picked up her prayer beads, eyes already shut.

A silver teapot, a snow-white lace tablecloth, a silver tray covered with pastries dripping butter. Cups and cups of yogurt, Xinjiang grapes, Indian candied fruit, Arabian dates, Kashmiri apricots, apples from the estate. No one ate much. Now and then Big Sister took a small cake, languidly broke off a piece, and gave it to the little dog. Her fingers were covered in butter. When a servant brought in more pastries, the dog feigned disinterest and snuggled up to me, drooping its ears. Laughing, Little Brother and Little Sister threw pieces of candied fruit at each other, then began to throw them at a passing servant.

"Don't do that," I said to them in a low voice.

Governess appeared at their side. "Sit still. Second Young Miss does not permit you to play in your own house," she said to them enigmatically. "You must listen to her." Her sunken eyes gave me a sidelong glance.

My nanny gestured to me, covering her mouth with her hand.

I ran to her. "Why should I keep silent?" I asked angrily.

"Speak softer, Miss." Looking around and lowering her voice, she said, "Old Master cast off the family and abandoned us all the day you came out of your mother's belly. Now your mother is one of the wives in this high-ranking official's residence." She picked a leaf out of my hair. "You must be obedient so that new Master and Governess will like you."

An apple rolled to my feet. Little Brother and Little Sister were shouting and leaping in the bushes. From the corridor a pair of horrible sunken eyes was watching me above lips that wore a cold smile. I wanted to raise my foot and crush the apple. Despite myself, I picked it up.

She walked out of the temple at her teacher's side, filling her lungs with pleasant, cool air. Her heart was bursting with an inexpressible sense of accomplishment. The sky was so blue it seemed to be drawing her up to heaven, the realm of the Buddhas. Walking down the steps, supporting Teacher by the arm, she noticed the ache in her own legs. All day, she had been sitting cross-legged on the thin cushion, answering one question after another, until she had smoothly passed the oral examination. Now she would be a *chuzan,* permitted to study the *Sutra of the Heavenly Guardian* with a teacher from one of the three great temples in Lhasa.

"Most of us live in ignorance," Teacher said in a low voice. "As we practice compassion, our ignorance dissolves. But one must also study hard to clarify the spirit."

The clear chanting of the sutras, the ring of the bell, the mysterious, dark wisps of smoke from burning juniper boughs, the simple grace of the robes—marrow and pith of the temple. More and more she would know, would comprehend all. As she stepped from the last stair onto the soft earth, the familiar yet haunting song came drifting down from heaven.

> *I, Su Wu, hostage of a western tribe,*
> *Cherish my Han god,*
> *Finding no shame in loyalty.*
> *Gulping sleet, chewing hides,*
> *Nineteen years I have endured*
> *Earth of snow, heaven of ice,*
> *A shepherd in bondage*
> *On the shore of a frozen sea.*
> *The insignia has rotted*
> *On my envoy's banner,*
> *And I am captive still,*
> *Finding in old trouble troubles ever new.*
> *My heart is firm as iron.*
> *At midnight I hear the alien flute*
> *High up on the fortress wall*
> *Bitter in my ear.*

Translation by Herbert J. Batt

Three Poems

Translator's Note

I met Meizhuo *(me sgron)*, a Tibetan writer and poet, in summer 1999 while I was working on a research project in Amdo (formerly in northeast Tibet and now incorporated into Qinghai and Gansu Provinces). Since she works from her home, we agreed to meet at her small, two-bedroom flat in Xining, the capital of Qinghai Province. For some reason, I had imagined her to be a physically strong woman, and so I was surprised to discover she is petite and elegant. Meizhuo's flat was small but immaculate, and awards for her writings were arranged neatly on a cupboard against the wall. After drinking some cups of tea, she lit a cigarette with her delicate hands and began to tell me about her life.

Tibetan writers who express themselves in Chinese have received little attention outside of China in recent years; because they write in Chinese, they are considered by many exiled Tibetans to be collaborators or sympathizers with the PRC government. But some Tibetans in China, such as Tashi Dawa, are seen as exceptions. His skillful fiction manages to be creative and imaginative despite his use of Chinese and the conditions this imposes on his work. Less well known but also noteworthy among this new breed of Tibetan writers is Meizhuo.

Born in 1966 in Taktsang, Amdo, Meizhuo lived in various places in the northeast provinces before her parents, both government employees, were stationed in Xining. After graduating from Xining Teachers' College *(qinghai shifan daxue),* Meizhuo was assigned to work at Xining Film Institute *(xining dianying gongsi);* later she was employed at the Literature and Art Association (Wenlian). At the Film Institute, she had, for the first time, many Tibetan colleagues and explored her interest in Tibetan culture. In 1987 she published her first short story and, since then, has written in many genres, including poetry. Because she was the daughter of a high-ranking cadre, her stories received much attention when they were published and she felt great pressure from many quarters. Her breakthrough as a writer came in 1997, when her novel *The Clan of the Sun (taiyang buluo)* won the national award for minority writers.

Like many of her generation, Meizhuo was educated in a Chinese university and therefore can express herself more fluently and accurately in Chinese than Tibetan. When I asked her if she speaks Tibetan, I could sense her unease. Since her childhood, she told me, she had spoken to her parents in Chinese and they had replied in Tibetan. Glancing sideways at me, Meizhuo said that she had tried to learn Tibetan from a teacher, but for various reasons had not continued the lessons. She was relieved and consoled by my comment that many young Tibetans in Switzerland are in the same position.

Because of her father's senior position in the government, Meizhuo had access to historical documents that enabled her to expand her knowledge of Tibet and its history. *The Clan of the Sun* is set in the republican or warlord period (1911–1949). During the last years of this period, from 1938 to 1949, Amdo was controlled by the Chinese Muslim general Ma Bufeng. As we discussed the Muslim-Tibetan war of the thirties and forties, Meizhuo became very agitated. The conflict still has deep resonance for Tibetans living in Amdo today.

A saga of two clans, Meizhuo's novel depicts the ambiguous relationship between Chinese civil servants and Tibetans. Suobai, the chief of the Yida clan, realizes that none of the Tibetans is represented in the government. Consequently, he attempts to establish a school in the village, believing that Tibetans might eventually gain better employment and equal treatment by the Chinese through better education. The resulting conflicts illustrate how traditionally minded Tibetans resist the outside world and how modernity inevitably intrudes in their lives.

As with many Tibetan writers, Meizhuo feels that her culture is misrepresented or distorted in contemporary Chinese fiction. Hence, she feels an obligation to portray Tibetan culture and customs from a more authentic viewpoint. *The Clan of the Sun* attempts such a portrayal. Throughout the novel, the narrator describes in detail the decoration of a prayer room, the process of searching for a new incarnation, the depiction of deities in certain Buddhist scroll paintings *(thangka),* and the concept of hell. Such long and elaborate descriptions are meant to be authentic representations of Tibetan culture.

Meizhuo is obviously familiar with these cultural references, but Tibetan readers sense in her work a certain alienation from them. This might be because her audience is primarily Chinese rather than Tibetan. Nevertheless, she experiments with language in ways that only Tibetans can fully understand. Thus, at the heart of her work is an ambiguity and a question: who does Meizhuo truly write for, Tibetans or Chinese?—Y. D.

The iron hoof has burned on the fertile wild land
But you, you have chosen the high plateau
Like now, like a hungry animal, like the intoxicating lake,
    to wander around
you are destined for the grassland.

The highland is also destined by the totem
The numerous falling eagles
The snow lion hidden in the forest.

On the map, the wings and hooves you have amassed
shrink into a deep red color that no one can repeat
The color of the sun, the color of blood,
a color that the next generation will never understand and tolerate.

Even among those who are not to endure, you have endured it.

A long time ago, I was crossing the border of your territory
spreading ancient love,
looking for your beautiful blue sky.

At last I understood,
your lineage is our natural dwelling which we cannot change
Before becoming proud I was haunted by feelings of inferiority.

Tears are hindering my sight
I cannot see the charm and gentleness that are written
    a thousand times inside me
I cannot see the magpie that consoles a lonely traveler.

Year after year, you were alone at the edge of the highlands
Charmingly naive you disrobe yourself
amazing a race with your transcendence above the worldly

You have taken a consort from far away,
and received also your own people's venerated Buddha
you defended the isolated life
you also brought faith through simple prayer

The country which has risen from the sea,
without gaining strength has become old and feeble.
Is the fire burning in your heart?

Occasionally there are those who awake from your ancestral line
Like you they wake and like you they fall,
At those times you cannot talk, you cannot express the agony
But I am in agony
I repeat my confession many times
I am in agony

TSEYANG GYATSO: MY KING

In the foothills of the Himalayas,
in Tawang,
amid the hardships of three hundred years ago
a child was born to bear the holy spirit
It was you!

It is you
the ocean of compassion and wisdom, precious and of Buddhist lore.
When you embraced the holy spirits
you held your people's faith
you embodied hope but you could not fulfill our hopes
you could not avoid the calamities of desire.

My King, it is you!

The undeserved disaster which befell you
after twenty-four years of winter,
on a day without snow
when the holy spirit left and floated away
At last you had your fortunate escape
At last you could rest in peace.

Ceaselessly, we rock your grave
but there is no one who can receive your precious fallen ashes.
The sentiments which Lacanghan could not destroy
rise slowly above the horizon
The magnificent stars lingering in the sky refuse to vanish

Let us prostrate ourselves
We are sincere and faithful
Like you, we touch our foreheads to the ground with true admiration
day and night, we pray to you.

Thus, my King,
year by year you floated in the wild land of Tawang
You drifted above the gleaming wheat
You floated in faraway places.

Thus, my King, on a winter day without snow,
    after three hundred years
without my noticing you floated to my place
I stretch my hand
and feel the eternal pain you suffered when you fell

MILAREPA: SONG OF A SAINT

I long to go to the eastern holy land
If you pray to me with faithfulness
With tears that are as sincere as your heart
I will prostrate myself before the stupa

Let us bathe in the water of compassion
Nearing dawn, when the sun rises,
we raise our purified faces
With folded hands we touch our foreheads
And so we come to your homeland
of Nyangyul Gongthang.

The house you lived in during your childhood
followed your father into emptiness.
From his grave, your father's concerned eyes
helplessly witnessed his wife and children become beggars.

You offer your body, mind, and speech
Calling for wind and rain, you invoke magic to create hail
overjoyed by revenge yet full of regrets.
Weary of life, you want to escape it
you become the cause for the ultimate unification of faith.

Therefore you are saved and save others
You withdraw from the cycle of life
You eat nettles and drink morning dew
when your whole body shines green,
you seek and attain the ultimate experience

Your followers, eyes full of tears, prostrate themselves before you
their eyes, rejoicing, have become your legacy.

I only desire to hear your name,
just hear your name.

In this way you set yourself alight
You are as magnificent as the rain and rainbow
Your crystal stupa has encompassed
The sacred sound of your golden bell and silver drum
All your wisdom and your sacred *vajra*

I fail to understand your ascetic life
but still beg you to absorb me within your compassion.

Translations by Yangdon Dhondup

Two Poems

LAND OF SNOWS

The Sun God strokes a miraculous silver comb across the earth
To form a Pure Land of snows that ferments the moon in a vat of ice.
When you find the lake hushed as the aqua sky
Don't you know it is His melody
    blazing its way through frozen rivers and peaks?

This glacier's ice stores the feelings of a lifetime!

That is why morning and night go on
    pulling the multicolored streamers of sun and moon,
And I clear the dust storm's mud
    and carry fresh water to my little plot of ground.

THE POTALA—THE VENTURER'S MOUNTING-STONE

Silver under the moon, a pagoda towers to heaven;
Golden stones dazzling in the sun, radiant with wisdom.
The constellation of the ten cultures, its thousand halls;
Thirteen-storied temple, messenger of thirteen centuries.

This red-and-white palace is no facade embellishing the snow city.

O venturing sons of the ages, know the will of the ancestors:
The steles at the Potala gate
    are mounting-stones for you and me
      to vault into the stirrups of our dreams!

Translations by Herbert J. Batt

Pipiting, July 26, 1988
The last sunbeams hit Pipiting gompa, *at the foot of the mountains.*
Photograph by Karl-Einar Löfqvist

Tomorrow's Weather Will Be Better _____

1

He drove his ox and his shaggy donkey, loaded with sacks of dung, along the rough, winding mountain path toward the little village that lay on the hill ahead. On his own back he carried a sack of sheep dung. From the neck of the ox hung a copper bell, from the donkey's neck an iron bell. With each lumbering step of the animals, the bells rang a contrasting harmony, splendid in the mountain stillness.

The cord of the dung sack cut into the sun-darkened skin on the back of Kelsang Tashi's neck. He had looped the crimson tiestrings of his winter hat into a knot like a flower beneath his chin, so it swayed from side to side like the bells hanging from the animals' necks. Pearls of sweat sprang from his forehead and temples and ran down his cheeks, onto his jaw. When the trickling sweat stung his eyes, he wiped them with the cracked palm of his dirty hand.

For fifty years he'd been carrying loads up and down this rough mountain path. Now his knees were swollen, and he hobbled like a cripple. He so accepted his body's declining strength that he didn't give it a thought.

Long before the first cockcrow, Kelsang Tashi had gotten out of bed, scooped some *tsampa* into his leather pouch, and gone out into the pitch dark. Trotting through the still of night with his ox and donkey, he had only taken a couple of hours to reach the pasturelands where the nomad herdsmen grazed their livestock. Everything was asleep, except for some mountain sparrows hopping about and some voles running playfully through the grass. He filled the large sacks with yak dung, and the smaller one with sheep dung. Hungry, he took out the *tsampa* from his pouch, only to discover it had frozen into lumps of ice.

It was cold, and Kelsang Tashi's stomach ached with hunger. He forced himself to gnaw one of the frozen chunks. Though he could hear his teeth grinding the ice, he couldn't taste a thing. He stuffed what was left of the *tsampa* back into his leather pouch, loaded the ox and donkey, swung the sack of sheep dung over his shoulder, and hurriedly set out on his way home.

Save for the steady clomping of his ox and donkey and the ringing of their bells, the familiar road was silent. The mountain was still a black shadow in the east. Smoke from cooking fires rose from the chimneys of the little houses in the village where his neighbors were boiling water for tea and cooking their morning gruel. Nobody had come out yet to drive sheep and oxen to pasture. *The sky gets light so early now,* he thought to himself, *and I'm already back from the pastureland with my load of dung.* He felt so happy, so proud!

Like many young men, Kelsang Tashi's elder son had gone to the city to work as a construction laborer in order to save money to get married. Last year there had been a long drought, so the harvest had been a very poor one. It had been difficult just making it through the winter, so he hadn't been able to afford to get his son married and to bring his bride into their home. He felt remorseful and remembered a proverb: "If last year's crop was poor, this year's will make up for it." He regretted the way he'd gone about his work last year. Resolving to put more energy into it, he'd begun early, just a week after New Year, gathering dung with fervor. He had a goal. No matter what happened, this year he would have a good harvest and bring a wife for his son into their home. Mother had suggested sending their elder daughter out into the fields to help him, but when he imagined her working out in the bitter cold, he rejected the idea. "Never mind," he said. "It's too cold today. There'll be plenty of work for her when the time comes."

Two weeks after New Year, the other villagers went out to work in their fields. They saw how he rushed about, but nobody outside his family knew the hour he woke up or went to bed.

Returning early now, he unloaded the sacks of yak dung onto the manure pile in his field, covered the pile with a layer of earth, and then carried the sack of sheep dung to the house. As usual, his older daughter came out to take the sack from him so that he could rest his back.

As soon as he stepped inside the door, he drank off the rice wine his wife had ready for him—three bowls, one after another.

"Father, you didn't wash your face," his daughter reminded him. "It's all sweaty."

Kelsang Tashi just laughed, said nothing, and wiped off the sweat with his hand. His wife brought him a bowl of freshly kneaded *tsampa* in one hand and a bowl of warm *tsampa* porridge in the other, only to see him already twisting sheep's wool into yarn. It seemed to her that his hands always itched for something to do.

To save time, he wolfed down the *tsampa* and gulped down the porridge. Then he picked up his farm tools and went back out to his field, followed by his elder daughter and younger son.

The sky was overcast, melancholy. The wind blew in cold gusts, and their frozen bones ached. Plowed last autumn, the soft soil swirled in the wind, forcing them to close their eyes. They wrapped strips of cloth around their faces, but their eyes were left uncovered and unprotected. They rubbed their watering eyes continually. By the time they went home for lunch, their clothes and hair were covered in pale, white dust, and a layer of it covered their faces like makeup. Anyone who saw them would think they were stage actors. But there was nothing comical or happy about their appearance. They formed an image of hardship long endured.

Every day Kelsang Tashi and his children tirelessly dashed back and forth across his field, spreading manure, watering, plowing, sowing, and weeding. Often, he rose long before cockcrow and set off with his donkey to collect manure and firewood at the top of the mountain. Occasionally, at his wife's urging, he would take his elder daughter with him. He would always arrive home at dusk, just as the village herd boys were driving their livestock back in from the pasture. He would put away his tools, drive his sheep into their fold, and put the ox and the donkey into their shed with hay and grain for them to eat. When his wife saw him go on working after he came home, she would say with feeling, "Kelsang Tashi, first come drink a bowl of hot tea, won't you?" He would look up at Pema Dolkar and calmly reply, "Don't worry, I'll be finished soon." However, as soon as he completed one chore, he would find another to do; thus, he never drank his bowl of tea until the sun had gone behind the mountain.

The first thing he would do when he finally walked in the door at the end of the day was say, "*Brrr*, it's cold," rubbing his hands together as hard as he could to warm them. But no matter how cold the weather, you could never tell it by his face because there was always sweat on his forehead. He would go to the kitchen to stoke the fire, then light the kerosene lamp, rub the dust out of his eyes with his sleeve, take the wet cotton cloth his daughter handed him, and give his face a wipe.

His family was known in the village for always eating supper after dark. A doctor would have said that eating so late was unhealthy. Busy with their work, the whole family sat together by the light of the kitchen fire until there was no sound outside but the occasional bark of a dog. His little daughter liked to snuggle up against her mother's breast as the woman sat with her older daughter, twisting sheep's wool into yarn.

Once, when his younger son sat watching idly, hands folded around his knees, Kelsang Tashi said to him, "Sitting with your hands folded, looking around—what fun, eh?"

Half-jokingly his son replied, "But if you don't have anything to eat, your guts will stick together!" He looked at his father and burst out laughing.

As it grew late, the children would doze off. "It's getting cold," Mother would say, tired herself. "If we don't go to bed soon, we'll have to burn more firewood. Isn't it better to go to bed now?"

"If I don't get work done when the nights are long," he would reply, "how will I get everything done in spring, when the nights are shorter and there's even more to do? If a man just eats and sleeps, he's no better than a corpse."

2

Kelsang Tashi resolved to bring in a good harvest this year so that he could get a bride for his son. When spring came and the nights grew shorter, he still made his younger son and older daughter get up before dawn, just as if it were winter, to go out and spread manure on the field. When his neighbors saw the manure spread out, as if it had been defecated by a passing flock of migrating cranes, they were absolutely astounded. "That manure didn't run onto the field all by itself, did it?" they whispered to each other. "Kelsang Tashi must not have slept all night!"

An old proverb says, "If you don't make the dust fly working in spring, autumn will bring you no shiny, dark grain." Whenever Kelsang Tashi saw anybody performing his spring work casually, he recited this proverb. His mother had given him only two hands, but if he didn't work as if he had more, wouldn't those two hands be useless if there were no harvest?

The surrounding hills were still overcast and gray, as though not yet awake from their dreams, and the grasslands and trees around the village looked like his hair, streaked with the white of the remaining snow. But the time for spring sowing had arrived, and while his hair was getting whiter and whiter, it would not be long before the gray of the earth would be turning green and vital—newly alive.

Swiftly, he walked to the field with an old-fashioned wooden plow on his back, driving his ox with the bell around its neck. In keeping with tradition, he festooned the horns and tail of the ox with red tassels and a flowered nine-eyed belt. He gripped the plow handle, broke into an old mountain song, and began to plow. Behind him walked his daughter with a leather seed bag slung over her shoulder, scattering the seed into the furrow.

She didn't know how many hours had passed or how much ground they had plowed when she saw the exhausted ox begin to pant and drip white froth from its mouth. The sound of the tinkling bell grew fainter and fainter. Father himself was worn out, dripping with sweat under the burning sun. He had already taken off his jacket. Now he stripped off his dusty, sweat-soaked shirt, threw it aside, hitched up his woolen trousers, and trudged ahead, naked to the waist and oblivious to the sun. His feet sank deep into the mud with every step, and beads of perspiration ran down his jaw. He raised his whip to urge on the old ox and sang out in a hoarse voice a plowman's song:

> *If the ox doesn't stick to the edge of the furrow,*
> *I follow behind the plow in sorrow . . .*

When he had finished singing, his weariness and melancholy seemed to have vanished. The song's melody gave voice to his work. But no matter how he urged his old ox on, it could continue no longer. Finally, it lay down on the earth like an old man who had carried a heavy load across the grasslands without anything to eat—too weak even to stand. Thrust deep into the earth, the plowshare stood motionless. The yoke lay still across the animal's neck. Kelsang Tashi raised his whip and lashed the ox's rump for all he was worth while his daughter tugged on the harness to pull the ox to its feet, but the animal was oblivious to its master's cries. He became disheartened and angry. Then he looked up and saw, not far off, the young fellow with whom he had quarreled at the irrigation canal the previous day. He remembered that when he returned home after the argument, he had regretted it. There just wasn't enough water for everyone's field. He blamed himself: why didn't he have the power to somehow find water? Today, that young fellow seemed terribly pleased with himself, grinning and jeering. He sang loudly, plowing swiftly behind a powerful young ox. Kelsang Tashi grew all the more angry and lashed his ox fiercely, then flew into a rage and began kicking the animal—all for nothing. His daughter felt sorry for the ox and pleaded with her father; finally, he stopped. Father and daughter unharnessed the ox and took off its yoke, and the old animal rolled over, exhausted, on the ground. In its eyes were bean-sized tears.

Kelsang Tashi sat on the ground, staring apathetically across his field as he wiped the sweat off his face and neck with his dirty shirt. He at last drank from his plastic bottle of *chang* in a single gulp. Taking a pinch of snuff, he anxiously noticed how dry the soil was under the blazing sun. He had no second ox to harness. *If only I were an ox*, he thought to himself.

The young lad had quickly finished plowing his field. When he saw old uncle Kelsang Tashi sitting helplessly, he walked up to his daughter and said straightforwardly, "Kunsang, get your seed, and I'll help your family plow the rest of your field!" The young fellow lashed his ox onward, and Kunsang fell in step behind him, casting the seed. Talking and laughing together, they soon had the job done.

Kelsang Tashi was in a quandary. *The young man saved me from disaster, like hot coals in a snowstorm. I should be grateful. But do I have to depend on someone else to finish my spring plowing? Did I give up? Am I good for nothing? It's degrading! I'm so ashamed!* Of course he knew that spring plowing is critical. If the land isn't plowed in time, it means disaster. Suddenly an old proverb came to mind: "Why complain that your belly's bloated after a good meal?" And this gave him comfort.

The sown fields changed color, and the green seedlings began soaking up moisture. The women busily hoed and weeded, enabling the men to relax for a few days.

Hearing *"Cuckoo, cuckoo"* in the woods, people said, "The cuckoo has cleaned out the poison that the squirrel and the woodpecker put in the water! All the animals can drink the water now and get strong again after winter." The poets rightly call the cuckoo the herald of spring.

The sky, as if jealous of the multiplicity of colors on Earth, became a deeper azure. You could see far into the distance, just as in autumn. The clouds—clear, white, lazy, and carefree—floated high up in the sky. But the sky spirit refused to send rain. It was the beginning of the spring drought. The villagers put on straw hats or wrapped cloth around their heads to keep the heat off. Even then, the sunlight reflecting off of the ground scorched them.

The cuckoo's call seemed to turn mournful, like a long, tragic sigh. Kelsang Tashi complained, "Go on and cry! Your coming has turned the sky blue and frightened away the clouds." But he never cursed the bird. Though it and the drought arrived at the same time, the cuckoo couldn't know the sky spirit's will.

3

In the dry heat, under the broiling sun, each family relied on its tiny daily ration of water from the village leader to irrigate its field. They watered the young plants at night, even when there was no moon, dipping buckets into the water that trickled in their irrigation canals, then groping their way along familiar paths in the dark to get to the plants' thirsty mouths. They took care to not waste a drop and forsook food and sleep in their struggle to save their dry, young shoots. Even when the village leader allotted him no water, Kelsang Tashi couldn't stay inside. He walked around his field, inspecting the dying seedlings, and racked his brains like a man trying to save a dying person. Tormented by anxiety, he paced his field and sang a song passed down through generations:

> The sky spirit wears a blue suit
> But the seedlings wear monk's yellow.
> Turquoise rain dragon way down south,
> What's distracting you!

It was a melancholy song, sung from the bottom of his heart—a tragic cry of expiring hope.

Sometimes a rain cloud would appear, a shower would wet the mountains, and hope would spring up in Kelsang Tashi's heart. Then he'd be busier than a weather forecaster, praying to the Three Jewels for help: "Take heed and send rain to save us farmers." But the rain would lurk among the mountaintops like a wily animal reluctant to come down to the lowlands, and wind would scatter the black clouds. At these times, Kelsang Tashi's chest filled with hopeless rage and he cursed the vast, cruel sky: "Ah! The weather's never been so hot! You want to play the devil and burn us to death—go ahead!" Obsessively, from sunrise until sunset, he scanned the sky, which was always clear and azure—not a cloud anywhere.

Days, the sun was blazing. Evenings, a chilly wind blew through the vil-

lage, making it difficult for the people to sleep. Kelsang Tashi knew that
these were the signs of a drought. If the weather went on like this much
longer, there would be no hope for a good harvest. Still, he wouldn't sur-
render. Early each morning, he took his younger son and elder daughter to
see if the village leader would allot him water for his seedlings, which were
wilting in earth as hot and dry as sand in a frying pan. *Water is more precious than gold or silver,* he thought to himself in despair.

Sagadawa, the mid-April festival of the full moon, arrived, and the villagers prayed to the earth spirit for rain. That afternoon, rain fell on the
mountaintop but still refused to descend to the fields. Some men caught a
frog and a scorpion and set them fighting. If the frog beats the scorpion,
says an old proverb, it will rain; if the scorpion wins, the drought will continue. Meanwhile, crowds of villagers walked three miles to the creek. Boys
and girls splashed each other, men threw women into the creek, and everyone chased each other in the water until they were all soaking wet, like
birds after a bath. Some women grabbed Kelsang Tashi to throw him in.
The wetter he got, the better for the weather, he thought, so he didn't resist,
hoping that it would bring rain. Many girls were soaked, and he chased
them around.

The villagers played and splashed for hours under the scorching sun.
That afternoon, as they walked home from the creek, the sky—as if jealous
of their game—grew dark with clouds and began raining heavily. Kelsang
Tashi couldn't suppress his joy. He believed that their splashing each other
had worked. That night he couldn't sleep. He gazed out at his field, wondering whether the rain would last through the night.

Early next morning, when his wife saw that he was awake, she looked up
from her housework and said to him in a kindly way, "Husband, don't go
out this morning. Stay at home and have a good sleep." But Kelsang Tashi's
mind was on how the crops were thriving after the rain. How could he sleep
when he felt as elated as a child at New Year? Not hearing what his wife was
saying, he jumped out of bed, climbed into his trousers, pulled on his shirt,
and ran outside to see the change in the fields.

He couldn't hold back a cry of amazement. The trees and grass were
pale and yellow no longer. In a single night, the crops had changed color.
Everything gleamed with moisture. In the fields and on the hillsides, the
green plants swelled with energy and life. Kelsang Tashi's laughter was
sweet.

As usual, that day his face ran with sweat, like the waterways in the grasslands. His hands were covered with dirt. More than once his wife urged
him, "Take some time today and give your hands and face a good wash."
He raised a hand to his face in his usual way, gave it a careless wipe, and
laughed. "Yesterday we splashed each other in the creek," he said, "so I
don't need to wash. But I'll do it to please you, Mother!" He wiped his face
with cold water and washed himself quickly, then rubbed his face with oil,

sat down, opened his snuff pouch, tapped some snuff onto his fingernail, and raised it to his nose. The only time he ever relaxed a little was when he savored his snuff; but today he could spare no time even for this because from outside his home a voice shouted that each household had to send somebody to a village meeting right away.

"Those people manage to find out the one minute I have for myself!" he exclaimed. He inhaled his snuff so hurriedly that he left half of it clinging to his nostrils, then he jumped up and ran out.

4

The rain filled Kelsang Tashi's heart with joy. He felt that the happy day when he would bring his son's wife into the home was close at hand. He imagined the wedding. They would hold the ceremony there in that room. Everything decorated, his friends all gathered for the celebration, he seated at the head of the table, holding high his wineglass and offering toast after toast to the couple. Much singing and dancing—a day to remember!

The drought had passed, but crops have many enemies who will attack without warning. A local soothsayer, an expert at preventing hail, explained a secret preventative method to the villagers: "Drive wooden stakes into the corners of the field. When summer hail comes down from the mountain, it will bump its nose on the wooden stakes and come no further." Because the villagers believed in the soothsayer's power, they thought his method would work. Kelsang Tashi and everybody else drove stakes into the corners of their fields. And no hail came.

Now, the men's work was done. Kelsang Tashi's wife and elder daughter went out to the field every day to pull weeds, and he looked for something else to do. It was the season for picking medicinal herbs, so he saw many villagers going up into the mountains to gather them. *My son's wedding is this year,* he thought to himself. *I don't have any other income, and I'm going to need a lot of money, so it would be a good idea for me to go too.* Once he'd made up his mind to do this, nothing his wife or his daughter said could dissuade him. His younger son said, "Father, you don't have to go alone. I'm young, I'm strong. I can help you!"

And so Kelsang Tashi and his son climbed the snowy peak five thousand meters above sea level. From morning to night, they risked their lives picking herbs. When they were hungry, they ate a few handfuls of the dried *tsampa* they'd brought with them. Every time they found a plant, they went wild with joy, as if it were a jewel. They stretched their hands into cracks in the rocks and turned boulders over until their fingers were cut and bleeding. The herbs grow above the snow line, where even in July there is heavy snowfall, torrential rain, and sleet. During storms, the shivering herb gatherers sought shelter in the gaps between the cliffs and worked hunched up against the freezing wind. When they slept, many of them crammed into a nomad's tiny hut. Everyone had come from far away, and no one had brought bedding. Each night, they huddled in coarse woolen blankets on the bare earth floor, keeping their clothes on for days, until their bodies were covered with lice and they itched so much they couldn't sleep. Kelsang Tashi had brought with him a precious antidote, which father and son diluted with water and washed with every day.

After braving danger for a week on the steep cliffsides, Kelsang Tashi took his dried herbs to the traders, who graded them medium quality and paid him one hundred *yuan* for seven kilograms. This was the most money he had earned all year. Ecstatic, he bought five bricks of tea leaves, enough for the whole family for several months; for his two daughters, four meters of cloth to make blouses with; and for his younger son, a pair of running shoes. The rest of the money he kept for his older son's wedding.

This year's harvest would be better than last year's. His crops had withstood the spring drought, and though the plants were not large or plentiful, he was satisfied. He felt grateful for the protection of the Three Jewels. After returning from gathering herbs, he placed a ring of bricks around the field to protect it from flooding.

From spring planting to autumn threshing, weather is the farmer's enemy. Even if there is no drought, there might be downpours, hail, frost, or prolonged drizzle—one possible calamity after another. From earliest times, humans have wished to control the weather, but the sky has always resisted.

As the time for the horse-racing festival drew near, the crops turned golden yellow, and faith and hope filled Kelsang Tashi's heart.

One day, when the setting sun's rays shone through clouds above the mountain, the whole sky suddenly grew black, thunder rumbled, the wind howled, and lightning flashed across the heavens. Kelsang Tashi fidgeted as if there were a stone in his shoe. The last thing he wanted was hail. He gazed at the sky. Rain began to pour. He shouted, "Beat it!" If only his words could control the heavens! But they had not the slightest effect. He turned once more to the Three Jewels, praying for their protection. At this very moment, he heard an enormous crackling sound and something hard hit his face. The villagers rushed out of their homes, dazed and bewildered. The mountain peak had turned white. The soothsayer famed for preventing hail shouted at the clouds from the top of his house, "Scat! Scat!" An elder cried out, "If these women keep screaming, it will bring down the hail!" and told the women to be quiet and stop cursing. But nothing—not the stakes in the corners of the fields, the experienced soothsayer, or the screams of the women—had the power to restrain the great hailstones that poured down like a warrior host from the sky. Miserably, the terrified villagers smelled the crushed grass, trees, and crops. Kelsang Tashi heard the sound of sobbing.

Though the hail finally stopped, the rain kept pouring. A vast sheet of water stretched in all directions. The men went to check their fields. Some searched with flashlights for the source of the floodwater, but in vain. And since they didn't know where it came from, how could they stop it? With a few other older men, Kelsang Tashi staggered back from the fields. Soaked and torn, his clothes hung from his arms and legs.

His wife rushed out and asked, "The crops? The crops?"

"Finished," he replied, heartbroken. "Nothing in sight but the flood."

"If hail and floods come, what can we do?" His wife tried to console him. "As long as people are safe."

The water gushing over the fields resounded in Kelsang Tashi's ears all night. He thought of his plans, his hopes, his futile efforts. He didn't sleep all night.

At dawn, his head felt heavy and his body weak. Groaning, he said, "What's wrong with me?" He struggled out of bed and pulled on his soaking clothes. Though the sky was gray and rain still falling, he ran to his field. He saw the near-ripe crops battered and crooked, as if trampled by a herd of animals. He stared vacantly, listening to women weep as if their families were dead. Then his mind went blank, and he started to faint. Suddenly he heard his daughter Kunsang call his name. He came to himself. He was crying, but he wanted to spare his daughter his suffering. He gazed at the twisting, rugged mountain road in the distance and said to her, "It's no use grieving. When a wife loses her husband, he's lost forever. When we lose a year's harvest, we can make it up next year. It's no good grieving. There's a saying, 'Tomorrow's weather will be better.' If we throw ourselves into our work and fight nature, we'll have a great harvest next year. Wait till everybody sees the great luck we'll have then!" And so, everyone waited for the next year's good fortune.

Translation by Yangdon Dhondup

from "The Lightning Field" _____

6

a patch of virga/a verse paragraph
slant marks/slashing the sky/silvered in a shaft
of sunlight/pellucid virgules marking time
and pitch in a run of silent recitativo
no skittering drops/no rivulets of rhyme
shearing off the windshield/dripping from eaves
from leaves/self-contained/this sheet of rain
evaporates/is throttled/bottlenecked
in the sky's throat/never nears/never
grazes/never wets/the tantalized ground
virginal downpour/suspended mid-fall
coitus interruptus/a phone call/a second
thought/a punctured tire/a pummeled breast
no/no/no/no/no
the milk/won't come/the seed/won't plant/the womb
nulliparous/swells anyhow/the rain
falls/and does not fall/stalled/the drops
make no discernible sound/a sob/a soughing
at the wheel/to our right/never overhead
never in reach/always down the road
an etching/scraped/scraped out/scarring the sky
a series of caesuras/a fractured field
a field of splintered bones/of lines broken
into spits smaller than feet/smaller than
a fetus/embryonic/the arrested rain

9

At the center of the world, a seismic hole
cut out of a jade disk inscribed with signs
delicate as a sandpiper's tracks at low tide;
a wrought-iron bed in a bare room, a star
of Zion patchwork quilt; your hands, my hips;
falling asleep still joined; every trap
sprung free. Smegma, at the umbilicus,
and bitter ululations for the dead,
love's untranslatable glossolalia
welling up in my throat, tonguing my ear.
Is it a faulty o-ring causes leakage
between worlds, the mystic's watery eye,
the desert altar's perennially trickling spring?
No amount of celestial calculations
can explain that bolt from the blue, that pure
engine of divine kindness that brought us
face to face. At the center of the world,
two molted eagle feathers: one that stands
in a bud vase filled with salt; one held up
by a screw eye. Looking across the room
as caravans of clouds, slow wagon trains,
lumber across the window's quartered plains,
I want to rouse you out of your light sleep,
let you demonstrate, as the clouds drift,
how thoroughly you penetrate my world.

10

Remember the row of *lux perpetua* candles
lining your bedroom's brick-propped plywood shelf,
each votive wrapped in waxy red-striped paper
stamped with the Virgin's upturned suffering face?
And how, hidden behind the left-hand speaker,
you had a box—no, a *carton* of condoms?
Looking knee to knee at Vermeer's *Lacemaker,*
you showed me how you saw in the loose strands
that overflow the velvet sewing box
an image of the imagination's bounty.
I said that I saw thread, a pair of hands,
a girl's head bent down in taxing concentration,
her own handworked collar framing her face.
I remember you walking backwards into your room,
drawing me with you, toward you, by both hands,
the bundle of fifty yarrow stalks I'd brought
still splayed out on the front-room's floor, one stalk
still set apart to stand for the Infinite,
"beginningless beginning and endless end,"
according to the xeroxed instruction sheet.
Not then, not yet, not that first night, but later,
now, I see how liminal and charged
we were in the laced and spiky candlelight,
bending to meet the mattress on the floor,
to meet like changing lines in a full embrace—

Evidence

It was a year ago last July, the sixteenth. A Tuesday. I still worked at the bank, in collections, and Frank and I were still together. I'd spent my lunch break at the lumber store buying a pine board he had promised to cut into shelves, and when I returned, the message was on my desk. Frank had called from the hospital. It had to do with our son. Frank had asked that I drive directly over. Although the message didn't say it, I think I knew what it was—Jeremy was dead.

But no, I didn't really believe that. I knew it was what all mothers think on the way to the hospital to see their children. I was setting myself up, giving myself the worst possible news, so that when I saw him with a strep throat or simple fracture, there would be that sudden joy. But when I arrived, I was stopped by a doctor outside the room the nurse had solemnly directed me toward. The doctor was a small man with a lot of black hair on his neck and the backs of his hands. He said, "Mrs. Karen Asher?" and I nodded. Then he took me into another, empty room. Although I resisted at first, the doctor's hand on my shoulder kept me moving.

It had happened at summer school, on the playground. He told me there had been no warning signs. One moment our son was waiting impatiently in the hot field for the kickball, and the next, he was on the ground, not moving. It took a while to understand. The doctor was talking about blood vessels in the brain, a rupture. "A stroke?" I asked with a calm that would have surprised me if it hadn't been for the numbness. "Seven years old and a stroke?" It wasn't making sense. No, the doctor said. A brain aneurysm. I nodded, wanting to make it clear that I understood. I'm not sure why, but what I wanted above everything was clarity. When I first saw the doctor, my fingers had trembled against my slacks, but as he talked, the shaking slowed and became dense in my blood, like lead—that was the numbness. The doctor emphasized again that there were no previous symptoms, nothing anybody could have done, and I continued to nod, hardly hearing but thinking to myself, This is what shock is like. I said, "Thank you," but I was thinking, Later, when all this sinks in, I'm going to wish for this empty feeling again, I'll want to be empty. Then I noticed the sound from the next room, where they were holding Jeremy's body.

Again guided by the doctor's hand on my back, I stepped into the room and saw Frank. His face was buried in the white wrinkled sheets that covered our boy to the neck, and his shaking body looked like it wanted to climb up and over the bed. I could hear his muffled crying, like a soft humming, and from behind me, a nurse paging someone. Past his shoulders I saw Jeremy's face. His eyes were closed, and his red mouth had gone purple and hung half-open. His white hair was camouflage against the white pillow. I remember standing there beneath those buzzing fluorescent lights, staring at Jeremy, and Frank on top of him, and all that came to me was that I didn't like his mouth open like that. It was something I had told him, that if he left his mouth open, the flies would land on his tongue. And when he got older, I told him it made him look stupid. And standing there in the hospital, I thought, That boy of mine looks stupid. I wish he'd close his mouth.

Since we had driven in separate cars, I went home from the hospital alone. I was thirsty. Because of that lumber Frank had wanted, I hadn't eaten anything. The board stretched from the hatchback door to near the windshield, balanced against the headrest. Whenever I accelerated, I saw the wood tremble to my right, above the empty passenger's seat, and I tried to decide if it was a dangerous thing, this board shaking beside my head. But I could not make up my mind.

I got home before Frank, and I remember balancing the board awkwardly against my hip as I jiggled the key in the front door, and then getting in, leaning the board against the couch, and rushing to the kitchen for a glass of water. Only after gulping for a long while did I stop and set the glass down. My son was dead. I had seen the evidence: his body in the hospital, those purple lips. Not everyone who has lost someone has that privilege. I walked into the living room and found a few of his toy cars half-hidden beneath the couch. I took them to his room. The late afternoon light was angling through the window, and the floating dust glowed in a way that seemed all wrong; it didn't work with what had happened. So I threw the toy cars onto the bedside table and closed the blinds, bringing on the dark. I pulled the door behind me. I sat in the living room, waiting for Frank, and then got more water. I wanted a cigarette. I hadn't smoked since I was twenty, when I first found out I was pregnant, but I wanted it all over again, and the urge was the same as eight years ago. I drank my water instead. Then Frank showed up. His heavy eyes were swollen and red, and his cheeks were scarred by tears. He stood holding his arms out, as if he were wet, exactly like a child just in from a thunderstorm. When I went to hug him, he began to cry again, and I walked him back to our bed, took his clothes off, and fed him aspirin, which he washed down with beer. I stroked his head until his shaking subsided, then left the bedroom, closing the door behind me.

I never expected to be Frank Asher's wife. All I knew about him in high school, back in San Antonio, was that he was my boyfriend's friend. Other than that, he spoke little, dressed in tan slacks and too-tight shirts, and seemed interested in nothing in particular. He did his school work well enough, had a couple friends, and hardly ever drank. He was unremarkable in every way. But he knew my boyfriend, Jim Royce, and that was how he knew me.

I'd been with Jim for the better part of a year when he introduced me to Frank at a football game. I don't remember it, but Frank insists we met then, during our junior year. The first time I remember meeting him is sometime during my senior year, after Jim had gotten another girl pregnant and was busy making wedding plans. Only then did I notice Frank Asher, who'd had a crush on me, he said, from the moment he'd met me at the football game. So I let him have me. He asked three times before I agreed to marry him. We were nineteen by then. A year later, I was pregnant and Frank got an offer from an old friend to work at a new auto-parts plant in Balaam, out in West Texas.

You can learn to live in any town if you put forward the effort. The move was not difficult for me—my mother had moved to California with her new husband, and the rest of my family was spread out across the United States—so there was nothing pulling me back to San Antonio. But in San Antonio I knew the streets like my hand, and whenever I wanted to slip away, I could just drive out of town on u.s. 90 West, to Hondo, and from there get to the middle of nowhere. But in Balaam, I began to realize, I was already in the middle of nowhere, so there was nowhere to go when I needed to get away.

Not that I needed to escape often. Jeremy kept me busy, and when he started school, my job at the bank took up any extra time. When I think of it now, it seems that those first eight years in Balaam with Frank and Jeremy were years without reflection, filled with movement and errands and responsibilities. For a while I even filled my time with community service, meeting with other mothers in the neighborhood to petition for a playground. I wasn't the organizer, but I was involved, and I kept so busy that when we finally got the word that we had the playground, I experienced a mild panic attack: my breaths went shallow, and the other women had to hold on to me and fan my face with official documents. They all said it was the heat, us standing on the steps of City Hall on a hot June day, but I still remember what I thought as my knees trembled on those concrete steps: What am I going to do now?

Even on that Tuesday afternoon of Jeremy's aneurysm, I was running errands, buying that ten-foot length of pine for Frank's shelves. I skipped my lunch to get this piece of wood, and although it's not such a strange thing on its own, I tend to look at all those years like this. Me filling up an hour lunch break with a trip to the lumber store. Me skipping breakfast to get Frank and Jeremy ready for the day. Me unable to sit still and relax even when I had lots of dead time. I still don't know how to do that.

The same thing happened when Jeremy died. Right away, in the hospital, without time to even understand what was happening, I went over to Frank and held his shoulders, trying to keep them still. He didn't say anything, only pressed his face deeper into the sheets, as if I weren't there. Later, it was me who had to talk to the funeral people, and talk clearly so that it would be done right, so that the flowers would be purple, which had been Jeremy's favorite color, and the preacher would be on time. Even though Frank beat me to despondency, I was not angry. I liked to hold things together. It made me feel useful in a way that tears could not.

I came prepared with a purse full of tissues, but the funeral passed without a breakdown. A few times, though, I did feel on the verge of tears and tried to nurse that feeling, but then Frank's soft, choking sobs would sound and distract me from my efforts.

Besides Frank's crying, what I remember most from the funeral are the children: maybe six or seven eight-year-olds, some of whom I'd met before. One of the strangers was a dark little girl with straight black hair to her shoulders who was crying. I watched her throughout the service, this little girl I'd never met, probably never even heard of, crying in public for my son, whom she knew, if at all, only from a distance. It really made me sick. It seemed to me that this little girl, crying away like Frank, was turning the whole service into bad theater. Who was she to grieve? Frank deserved to—I knew that—but this dark girl? Her mother stood behind her, patting her shoulder, squeezing her sympathetically, obviously falling for the ploy, but not me. Frank's mother had come into town, and she was crying as well. I wasn't crying, but I at least deserved to. I wanted to march over and slap that girl's tearstained face and demand an explanation. I wanted her to admit that she had never known Jeremy, that she was only crying for attention. What I wanted was her shame.

After the service I saw her again, a little ahead of me in the crowd, and without thinking, I hurried until I was right behind her. Her mother was farther up and didn't see when I pressed my foot against the edge of the girl's shiny black shoe. With her next step, she lost her balance. I walked on, hearing with satisfaction her faint moan as she hit the brown grass and called, "Mommy!"

Frank took the week off, which only made sense. I did too, but by Monday I was worn out. We were zombies in the house, walking slowly from room to room, usually avoiding Jeremy's, not speaking. Half the time, Frank hardly recognized me. When we did talk, we did a lot of apologizing, like when we turned a corner and found ourselves face to face. This happened too much. The house was so small. It seemed I was always returning from the kitchen to find him slumped in front of the television, his face in his hands, or curled up on the bed, shaking. He couldn't do the simplest things for himself. He forgot to brush his teeth in the mornings and went days without a shower. On Sunday, I asked if he might want me to draw him a bath, and he stared at me with this blank look, as if he'd never heard of a bath before. And those tears, they were what really ate at me. No matter how far away I got, I was always close enough to hear them. My teeth would set, my jaw tightening. Or I'd feel sick and guilty, like a voyeur. Why couldn't he pull himself together? On that Monday morning, six days after it had happened, when I started dressing for work, Frank looked at me, baffled, and I explained, "Something to distract me." I don't know if he believed it, but I think he was too weak to question. Partly, it was true, for what I wanted more than anything was a distraction, but what I didn't tell him was that I was still able to function. Even during those quiet moments when I dwelled on Jeremy, pictured his white bangs and pink complexion, saw him dropping in a hot field of brown grass, the death hardly seemed a blow. Frank wept when his coffee was cold, and whenever he saw Jeremy's picture.

The office wasn't much better. Irene and Sandy and the rest of them gave me these long, sad looks and meaningful sighs, and they whispered back and forth. I heard Ted's lowered voice when I passed the staff lounge: "It'll hit her sometime, it's bound to. And when it does . . ."

"You're not kidding," someone replied.

Later in the week, Ted stopped by my cubicle and knocked on the wall. He came in and sat across from me with a somber expression. "How're you doing?"

"Fine," I said. "I guess."

He nodded, looking around my little space, and rolled his lower lip in a thoughtful pout.

"Ted?"

"Yeah?"

I opened my hands. "Did you want something?"

I'd always liked working for Ted, though we had never really hit it off. We worked together well, but beyond that, we didn't share much, and so it surprised me when he kept nodding and said, almost to the wall, "Did you know I lost a daughter ten years back?"

He said it matter-of-factly, as if it were nothing much. "No, Ted. I didn't."

He looked at me finally. "No, I guess you wouldn't. I don't tell people much, but it seemed like . . ." He shrugged and smiled.

"Sure," I said.

"Her name was Elizabeth."

"Oh."

"I came out of it a lot faster than my wife, but it takes women longer, you know. Nothing to be ashamed of—they've clocked more time with the children. It only makes sense."

"I see."

He didn't say anything after that, just sat limply, staring past me, past the wall even, and I let him. It did make me uncomfortable after a while, him just sitting there, but I thought he deserved that much. When he finally came out of it, he looked up at me and said, "You know you can take whatever time you need."

"Yes."

"Paid, and everything."

I smiled. "I don't need it, Ted."

He nodded, and I saw his eyes had pinked a little. "I better go."

I said, "Sure," and watched him leave.

One night, while Frank and I were in bed waiting for sleep, I listened to his breathing in the dark—that hot, insistent rhythm of insomnia—and I slid closer and laid my head on the bony peak of his shoulder. Without speaking, he kissed my forehead.

I heard the groan of his neck as he turned to face the ceiling again. I kept my head on his shoulder because it felt nice, and stroked his chest, running my fingers lightly through his curly hair. He did not move. I hadn't expected him to—I don't know what I was expecting. I nuzzled my breasts against his arm and listened to his steady breathing as I slipped my hand lower, over his bellybutton, to the elastic ridge of his underwear. I pushed my fingers beneath; his breathing shifted. It didn't take much stroking for him to become hard, and his breaths quickened in the darkness as he stiffened in my hand. I turned to face him and kissed his neck, tongued it, then pulled at his far shoulder until he succumbed and rolled over. He was quiet about it, and fast, and I opened my thighs until they burned in the joints and I kept pulling him deeper; his thrusts became stronger and I felt him striking my back wall. Cool sprinkles of his sweat fell on my cheeks, and I opened my eyes when I felt him tremble and watched his face contort as if his muscles had lost all control, and then it was over.

Heavily, he fell onto me, then lifted himself and dropped down beside me. We both stared at the ceiling, our breaths strong and rapid, and then he cleared his throat and moved away. There was a click, and the room was suddenly filled with light. He was sitting on the side of the bed, facing away from me. His pink back glowed with perspiration. He rubbed his eyes slowly. I waited.

"What are you doing?"

"What do you mean?" I pulled the sheet up to my chin.

He wiped his eyes again and turned to me, and when he put his hand down, I saw that his eyelids were swollen; he shook his head. "How can you?" He was exasperated. "So soon."

I rubbed my own eyes, but only to hide my face from him. "I don't know. I'm sorry," I said. "I don't know what came over me." I rolled over so that I faced the wall, and after a while, he put out the light and went to the kitchen. I don't know how long it took him to have a drink and come back, but it was enough time for me to see that he had misunderstood—he must have.

The sex had nothing to do with Jeremy, not directly. It was not about him; it was about us, Frank and me, and what we had left. As I lay there, feeling the cold, wet spot on the sheets, I thought that I should tell him this, that he would surely understand. But when he came back to bed, I let it go. It could wait until morning. The next morning, though, I was no longer sure of what he did and did not understand, and I said nothing.

Frank asked for more time off. His supervisor, as you'd expect, was understanding and gave him another five days. I mentioned one morning in passing that since he had this time, he could build those shelves I'd bought the lumber for. Frank looked at me when I said that, as if he hadn't heard. "To distract you," I said. "It might help." He nodded in the slow, confused way I'd grown used to, though he never did build them.

At the office, all the stares and whispers and the way people waited like impatient spectators were beginning to suffocate me. A couple of them put Hallmark cards on my desk: *Our deepest condolences to you and yours* and *God shall wipe away all tears; and there shall be no more death, neither sorrow, nor crying, nor pain: for the former things are passed away.* They crowded around me throughout the week with their sentiments and prayers, and my steady claustrophobia began to turn into anger. And there was always Frank. He appeared so passionate beside me, with his tears and grief and all his loud noises. He was a spectacle, so much that even in the privacy of our small home, I felt embarrassed by him, as if the neighbors were pressing their ears to the wall. I even wondered if he really felt as strongly as he acted. I knew he was devastated, but I was beginning to suspect that he was using the pain to draw attention to himself, like that little girl at the funeral, to get my attention and the attention of his mother, whom he talked to daily on the phone. But then I'd see myself like my co-workers saw me, the way they had to see me, and I'd get upset with myself for not crying, for being such a bitch to my husband, for thinking such horrible things. It was natural, I knew, for me to break down in my cubicle and start bawling over the computer, but my body just wasn't cooperating.

One night, after Frank went to bed, I took a picture of Jeremy into the bathroom with me. It was a year old and taken from above him. Jeremy's round, dimpled face squinted up at the sun. I sat on the sink counter and put my feet in the basin, leaning against the mirror. I stared at his smiling face, at his shiny pink nose. I whispered to myself: Jeremy is dead. My son is dead. My only child is dead, and I'll never be able to hold him again. He'll never know how much I loved him. I repeated this for nearly an hour, trying to concentrate, squinting sometimes, but my attention kept being diverted by my reflection, my voice in that little room. Around midnight I gave up.

Another time, I overheard Frank talking to his mother on the phone. He was in the kitchen, trying to keep his voice low, but his words echoed along the linoleum floor and into the living room, where I sat on a chair, leaning into the sound.

"No, Ma," he whispered. "Of course she loved him. Christ. What do you think she is?" Later, he added, "Ma, that's my wife you're talking about."

I drove out to the mall in Brownwood, partly to get some sorely needed towels from the outlet store, though mostly to get away. When I walked past the girls' department, I saw a ten-year-old with red hair talking to her mother in a tight, very bossy voice. Holding a pink skirt over her jeans, she said, "Helen, I am *not* about to wear this!" The mother shrugged and took the skirt away, saying, "Well, honey, you just need to find something yourself." I felt sick.

It wasn't the girl's attitude, but the way she called her mother "Helen." It reminded me of how Jeremy, during the last year or so, had begun acting like that little girl. He always wanted to do things for himself, and sometimes he would push me away when I came to help him dress. And I wondered if maybe it was a short leap from that kind of behavior to this little girl calling her mother by her first name. And then I remembered one moment in particular, when Jeremy's face had gone red and stony and he yelled, "I can dress myself!" And I realized that the time I was thinking of, the morning when I'd gone into his room to hurry him so he wouldn't miss the bus, was the morning of July 16, his last day alive.

I looked away from the girl and her mother and walked out of the store, into the bright mall. I was shaking. Mothers and fathers were pushing carriages, and an old woman in an electric wheelchair buzzed by. I went into a drugstore, bought a pack of cigarettes from a teenager in a green cap, and took some matches from the container beside the register. I went back into the mall and found a bench and opened the pack. My fingers kept fumbling with the plastic wrap; I grunted under my breath until I had gotten a cigarette free. I lit my first cigarette in eight years and sucked in the smoke. I wasn't thinking about the cigarette at all. It was as if the cigarette weren't even there; it only existed so I could take the news that on my son's last day on earth, he had been angry with me. He had thought me an overbearing mother. He had hated me with the intensity only children can muster.

The smoke hit my lungs and burned there, and for an instant it did feel good. I felt the sensual pleasure that cigarette smoke had given me, the comforting weight in the chest—but then the burn took over and my insides itched, and I coughed and hacked and spat into my palm until it was all out of me.

Frank went back to work, but it was obvious from the apathetic shrugs he gave when he came home at night that he wasn't really working; he was only transporting his body to the plant each day, forcing it to go through the motions, imitating work. That was when I decided to take a day off.

I got Frank's tools from the shed and cut the lumber on the back deck. In one of his books I found descriptions of how to do it. I measured out three-foot sections, threw away the extra foot, then sanded the rough edges. So there would be enough support, I measured to find the studs, and then I mounted the three pine shelves to the living-room wall. By the time Frank got home, I had cleaned up everything and put the tools away. He came in quietly, like he'd been doing for weeks, took off his jacket, and wandered into the living room. He saw the shelves; I was standing a little behind him. He did not move. He froze right where he was.

"Did I cut them all right?" I asked him.

He said nothing, but stepped closer and ran his thumb along the edges.

"Maybe I should have stained them," I said. His silence was disturbing.

After a while, he looked at me. I saw how his eyes were wide and more green than brown in the light from the windows. And then I got this feeling he was playing a game, trying to stare me down.

I leaned forward. "What?"

He walked past me and to the bedroom. I waited. Soon he returned, buttoning his jacket, and his eyes had that look I'd seen too much of over the past weeks. Without a word, he passed me and went to the door and left. I watched from the window as he drove away.

For the rest of that evening, I alternated between the bedroom and the living room, where I peered out the windows into the darkness, returning to the bedroom along the same path Frank had endlessly followed during those first two weeks. I checked the shelves now and then to make sure they were still stable, and when it became clear that Frank was going to spend most of the night out, I sat in the living room and watched television. There was the last of the news, a forecast of showers, and then a sitcom I'd heard of but never watched before. It was a family show, except there was no mother. There were three men who raised four children, ranging from toddler to teenager. How they came across those four children, I don't know. I turned off the television and tried to go to sleep.

Frank returned after one in the morning, smelling of liquor and cigarettes, and fell heavily into bed beside me. I pretended to be asleep. When he started snoring, I went outside.

The day's heat had mostly disappeared, and a cool breeze from across the plain that surrounds Balaam followed me into the car. I drove out of town and took 190 farther west. When you're that far away from major cities, the highway turns black and headlights can only do so much. I rolled down the window and drove for a long time. I thought about all of it—Jeremy, Frank, even my job—without coming to any decision. I didn't even know if there was something to decide. Then I remembered Jim Royce from high school and how much I'd loved him. He'd been the first boy I'd ever slept with and was kinder than most, even though he wore a wide white Stetson and strutted around like a cowboy. He would bring little gifts to school for me—Hershey bars, country-music tapes, sometimes even flowers—and he had the clearest skin I'd ever seen, with just enough Mexican in him to keep it permanently tanned; his shoulders were broad, and he had a strong nose. And then I remembered the time he told me he had gotten Shirley Hubbard pregnant. It was between Geography and Gym, and he pulled me out through one of the side doors of the building so that we could be alone. I only nodded quietly as he touched my elbows and said he was sorry. Then, after an awkward pause, I cussed at him loudly, turned, and walked back into the building, dry-eyed and furious. And that was all I did, until I got home. Then I cried off and on for the next three weeks, not knowing when it would start or stop. I felt so out of control during those weeks, like an empty sock being tossed by the wind.

I couldn't help but compare that to the way I was acting now. I had experienced that complete shattering, where your insides shake like they're breaking apart and wave after dark wave of misery takes control of your eyes and thoughts and shoulders. Why not for my son? I knew I was a good mother, always had been. I'd read to Jeremy at night while Frank watched television. I took him to soccer and baseball when Frank worked late; I cleaned his cuts.

No explanation made sense. For a while I thought it had something to do with my own mother, absent throughout my high-school years and always chasing down new husbands, or my father, who left when I was two, before I'd had a chance to know him. But these were excuses. And then I thought it had to do with the time Frank and I were first trying to conceive. It took a long time, half a year, and then it happened: I missed a period. Almost two weeks passed, and it was a day-by-day thing, our excitement building, Frank getting home each evening with that question—"Today?" —and me smiling and shaking my head. But then the period did come, and the bleeding was painful, heavy. Sitting on the toilet with my head in my hands, the cramps rippling through me, I was sure that our child had gone with the blood into the toilet. I believed it even though I never saw any proof, only the blood. I thought that perhaps this or my parents was why I could not cry for my dead son, but neither explanation made any sense and still doesn't. Then it occurred to me that if there were a reason I was not grieving, maybe it was something I did not want to know.

By the time I got to Bakersfield, it was three in the morning, a light rain was falling, and the twenty-four-hour gas station on the outskirts of town had closed.

Frank was already gone when I returned later that morning. I called in sick—Ted made understanding sounds, as if this kind of grieving were our secret—and spent the day cleaning up. I vacuumed the whole house and dusted and aired it. I went to the grocery store, pushed my cart through the bright aisles, and blinked at the people who passed me. When I looked at them, I had the feeling that none of them understood anything. None of these strangers knew what pain I had in my life.

I bought some flowers for the dining room, and some leafy plants to use as bookends on the new shelves. I made a large lasagna and got an expensive Portuguese red wine Frank once said he liked. By five, everything in the house was clean and the wine was breathing and the whole house smelled thickly of lasagna. I changed into a dress.

He got home a couple hours late, and from the way he blinked when he came into the house and swayed, and held his head as if he had a headache, it was obvious he was drunk. But he was quiet.

"Would you like something to eat?" I asked.

He looked at me momentarily before going to the shelves. He stood in front of them, his eyes wandering over the green plants and books, as if he were reading titles. And then, with an unsteady arm, he swiped each shelf clean, pushing plants and dirt and books onto the carpet. I stepped back. He gripped the sides of each shelf and yanked hard, ripping each one out of the wall. The nails pulled against the studs and screeched when they came out. Breathing heavily, he twisted and pulled until they had all come free, and then he collected them under his arm and walked out the front door. I stared at the wall, at the open sores where pieces of wall had been torn out. Then I went to the window. He was throwing the shelves into the back seat of his car. And then he was driving away. His wheels made a noise when he took the corner.

I have not seen Frank for a long time now. I hear through mutual friends that he's moved out of his mother's place and has his own apartment. And I'm glad for him since it shows he's making headway. When he left Balaam, he told me to keep the house for myself, but the size of it troubled me, and when I sold it, I sent him half the money in an envelope addressed to him in care of his mother.

We did finally talk things over. He apologized for the mess he had made, and I apologized for my mothering. He looked up at me and said, "What?"

We were in a diner, and he had spent the past week at a motel.

"My mothering," I repeated.

"Honey," he said, moving his hand to my side of the table. "You were a great mother. That's not the problem here."

"But it is," I said calmly. I'd had a while to think it all through. I had dwelled on it for so long that I was able to finally see what I'd been hiding from. "I didn't love him," I said slowly so that he wouldn't make me repeat it, but it didn't work.

"What?" He pulled at his lip with his thick fingers. "What are you talking about?"

I forced a smile, felt it shiver there on my face. "I finally understand," I said. "It wasn't really love." My smile was disintegrating.

How do you explain to someone that you've followed a series of clues that have led you to your own crime? Over the weeks, I had watched the evidence accumulate against me. The lack of tears, my mother-in-law's suspicions, and especially the stares from everyone—they all gathered together during the week Frank spent in his motel room, and they convicted me. By that afternoon, I had accepted their verdict.

Frank stared for a long time, and when he finally did speak, it was to the waitress: "Can we get the bill?" The next day he began moving his things out of the house and to his mother's in San Antonio. I helped him pack for an hour or so, but after he told me three times that he could do it alone, I took a drive out to Bakersfield again. It was early afternoon, a Sunday. People were filing out of the low Church of Christ building just off the highway, and I turned into the parking lot and watched them for a while. Men were in suits too heavy for midsummer Texas; women pinned white straw hats to their hair. Finally free of the dull service, children scurried around and ducked their parents' slaps.

I don't know how long I was there, watching all of them greet each other and say their farewells, but suddenly, a man in a suit was tapping on my window. I blinked until my vision came back. The parking lot was empty.

"You need any help?" he asked when I rolled down the window.

He looked the way I imagine Jim Royce looks now: sort of wide and proud, but broken beneath the surface, broken like Frank. He squinted against the sunlight, and I looked up at him without speaking.

He pointed a bent finger at my face, then tapped his eye. "Are you all right?"

I wiped beneath my eyelids, felt the dampness, then continued to stare at him silently until he became uncomfortable. He looked up, past the car to the highway, trying to appear collected, then turned back to me. He opened his mouth hesitantly, as if to speak, but I said, "No." I started the engine and nodded at him. "I'm fine." I drove straight back to Balaam.

■ **FICTION**

Ask the Sun by He Dong. Translated by Katherine Hanson. Seattle:
Women in Translation, 1997. 112 pages, paper $12.95.

"Not so very long ago the Middle Kingdom had a sun whose name was Mao
Zedong. He called China's children morning suns. Today I ask the sun." This epi-
graph begins *Ask the Sun,* a lyrical collection of short stories by Chinese poet and
short-story writer He Dong, who lives in Norway, where she is a researcher at the
University of Oslo. Born in Beijing in 1960, He Dong describes what it was like to
be one of Mao's many "children," to grow up under the influence that he radiated
across China. She is part of that generation whose childhood was marked by the
sudden disappearances and reappearances of family members, by public humilia-
tions and abrupt reversals of status, and by constant surveillance and self-censor-
ship. It's no surprise that Mao's children became adults who ask the eternal question of childhood: *why?* The only person who can answer them is dead, so the
question hangs in the background, like a dark sun, like the indelible memory of
Mao himself.

"Time," says the narrator of the volume's first story, "Nine," "has carried me
into a new phase. I am living a quiet and peaceful life, but this phase is also marked
by something else: The memory of an enemy." She is seven when the Great Proletarian Cultural Revolution begins and her parents and brother are banished to the
countryside. She is left with her seventy-three-year-old grandmother in a neighborhood terrorized by a housewife named Aunt Huang, who zealously seeks out
"counter-revolutionaries." The young girl struggles to help her nearly illiterate
grandmother read and memorize Mao's "Little Red Book." But when the grandmother makes a small mistake during a mandatory study session, Aunt Huang
furiously brands her a traitor to the state and punishes her harshly. The old grandmother sorrowfully and violently bangs her head against the hard wood floor nine
times to atone and to protect her granddaughter. And in that way, the girl learns to
hate. Although she gets her revenge, her childhood has been scarred by a brutal
political system that makes children witnesses to its crimes.

The other five stories in *Ask the Sun* are equally moving and lyrical. Like her
characters, He Dong is tender but never sentimental, political but not didactic,
strong but not at a loss for deep emotion. She writes with a deceptively calm and

spare eloquence, casting a burning look back at a history both personal and political. *Ask the Sun* is the work of a bright talent, a storyteller who retains a remarkable innocence and purity for all of her worldly wisdom.

LEZA LOWITZ

■ **LITERATURE & CULTURE**

The Voice That Remembers: A Tibetan Woman's Inspiring Story of Survival by Ama Adhe as told to Joy Blakeslee. Boston: Wisdom Publications, 1999. 272 pages, paper $14.95.

The Voice That Remembers, Ama Adhe's moving account of the Chinese invasion of Tibet and her twenty-seven-year imprisonment for organizing a women's resistance movement, is both deeply disturbing and inspiring. In striking contrast to her horrific experiences as a prisoner—torture, rape, starvation, forced labor, medical experiments, beatings, and interrogations—the tone of her narrative is calm and matter-of-fact.

As the title suggests, this book is not only about Adhe but also about remembering those who did not survive, "whose bones have become part of a land now tread by strangers." She weaves her personal story with those of fellow prisoners, friends, and family, including her brother Jughuma, who helped protect the Dalai Lama during the events that led to his exile. Her story is also the story of Tibet as a country and the desperate struggle to save its culture and religion from destruction.

Adhe was born in 1932 in the eastern Tibetan region of Kham. The book's first section, "Before the Years of Sorrow," describes her childhood in the mountains and vividly portrays family members—many of whom would lose their lives under Chinese rule. "Even now as I close my eyes," she begins, "I can recall my first memory—laughing, spinning, and falling in fields of flowers beneath an endless open sky."

That relatively carefree life, steeped in Tibetan tradition, did not last long. In 1950, when Adhe was eighteen and newly married, the Chinese invaded Kham. She describes the methodical way in which they took control: lulling the people into a false sense of security by feigning respect for their religion and promising to stay only a short while. These promises were broken when the Chinese built an airstrip and roads and brought in more soldiers. By 1955, the Chinese had declared religion useless and begun the systematic looting and desecration of Buddhist monasteries. Many monks were killed. Others were arrested, publicly humiliated, imprisoned, and forced to cut down sacred forests or slaughter animals—both of which were against their religious beliefs.

The Chinese presence in Kham had a profound effect on Adhe's personal and religious life. Shortly after speaking out against the Chinese, her father died in a hospital under suspicious circumstances. Next, her husband was poisoned and died before her eyes. Now alone, she had a young child and was two months pregnant. "I didn't know what to do," she writes. "My sorrow turned to anger and then to a conviction of determined responsibility."

This determination led Adhe to create an underground network of Tibetan women who gathered information for the men fighting in the mountains. Under torture, one of the resistance members confessed Adhe's participation, and the Chinese arrested her. She gives a gripping account of the soldiers arriving at dawn to drag her away from her crying three-year-old son and one-year-old daughter. She would never see her son again, and when decades later she was eventually reunited with her daughter, they would not recognize one another.

In prison, Adhe was interrogated and tortured. Her brother-in-law Pema was shot in front of her, his blood spilling on her dress as she begged the Chinese to kill her, too. They refused, saying, "If we kill you . . . it will be over too quickly. We want you to suffer for the rest of your life."

For the next twenty-seven years, Adhe was tortured, starved, beaten, and shunted from one foul prison to another. "When one is imprisoned," she writes, "the smallest sound takes on a magnitude of importance. The sound of approaching feet can mean that someone is about to be tormented. . . . The sound of a bird means that it is light outside." She expresses her sorrow over Pema's death with the same subdued, unrelenting force: "Before his execution, I always knew that he was alive because I could hear the sound of his chains whenever he moved about in his cell. From that day, there was no such sound."

Adhe describes how the prison guards would make a point of sitting on sacred *thangka,* using holy scriptures as wallpaper, and humiliating the lamas. She also saw trucks outside the prison walls, carrying away valuable objects from the monasteries, taking the wealth of Tibet to China.

Adhe continually defied her Chinese captors, finding ways to sneak extra food to the imprisoned lamas and to exchange information with her cellmates. Because of this, she was repeatedly punished and was detained for several years beyond her original release date. As I read the account of her long incarceration, it seemed impossible to me that anyone could have survived such brutality. Remarkably, Adhe not only survived but retained her faith and compassion, along with a deep commitment to tell the stories of those who would never be able to do so.

Adhe's release from prison was not a joyful moment. Going home, she saw that the mountains of her childhood had been stripped of their sacred forests and the monasteries destroyed. When she arrived, she discovered that many of her friends and family, including her son, had died under the Chinese.

In 1987, Adhe and her second husband managed to cross the border into India, where she now lives in exile, in the same town as the Dalai Lama. It was he who urged her to record her story in a book—"for the sake of the living and the dead," he said. About a year later, a human-rights worker invited her to attend the first international hearing on Tibet, which was held in Bonn, Germany, in 1989. Although she feared for her relatives still living in Tibet, she decided she had to speak out on the plight of Tibet. Since then, she has continued to be an outspoken advocate of human rights.

While imprisoned, Adhe had begun piecing together a mattress, starting with strips of fabric torn from the inner lining of her own frayed *chuba*. Gradually, she added scraps she collected from the clothing of prisoners who had died—some of them close friends. She worked on this mattress throughout the years of her incarceration, carrying it from prison to prison, and kept it with her even after she was released. It is one of the few material reminders of her imprisonment and of those who did not survive. "I am free now," she writes. "There are no guards outside my door. . . . Yet an exile can never forget the severed roots of beginnings, the precious fragments of the past carried always within the heart."

SHARON MAY BROWN

The Hundred Thousand Songs of Milarepa. Translated by Garma C. C. Chang. Boston: Shambhala, 1999. 730 pages, cloth $55.

Tibetan Buddhist poet and anchorite Milarepa is as beloved by common folk and artisans throughout the Himalayas as Saint Francis of Assisi is by southern Europeans. Like pious Francis, Milarepa practiced what he taught, voicing his eleventh-century religious joy by spontaneously composing sacred songs that still resonate in and for our time. And like the Italian mystic, Milarepa has been acknowledged as a saint, although, as this now classic rendering by Garma Chang of *The Hundred Thousand Songs of Milarepa* suggests, his transcendent odes, canticles, litanies, and consecrations may remind today's readers of a modern example of the wandering bard: Walt Whitman.

Known in Tibetan as the *Mila Grubum,* the sixty-one stories comprising this epic biography unfold for our edification in the manner of a miracle play. Covering an exhaustive range of spiritual problems, solutions, and instruction, the stories were drawn from the life and travels of this yogic ragamuffin *par excellence.* Their original author—known to Tibetan scholars as the Insane Yogi—was a student of Gampopa, the chief disciple of Milarepa and himself the author of *The Jewel Ornament of Liberation,* another core Tibetan Buddhist text. As Chang informs us, the stories are organized into three streams: descriptions of Milarepa's extensive encounters with "malignant" spirits and demons; accounts of the master among his disciples; and assorted apocrypha, including advice to physicians, beer-drinking songs, evidence of spiritual accomplishment, heartfelt advice, and the like. A vast compendium of medieval Tibetan cultural lore, the *Mila Grubum* is as sumptuous a feast for Western readers as *The Canterbury Tales;* a holy book as well, it continues to serve as a fountain of wisdom in Tibetan Tantrist practice.

This edition arrives not unknown to readers of English. A previous edition was published forty years ago and still appears from time to time at antiquarian booksellers (and often at higher cost than this far more exquisite, new edition). Garma Chang wrote his peerless translation in the 1930s, during an eight-year tenure in Buddhist monasteries in the Kham region of inner Tibet. A scholar of China's Hua Yen Buddhist tradition, based upon the Avatamsaka Sutra, Master Chang is equally renowned for *The Buddhist Teaching of Totality* and was compiling—alas, at the time of his death—a dictionary of Buddhism for Western readers. Nonetheless, in fathoming the *Mila Grubum*'s manifold obscure passages he left us with an encyclopedic *tour de force* of primary Buddhist doctrine, terminology, psychology, and technical instruction.

Milarepa also comes to us with considerable advance notice. Henry Miller brought news of him to American readers in the 1940s, and later, in *Big Sur and the Oranges of Hieronymous Bosch*, he wrote of the Tibetan sage in the same reverent breath as he did Lao-tzu, Socrates, Siddhartha Gautama the historical Buddha, and Jesus of Nazareth. Indeed, Miller borrows from Milarepa in the epilogue to one of his own tomes: "It was written; and it had to be," he reminds. "Behold to where it has led." Ten years later, Allen Ginsberg—an ardent Buddhist practitioner in the Kagyu lineage originated by Milarepa and his guru, Marpa the Translator—also began patching in references to the wily Tibetan master, and he continued to do so for the next three decades.

Who, then, was this reclusive man, and what was the gift that enabled Milarepa to excite such uncommon interest during the past eight hundred years? As the stories of the *Mila Grubum* recount, Milarepa was a peasant who, devoted to the Buddha, sought teaching from Marpa, a farmer-yogi of ferocious temper. Initially rebuffed, Milarepa was subjected to performing herculean labors: building heavy stone houses, then demolishing them. Following a period of deep meditation in seclusion, he was finally embraced by Marpa and initiated into all the knowledge and miraculous powers that his master, a translator of Indian texts, could teach him before sending him out as an itinerant yogi and instructor of the *dharma*. Where fact and legend meet is hard to say, but through his lifelong wandering and preaching, Milarepa emerged as the prototype of a mountain guru, a living Buddha, an extreme renunciate with more than a little of the coyote trickster in him.

Part folklore and fairy tale—the very stuff that spawned the hugely popular Lobsang Rampa novel series of the 1960s—these stories from the *Mila Grubum* marry the fantastic, the ineffable, and the practical. Their subject, reworked again and again, is the Mahamudra path.

As Chang informs us in the brilliant notes that conclude each story, Mahamudra is the great gesture or symbol of the nonexistence or insubstantiality of the self and all beings and things. It is not so much a principle as a practice—what is known to Buddhists as the School of the Whispered Transmission. "According to Mahamudra," Chang explains, "the primordial nature of mind is not only 'void' in its essence, but is also an illuminating self-awareness embodied in the Void."

In "The Tale of Red Rock Jewel Valley," songs are sung to an astonishing array of ghosts, demonesses, slack-jawed peasants, disciples, and sundry bejeweled landlords. Here Milarepa recognizes "that all phenomena are of one's own mind" and "mind itself is a transparency of Voidness." Through this Voidness, he says, we are led to full realization of the *dharmakaya* realm—what Ginsberg liked calling "nondiscriminating ultimate reality, equivalent to the nonconceptualizing awareness of ordinary mind."

Call it mystic superhero hagiography if you want, but the punch lines in *The Hundred Thousand Songs of Milarepa* pack enough wattage to blow out the lights of the universe. And there's the spin: as *the* masterpiece of Mahamudra insight training, the *Mila Grubum* is never about negation but the ever-ripening amplitude of complete and fulfilling meditation. You've come across *wabi* and *sabi* in your Zen reading? That less is better, and well worn is neater? Well, that's also the ticket of admission to Milarepa's theater of the marvelous. A devotee of spartan tastes and the owner of a funny bone a mile wide, this *dharma* master keeps on singing good advice even as he leaves this mortal coil. And as eight centuries of peasant listeners have appreciated, no advanced diploma is necessary to achieve this version of salvation.

Like his guru Marpa, in whose name each story is invoked, Milarepa bypasses institutional religion in favor of a yogic life modeled after that of Buddha Shakyamuni. As Milarepa illustrates in "The Gray Rock Vajra Enclosure," what could one really expect to hang on to anyway?

> *In the beginning, nothing comes;*
> *In the middle, nothing stays;*
> *At the end, nothing goes.*
> *Of the mind there is no arising and extinction!*
> *Thus one remains in the Equality of past,*
> *Present, and future.*

What we see him advocating in this passage is the perennial Himalayan *guru-chela:* the master-student model of direct wisdom transmission. As he confirms in "A Woman's Role in the Dharma," we may reach enlightenment on the Tantrist path without the formal intervention of the clergy: "One may reach Buddhahood either as layman or monk. Without changing one's status, one may still become a good Buddhist."

Although we do not need the clergy while on this path, the need for a teacher of some sort remains. Some of the *Mila Grubum*'s loveliest accounts describe the manner in which disciples came to Milarepa. The six stories concerning Rechungpa, the leper disciple, and his struggles in overcoming temptation are the favorites of many: their message of the difficulty of overcoming the lust of the senses is timeless. The richness of Milarepa's preaching genius surfaces again and again as the stories wax and link together. We receive a treasury of instruction on such matters as the Twenty-One Exhortations, the Three Greatnesses, and the Eight Non-Fears—a veritable decoder ring for the lacunae essential to rounding out one's knowledge and practice of the *dharma.*

Whether it be an understanding of *karma* or of the bardo of death—or precise instruction in meditation or dealing with annoying distractions, fearful encounters, or bullies of every ilk—*The Hundred Thousand Songs of Milarepa* is just what the doctor ordered. If, that is, your notion of healing centers on joy and poetry, on unshakable self-discipline and overcoming fear or doubt, on simple magic, or on the belief of dying without regret. Here are Shelley and Keats for the having, and old Homer and Blake, Whitman and Ginsberg—all singing the body electric and infused with the compassion and happiness of the Dalai Lama. What a magnificent gift this book is! If there's justice at all in this precious home we call life, then may we all get to taste Milarepa's wild nettles and pure mountain water before we die.

TREVOR CAROLAN

The Dragon in the Land of Snows: A History of Modern Tibet Since 1947
by Tsering Shakya. New York: Columbia University Press, 1999. 574 pages,
cloth $29.95.

The Autobiography of a Tibetan Monk by Palden Gyatso with Tsering
Shakya. New York: Grove Press, 1997. 288 pages, cloth $24.

Tears of Blood: A Cry for Tibet by Mary Craig. Washington, D.C.:
Counterpoint, 1999. 380 pages, cloth $26.

The Dragon in the Land of Snows is the even-handed history of modern Tibet that's
been much needed. Without such a balanced account of the country's recent tra-
vails, Tibet has been in danger of vanishing twice: first into the grasp of the PRC,
which invaded and occupied the nation in 1950, and then into mythologized and
misinformed notions of Tibet's culture and people. Impressively researched and
written, *The Dragon in the Land of Snows* makes use of political documents and
sources that have not come to light before, and clarifies to a great extent such
difficult issues as the internal struggles of the Communist Party under Mao Tse-
tung, the dynamics of the Cultural Revolution, the mediating role of the Dalai
Lama, and the influences exerted by Cold War intrigues inside Tibet and throughout the region. It's clear that author Tsering Shakya is sympathetic to the plight of
his countrymen, but his account is remarkably restrained, seeking fundamentally
to be objective and leaving out, for the sake of dispassionate scholarship, the enor-
mity of the events that impacted the lives of Tibetans.

In a separate context, however, Shakya relates precisely the horrifying effects of
Chinese occupation on individual lives. *The Autobiography of a Tibetan Monk* is
the harrowing first-person account of Palden Gyatso, who related the details of his
life to Shakya during some three hundred hours of interviews in 1995. Tortured,
starved, and subjected to horrendous living conditions, Palden Gyatso endured
thirty-one years as a political prisoner of the Chinese. During his imprisonment,
which began in 1959 when he was twenty-eight, he never gave up his dedication to
Buddhist compassion for all beings—he had become a monk at age ten—nor
stopped resisting the cruelty of his Chinese captors and their relentless efforts to
break his spirit and "reform" his thoughts. In 1992, he escaped from Tibet and
made his way across the border into Nepal, continuing on to India. He not only
carried with him his eyewitness report of the Chinese depredation of Tibet and its
people, but also managed to smuggle out electric cattle prods, stun guns, handcuffs, and other torture devices frequently used by prison guards —proof against
the claims of the Chinese government that torture was forbidden in its prisons.

A third recent book that helps us understand the conditions in Tibet between
1950 and the present is Mary Craig's *Tears of Blood*. Clearly and forcefully written,
Craig's history unfolds not through the lens of international politics but primarily
through her interviews with numerous individuals who lived through the events of
the last half century; in this regard, her book is an important companion to the
other two reviewed here. Like *The Dragon in the Land of Snows,* it challenges the

official Chinese version of historical events; and like *The Autobiography of a Tibetan Monk,* its countermemory is rendered in the words of ordinary Tibetans who survived tremendous human-rights abuses.

All three of these books are necessary to an understanding of Tibet's past and present: some 1.2 million Tibetans—twenty percent of the population—were killed or died of starvation from 1950 to 1980; more than 100,000 people were sent to prison camps; and contemporary reports tell of hundreds of sterilizations and late-term abortions being forced on Tibetan women to ensure that the native population remains low. We can barely comprehend the depth of this tragedy. We require the strength and resiliency of a faith such as Palden Gyatso's—and of his fellow Tibetans and other survivors of the twentieth-century's holocausts and mass murders—to pass through these flames and remain human.

FRANK STEWART

About the Contributors _____

Alai was born to Tibetan peasant parents in Maerkang, Sichuan Province, in 1959. In 1980, he graduated from Maerkang Normal College and began teaching. He published his first collection of poetry in 1990. He now concentrates on writing fiction and lives in Chengdu, the capital of Sichuan Province, where he works on the staff of the magazine *Science Fiction World (kehuan shijie)*. The poems in this issue of *Mānoa* appeared in *Listening to Tibet (lingting xizang)*, published by Yunnan Renmin Chubanshe (Yunnan People's Publishing Co.) in China in 1999.

Hil Anderson has lived in Taiwan, where he researched contemporary poetry. He is pursuing a joint degree at Harvard University and Georgetown Law Center.

Herbert J. Batt has a doctorate from the University of Toronto and has taught at Shanghai Normal University, Shanghai University of Finance and Economics, and Beijing Capital University. The translator of numerous works from Chinese, he is editor and translator of *Tales of Tibet: Sky Burials, Wind Horses, and Prayer Wheels.*

Kevin Bowen is director of the William Joiner Center for the Study of War and Social Consequences at the University of Massachusetts–Boston. His most recent collection of poetry is *Forms of Prayer at the Hotel Edison;* with Nguyen Ba Chung, he translated from Vietnamese *Distant Road: Selected Poems of Nguyen Duy.*

Sharon May Brown photographed, researched, and wrote about Khmer Rouge atrocities for the Columbia University Center for the Study of Human Rights. Her photographs have appeared in the books *Seeking Shelter: Cambodians in Thailand* and *The Saving Rain.* Her story "Kwek," about a young boy who rebels against the Khmer Rouge, appeared in the summer 1999 issue of *Mānoa.*

Trevor Carolan is a contributing editor for *Shambhala Sun* magazine. He teaches at Simon Fraser University in British Columbia.

Tashi Dawa was born in Batang County, Sichuan Province, in 1959. His father is Tibetan, and his mother is Han Chinese; both are Chinese-speaking Communist Party cadres. His first fiction appeared in 1979; in 1993, he published the novel *Turmoil in Shangri-La (saodong de xiangbala)*. Regarded as the leading Tibetan author writing in Chinese, he has had his work translated into English, German, French, Italian, and Japanese. "Chimi, the Free Man" appears in *Tibet: The Mysterious Age (xizang yinmi suiyue),* published by Changjuang Wenyi Chubanshe (Yangzi River

Publishing Co.) in China in 1996. "The Glory of the Wind Horse" appears in *Listening to Tibet (lingting xizang),* published by Yunnan Renmin Chubanshe (Yunnan People's Publishing Co.) in China in 1999.

Yangdon Dhondup was born in India in 1970. She was educated in Switzerland and graduated in Chinese studies from London University's School of Oriental and African Studies (SOAS). Currently a doctoral student at SOAS, she is researching Tibetan authors writing in Chinese.

Xue Di was born in Beijing in 1957. Shortly after participating in the Tiananmen Square demonstrations in 1989, he left China and became a fellow in Brown University's Freedom to Write program. His published works include *Heart into Soil, Flames, Trembling,* and *Dream Talk.* He has twice received a Hellman-Hammett award, sponsored by the Fund for Free Expression, an affiliate of Human Rights Watch in New York.

Dpa' dar formerly worked for the Publishing and Translation Office of Gannan Prefecture, Gansu Province. He is now retired and lives outside Lanzhou. His work in this issue received an award for "outstanding poem" from the Gansu Provincial Literary Association. The poem first appeared in Chinese in the literary magazine *Gesanghua* and was later translated into Tibetan and published in the literary magazine *New Moon (zla zer).* The version in this issue was translated from a transcription of the Chinese original.

Geyang was born in 1972 in Dagyab, located in the Kham region of eastern Tibet. In 1989, at the age of seventeen, she graduated from Nanjing Meteorological Institute, and from 1996 to 1997 she studied writing at the Lu Xun Institute in Beijing. Her stories have won a number of prizes. She now works for the Tibetan Meteorological Bureau and reads the nightly weather report on Lhasa television. The story in this issue appears in *Listening to Tibet (lingting xizang),* published by Yunnan Renmin Chubanshe (Yunnan People's Publishing Co.) in China in 1999.

Dhondup Gyal began publishing in 1980 and is credited with founding modern Tibetan literature. In 1985, feeling that the fate of the Tibetan people was hopeless, he committed suicide. Among the works published before his death are a book of short stories, *Dawn Pillow Writing ('bol-rtsom zhogs-pa'i skya-rengs),* and *History and Specificity of the Tibetan Tradition of Narrative Song (mgur-glu'i lo-rgyus dang khyed-chos).* In 1999, his works were collected into seven volumes and published in China. The poem in this issue was originally published in *Light Rain (sbrang char)* in 1983. After Dhondup's death, it was reprinted in two editions of his work: the first published in 1994 by the Amnye Machen Institute in Dharamsala, India; and the second, a larger edition, published in 1997 in China.

Palden Gyal is the founder of the noted Tibetan literary journal *Jangzhon* and the independent newspaper *Tibet Times.* His collection of poetry in Tibetan, *The Offering and Other Poems (mchod),* was published by the Amnye Machen Institute. He now lives in Washington, D.C., where he works as a writer and broadcaster for Radio Free Asia.

Lauran R. Hartley is a doctoral candidate in Tibetan studies at Indiana University who is conducting research at Qinghai Nationalities College in Xining. Her translation of "Journal of the Grassland" first appeared in *Beacons,* the journal of the American Translators Association.

Ju Kalzang is one of the most widely acclaimed Tibetan poets today. After earning a master's degree in 1987 at Qinghai Nationalities College, he returned to his native home in the nomadic area of Golok, in Qinghai Province, where he now serves as director of the Nationalities Section of the Golok Prefecture Translation Affairs Bureau. "Tibet, Mother, *Mani" (bod ama mani)* appears in his collection *Gangs-'dabs-kyi sems-pa,* published in Xining in 1994; "The World Seen from Another Angle" *(gru-ga gzhan zhig nas mthong-ba'i 'jig-rten)* was originally published in *Light Rain (sbrang char)* in 1990 under the name Tig Ta (the pseudonym alludes to a bitter Tibetan medicine).

Yangtso Kyi was born in 1963 in the nomadic area of Qinghai Province. Though her primary-school education was several times interrupted by the need to tend her family's herds, she persisted in her studies and graduated from Northwest Nationalities Institute in 1988. Her story in this issue—her first and most important published piece—elicited many sympathetic and congratulatory letters when it appeared and has since been reprinted in major anthologies of modern Tibetan fiction. Formerly a community educator for a local women's association and an official translator, she now works as a legal researcher in the town of Chab-cha in Qinghai Province.

Andrew Lam is an associate editor at Pacific News Service in San Francisco and a regular commentator on National Public Radio's *All Things Considered.* He has won numerous journalism awards, including a 1992 Society for Professional Journalism Award, a 1993 Media Alliance Meritorious Award, and a 1995 Asian American Journalist Association National Award. He is working on his first short-story collection.

Sarah Lindsay is the author of *Primate Behavior,* a finalist for the 1997 National Book Award for poetry. She works as a copy editor for a magazine-publishing company in Greensboro, North Carolina.

Karl-Einar Löfqvist was born in Vilhelmina, a small village in Lappland, in northern Sweden. In 1986, he travelled to Asia and visited the Himalayan region of India, where he began photographing the Tibetan mountain people of Ladakh. In 1989, he exhibited these photographs at the Ethnographical Museum in Stockholm; he has also had exhibitions in England, India, and Denmark. He lives in Stockholm and continues to visit Ladakh.

Lenore Look is the author of *Arthur's First-Moon Birthday* and *Love As Strong As Ginger,* which was selected as a *Booklist* Editor's Choice in 1999. Her essays have appeared in the *Princeton Alumni Weekly* and in *Race and Races: Cases for a Diverse America.* A native of Seattle, she now lives in northern New Jersey.

Leza Lowitz is *Mānoa*'s contributing editor for Japan. Her most recent collection of poetry is *Yoga Poems: Lines to Unfold By.*

Meizhuo is from Amdo, formerly in northeast Tibet and now incorporated into Qinghai and Gansu Provinces. She published her first short story in 1987. In 1997, her novel, *The Clan of the Sun (taiyang buluo),* won the national award for minority writers. She also writes poetry and essays. Her poems in this issue are from *Collected Poems of Modern Tibetan Poets (zangzu dangdai shiren shixuan),* published by Qinghai Renmin Chubanshe (Qinghai People's Publishing Co.) in China in 1997.

Carol Moldaw is the author of three books of poetry: *Chalkmarks on Stone, Pencereden (Through the Window),* and *Taken from the River.* Her work has recently appeared or is forthcoming in *Agni, Field,* and *Paris Review.*

Tashi Pelden was born in Ranpa, in rural Tibet. In 1976, he left high school to return to his home village to teach in the local commune school. In 1985, he became a reporter and translator for the *Tibet Daily* newspaper, where he still works. He has published a novel and many novellas and short stories, all written in Tibetan. The story in this issue first appeared in the volume *Tomorrow's Weather Will Be Better,* published by Sichuan Nationalities Press in 1994.

Ronald D. Schwartz is a professor at Memorial University in Newfoundland, Canada, and a former honorary research fellow at the Centre of Asian Studies of the University of Hong Kong. His most recent book is *Circle of Protest: Political Ritual in the Tibetan Uprising.*

Sebo is the pen name of Xu Mingliang, a Tibetan born in Chengdu, Sichuan Province, in 1956. As a child, he moved with his family to Fenghuang, Hunan Province, an area of Tibetan, Miao, and Tujia minorities, as well as Han. In 1973, he enrolled at Liaoning Medical Institute in Shenyang, Liaoning Province, in northeast China. After graduation in 1975, he began practicing medicine in Motuo, later transferring to People's Hospital in Lhasa. He now works for the Sichuan Provincial Literary Association. The story in this issue appears in *New Tibetan Fiction (xizang xin xiaoshuo),* published by Xizang Renmin Chubanshe (Tibetan People's Publishing Co.) in Tibet in 1989.

Tsering Shakya was born in Tibet and escaped the Cultural Revolution by fleeing with his family to India in 1967. Now a research fellow in Tibetan studies at the School of Oriental and African Studies in London, he has regularly briefed diplomats in the British Foreign Office and the European Parliament. With Palden Gyatso, he wrote *Fire Under the Snow: The Testimony of a Tibetan Prisoner;* his most recent book is *The Dragon in the Land of Snow: A History of Modern Tibet Since 1947.*

Olen Steinhauer has just returned from a year in Romania, where he was on a Fulbright grant to research a novel about the country's 1989 revolution. His work has recently appeared in *Quarterly West* and *Paragraph.* He lives with his wife in New York.

Virgil Suárez is the author of over fifteen books of prose and poetry, most recently *In the Republic of Longing,* a collection of poems from Bilingual Review Press. Next year, his sixth collection of poems, *Palm Crows,* will be published. He divides his time between Miami and Tallahassee.

Tonga was born in Lhasa in 1962 and graduated in 1984 from Beijing Institute of Physical Education. His stories have been published in *Fiction Monthly (xiaoshuo yuebao)* and other prominent literary magazines. From 1986 to 1988, he studied in Nepal, receiving a degree from Tribuhuvan University. He now works for the Foreign Affairs Office of the government of the Tibetan Autonomous Region. The story in this issue first appeared in 1984 in *Tibetan Literature (xizang wenxue).*

Bill Tremblay is working on a manuscript entitled *Rainstorm Over the Alphabet.* Poems from that collection have been published in numerous journals.

Yidam Tsering was born in 1933 to Tibetan peasant parents in Tsongkha, on the outskirts of Xining, capital of Qinghai Province. In 1949, after the Communists took control of Qinghai, he entered a provincial cadre-training program, then joined a song-and-dance troupe as a performer, dramatist, and director. He has published numerous collections of poetry. The poems in this issue are from *An Anthology of Contemporary Tibetan Authors (zhongguo dangdai zuojia youxiu zuopinji),* published by Gansu Minzu Chubanshe (Gansu Nationalities Publishing Co.) in China in 1991.

Lhagyal Tshering was born in 1962 and is a teacher and researcher in Hezuo, Gansu Province. A collection of his poems was published by the Beijing Nationalities Publishing House in 1998. His work in this issue was originally published in *Light Rain (sbrang char)* in 1986. He recently coauthored a book on the history of Tibetan literature.

Janet L. Upton received her doctorate in anthropology from the University of Washington in 1999. Her dissertation focused on the role of schooling in a Tibetan community in Amdo. She is a program officer at Trace Foundation in New York, where she works on projects concerning minority higher education in China. She has written numerous articles and conference papers on Tibetan language, literature, and education in China.

Keith Waldrop lives in Providence, Rhode Island, where he teaches at Brown University. Among his books are *Potential Random* and *Light While There Is Light: An American History.*

Yangdon was born in Lhasa in 1963. After her graduation in 1985 from Beijing University, where she studied Chinese literature, she returned to Tibet and began working as an assistant editor for the periodical *Tibetan Literature (xizang wenxue).* In 1986, she began publishing her stories in that magazine—among them the story in this issue, which she subsequently expanded into a novel in 1994. In the same year, she returned to Beijing to work at the Chinese Center for Tibetan Studies, where she serves as an editor for China Tibetan Studies Press. The story in this issue appears in *Listening to Tibet (lingting xizang),* published by Yunnan Renmin Chubanshe (Yunnan People's Publishing Co.) in China in 1999.

bamboo ridge

JOURNAL OF HAWAI'I LITERATURE AND ARTS

Issue #77

ISBN #0-910043-60-4 (259 pages)
($10 + $3.00 book rate postage/handling)

Features:

- Poetry by the *Three Transpacific Wanderers* Albert Saijo, Gary Snyder, and Nanao Sakaki who read to a standing room only crowd at the UHM Art Auditorium last spring.

- New work by Ian MacMillan, Cathy Song, Eileen Tabios, Lee A. Tonouchi, and 34 others.

- Documentary photographer (and this issue's cover artist) Franco Salmoiraghi contributed an essay to accompany his photographs of Waialua town on O'ahu.

Here is a preview...

Thirty years ago, or even 10 years ago, you could imagine that Waialua would always be a sugar mill town. But in 1996 the mill was suddenly closed. It was the last one on O'ahu. Today, there are only a handful of sugar mills left on Maui and Kaua'i. Sugar in Hawai'i has been dying for years. It is perhaps as good as dead. Most of those immense landscapes of cane grasses are now fields of weeds or other smaller crops. The mills are rusting or dismantled. Only a few camps are left, mostly terminally rundown. The sugar towns no longer have a sugar-town future...

What about the people in the photographs? The lifestyle of a community is portrayed in the momentary click of a shutter as these people share a few moments or a fraction of a second of their lives for the camera. They have given a gift of memory to the future, to those who wish to see and understand something of the life they and their fellow workers led.

Bamboo Ridge is published twice a year. Subscriptions are $35 for 4 issues, $20 for 2 issues. Institutional rate: $25 for 2 issues. For subscription information, back issues, or a catalog, please contact...

BAMBOO RIDGE PRESS
P.O. BOX 61781
HONOLULU, HAWAI'I 96839-1781
(808) 626-1481
www.bambooridge.com   brinfo@bambooridge.com

Reimagining the American Pacific

From *South Pacific* to Bamboo Ridge and Beyond

ROB WILSON

In this compelling critique Rob Wilson explores the creation of the "Pacific Rim" in the American imagination and how the concept has been variously adapted and resisted in Hawaii, the Pacific Islands, New Zealand, and Australia. *Reimagining the American Pacific* ranges from the nineteenth century to the present and draws on theories of postmodernism, transnationality, and post-Marxist geography to contribute to the ongoing discussion of what constitutes "global" and "local." It is an engaging and provocative contribution to the fields of Asian and American studies, as well as those of cultural studies and theory, literary criticism, and popular culture.

"Lyrical and disruptive, Wilson's book masterfully dismantles multiple and contradictory imaginings of "the Pacific" and recovers the psychic longings, material histories, and politics that have variously produced the modern "Asia Pacific." This book wrenches American studies out of any lingering continent-bound complacency, gives a much needed broader scope to Asian American studies, and discloses crucial blind-spots in Asian area studies. Highly recommended for scholars in all these areas, as well as cultural studies in general." —David Palumbo-Liu, author of *Asian/American: Historical Crossings of a Racial Frontier*

320 pages, paper $18.95
New Americanists

Duke University Press
www.dukepress.edu
call toll-free 1-888-651-0122

Washington and Lee University

is pleased to announce

The Glasgow Prize
for Emerging Writers

$2,500

The Prize includes publication of new work in *Shenandoah*
and a one-week residency at Washington and Lee University.

Eligibility for 2001 Prize: all poets with one book.

To apply, send first book, samples of new work and vita
between February 1 and March 31, 2001

R.T. Smith
The Glasgow Prize
Troubadour Theater/2
Washington and Lee University
Lexington, VA 24450-0303
(540) 463-8908

Sponsored by the Arthur and Margaret Glasgow Endowment,
established in 1960
"for the promotion of the expression of art through pen and tongue."

MĀNOA

Take a deep breath

and discover the world—

Asia, the Pacific, and beyond

Photo by Wayne Levin

S tart your literary adventure with a 1-year individual subscription—two book-length issues at 30% off the single-copy price. **And if you subscribe with this coupon, you'll receive a free 18" x 25" *Mānoa* poster of gallery quality, featuring the underwater photography of Wayne Levin.**

Name _____

Address _____

City/State/Zip_____

❑   Enclosed is my check/money order for ❑ $22 (U.S.) or ❑ $25 (NON-U.S.) payable to the University of Hawai'i Press.

❑   Please charge to my ❑ VISA ❑ MasterCard.

Card No.   _____

Expires_____ Signature _____

MĀNOA • University of Hawai'i • English Dept. • Honolulu, HI • 96822 • U.S.A.
For a preview of your free poster, see www.hawaii.edu/mjournal/text/Tshirt.html.

12:2

(2/05) $1.